SEVENTH EDITION

The Little, Brown Essential Handbook

Jane E. Aaron

Longman

Boston Columbus Indianapolis New York San Francisco Upper Saddle River
Amsterdam Cape Town Dubai London Madrid Milan Munich Paris Montreal Toronto
Delhi Mexico City São Paulo Sydney Hong Kong Seoul Singapore Taipei Tokyo

Executive Editor: Suzanne Phelps Chambers
Senior Development Editor: Anne Brunell Ehrenworth
Senior Supplements Editor: Donna Campion
Senior Marketing Manager: Susan E. Stoudt
Production Manager: Bob Ginsberg
Project Coordination, Text Design, and Electronic Page Makeup: Nesbitt Graphics, Inc.
Cover Design Manager: John Callahan
Cover Designer: Kay Petronio
Senior Manufacturing Buyer: Roy L. Pickering, Jr.
Printer and Binder: RR Donnelley & Sons Company/Crawfordsville
Cover Printer: Lehigh-Phoenix

For permission to use copyrighted material, grateful acknowledgment is made to the copyright holders on p. 261, which is hereby made part of this copyright page.

Library of Congress Cataloging-in-Publication Data

Aaron, Jane E.
The Little, Brown essential handbook / Jane E. Aaron. -- 7th ed.
p. cm.
ISBN-13: 978-0-205-71876-4
ISBN-10: 0-205-71876-0
1. English language--Grammar--Handbooks, manuals, etc. 2. English language--Rhetoric--Handbooks, manuals, etc. 3. Report writing--Handbooks, manuals, etc. I. Title.
PE1112.A24 2010
808'.042--dc22

2010037752

Longman
is an imprint of

1 2 3 4 5 6 7 8 9 10—DOC—13 12 11 10

ISBN-13: 978-0-205-71876-4
ISBN-10: 0-205-71876-0

www.pearsonhighered.com

Preface

This small book contains essential information about academic writing, the writing process, usage, grammar, punctuation, research writing, and source citation—all in a convenient, accessible format.

You can use this book at any level of writing, in any discipline, and in or out of school. The explanations assume no special knowledge of the terminology of writing: needless terms are omitted, and essential terms, marked °, are defined in the Glossary of Terms. Material especially for writers using English as a second language is marked ESL. Examples come from a wide range of subjects, from science to literature to business.

The guide on the next page shows how the book works, and the complete table of contents inside the back cover details the coverage. The book has three main components.

The big picture

An overview of academic writing, writing arguments, writing in the disciplines, and document design begins the book. These chapters can help you define the context for your writing and make decisions about purpose, audience, research, revision, format, and other matters.

Editing

Many of this book's chapters will help you write clearly and correctly. You'll never need or use every chapter because you already know much of what's here, whether consciously or not. The trick is to figure out what you *don't* know, focus on those areas, and back yourself up with this book.

Checklists for editing appear on pages 30 (effective sentences), 50 (grammatical sentences), 84 (punctuation), and 104 (spelling and mechanics). You can develop a personal editing checklist as well by keeping a list of mistakes and other writing problems that your readers point out to you.

Research and documentation

When you need to consult sources for your writing, this book can help you find them, evaluate them, and cite them. Chapters 35–39 guide you through the process of research writing, and 40–43 detail the four most widely used styles for citing sources: Modern Language Association (MLA), American Psychological Association (APA), Chicago, and Council of Science Editors (CSE).

Finding what you need

The handbook provides many ways to reach its information:

Use a table of contents.

Inside the front cover, a brief contents gives an overview of the handbook. Inside the back cover, a detailed outline lists all the book's topics.

Use the index.

At the end of the book (p. 263), this alphabetical list includes all topics, terms, and problem words and expressions.

Use the glossaries.

"Glossary of Usage" (p. 239) clarifies words and expressions that are often misused or confused. "Glossary of Terms" (p. 249) defines grammatical terms, including all terms marked ° in the text.

Use a list.

"ESL Guide" (pp. 294–95) pulls together the book's material for students using English as a second language. "Editing Symbols" inside the back cover explains abbreviations often used to mark papers.

Use the elements of the page.

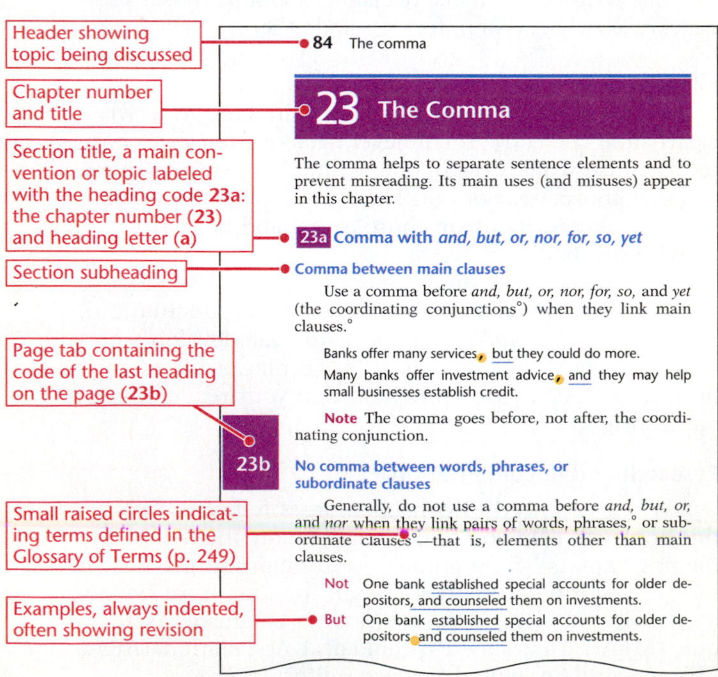

Supplements

- An exercise book provides more than seventy practice activities on grammar, usage, punctuation, research writing, and documentation. The double-spaced exercises allow you to work directly in the book.
- mycomplab The Web site *MyCompLab* (*mycomplab.com*) integrates instruction, multimedia tutorials, and exercises for writing, grammar, and research with an online composing space and assessment tools. This seamless, flexible environment comes from extensive research in partnership with composition faculty and students across the country. It provides help for writers in the context of their writing, with functions for instructors' and peers' commentary. Special features include an e-portfolio, a bibliography tool, tutoring services, an assignment-builder, and a grade book and course-management organization created specifically for writing classes.
- Students can subscribe to *The Little, Brown Essential Handbook* as a *CourseSmart* e-textbook. The site includes all of the handbook's content in a format that enables students to search the text, bookmark passages, integrate their notes, and print reading assignments that incorporate lecture notes. For more information, or to subscribe to the *CourseSmart* e-textbook, visit *coursesmart.com*.
- vango notes *VangoNotes* are study guides in MP3 format that enable students to download handbook information into their own players and then listen to it whenever and wherever they wish. The notes include "need to know" tips for each handbook chapter, practice tests, audio flash cards for learning key concepts and terms, and a rapid review for exams. For more information, visit *VangoNotes.com*.

Acknowledgments

We are grateful to the following teachers who offered advice for this revision: Chris Allen, Piedmont Technical College; Nancy Alexander, Methodist University; Michalle Barnett, Gulf Coast Community College; Barclay Barrios, Florida Atlantic University; Richard Bollenbacher, Edison Community College; Ronald Clark Brooks, Oklahoma State University; Jay T. Dolmage, West Virginia University; Gabriel Fletcher, North Central Texas College; Angela Messenger, Youngstown State University; Ellen Olmstead, Montgomery College; Amy Patrick, Western Illinois University; Tiechera Samuell, Three Rivers Community College; and Thomas Swartz, Western Michigan University.

Thanks also to my friends at and around Longman, especially Suzanne Phelps Chambers, Carol Hollar-Zwick, Bob Ginsberg, Anne Brunell Ehrenworth, and, at Nesbitt Graphics, Susan McIntyre and Jerilyn Bockorick.

WHY DO YOU NEED THIS NEW EDITION?

This edition of *The Little, Brown Essential Handbook* differs from the previous edition in countless ways. Here are five that make the book indispensable:

1. More help with college writing ▪ The expanded chapter on **academic writing** gives you more help analyzing your assignment and discusses the key academic skill of synthesizing your own and others' views. ▪ A new chapter on **argument** helps you formulate and state your opinion clearly and logically and includes a sample paper. ▪ A chapter on **writing in the disciplines** provides you with an overview of the concerns, assignments, and source documentation in all of your courses.

2. More help with the research process ▪ The chapter on **finding sources** covers all kinds of print and electronic sources you may encounter in your research. ▪ The chapter on **evaluating sources** includes case studies that show how you can distinguish reliable and unreliable sources.

3. Up-to-date, more accessible help with citing sources in your work ▪ Detailed explanations present the **most recent versions of MLA, APA, Chicago, and CSE documentation styles** and show you how to document a wide range of print and electronic sources. ▪ **Annotated sample sources** show you how to find and format bibliographic information in articles, books, and Web sites. ▪ **Color highlighting** distinguishes key elements of source citations in every style.

4. A better reference for ESL writers. ▪ The new "ESL Guide" at the end of the book provides an orientation to mastering standard American English and pulls together all the book's integrated ESL material.

5. Access to *MyCompLab* ▪ *The Little, Brown Essential Handbook* is even more useful when you combine it with *MyCompLab,* a Web gateway to resources on grammar, writing, and research developed specifically for writers.

PEARSON

PART 1

Writing

Checklist for revising academic writing

This checklist covers the main considerations in academic writing. For a detailed guide to this part, see the contents inside the back cover.

Purpose and audience (p. 4)

- ☑ What is your purpose? Does it conform to the assignment?
- ☑ Who are your readers? Will your purpose be clear to them?

Thesis (p. 5)

- ☑ What is your thesis, or central claim?
- ☑ Where in the paper does your thesis become clear?

Development

- ☑ What are the main points supporting the thesis?
- ☑ How well do the facts, examples, and other evidence support each main point?

Use of sources

- ☑ Have you used sources to support—not substitute for—your own ideas? (See pp. 6–7, 141–42.)
- ☑ Have you integrated borrowed material into your own sentences? (See pp. 142–49.)
- ☑ Have you fully cited each use of a source? (See pp. 150–56.)

Unity

- ☑ What does each paragraph contribute to the thesis?
- ☑ Within paragraphs, what does each sentence contribute to the paragraph's idea? (This paragraph idea is often expressed in a **topic sentence.**)

Coherence

- ☑ Will the organization be clear to readers?
- ☑ How smoothly does the paper flow?
- ☑ Have you used transitions to link paragraphs and sentences? (See p. 259 for a list of transitional expressions, such as *first, however,* and *in addition.*)

Language (pp. 8–9, 41–46)

- ☑ Have you used standard American English that is appropriately formal for your writing situation?
- ☑ Is your writing authoritative and neutral?

Format

- ☑ Have you used the appropriate format for the kind of writing you're doing? (See p. 21.)
- ☑ Have you included all necessary parts of the paper, such as your name, a title, and source citations?

1 Academic Writing

When you write in college, you work within a community of teachers and students who have specific aims and expectations. The basic aim of this community—whether in English, psychology, biology, or some other discipline—is to contribute to and build knowledge through questioning, research, and communication. The academic disciplines do differ in their conventions for writing (see Chapter 3, p. 17), but many academic papers share the features discussed in this chapter.

1a The writing situation

Any writing you do for others occurs in a **writing situation** that both limits and clarifies your choices. You will most likely have an assignment, and to fulfill it you will communicate something about a subject for a specific reason to a particular audience of readers.

Assignment

When you receive a writing assignment, study its wording and requirements:

- **What does your writing assignment tell you to do?** Words such as *discuss, report, describe,* and *analyze* ask you to explain something about your subject. Words such as *argue* and *evaluate* ask you to make a case for your opinion.
- **What kind of research is required?** An assignment may specify the kinds of sources you are expected to consult.
- **What other requirements do you have to meet?** When is the assignment due? How long should your writing be? What format does the assignment require—a printed paper? a Web site? an oral presentation?

Subject

Most writing assignments give at least some latitude for choice of subject. Consider the following questions to find your approach:

- **What subject do you want to know more about?** A good subject is one that you care about. Consider something that you want to know more about or that makes you especially excited or angry.

mycomplab

Visit *mycomplab.com* for more help with academic writing.

- **Is your subject limited enough?** Choose a subject that you can cover in the space and time you have, or narrow a broad subject by breaking it into as many specific subjects as you can think of.
- **Is your subject suitable for the assignment?** Review the assignment to ensure that the subject fulfills the requirements.

Purpose

For most academic writing, your general purpose will be mainly **explanatory** or mainly **argumentative:** you will aim to clarify your subject so that readers understand it as you do, or you will aim to gain readers' agreement with a debatable idea about the subject. The following questions can help you think about your purpose:

- **What kind of writing, or genre, does your assignment specify?** For instance, are you writing a case study, a review of others' writing, a position paper?
- **What aim does your assignment specify?** For instance, does it ask you to explain something or to argue a point?
- **Why are you writing?** What do you want your work to accomplish?
- **How can you best achieve your purpose?**

Audience

Most academic writing assignments specify or assume an audience of educated readers or even experts in your subject. Use the questions below to adapt your writing to the needs and expectations of your readers:

- **Who will read your writing?** What can you assume your readers already know and think about your subject? How can your assumptions guide your writing so that you tell readers neither too little nor too much?
- **What are readers' expectations?** For the discipline in which you're writing, what claims and evidence, organization, language, and format will readers look for?
- **What is your relationship to your readers?** How formal or informal should your writing be?
- **What do you want readers to do or think after they read your writing?**

1b Thesis and organization

Much academic writing is organized to develop a main idea, or thesis.

Thesis

The **thesis** is the central idea or claim in a piece of writing: the entire work develops and supports that idea. Often, a thesis starts out as a question that guides a writer's research and drafting. In the final paper, the thesis usually appears in a **thesis statement.**

Here are pairs of questions and answering thesis statements from various disciplines:

Literature question	What makes the ending of Kate Chopin's "The Story of an Hour" believable?
Thesis statement	The ironic ending of "The Story of an Hour" is believable because it is consistent with the story's other ironies.
History question	How did eviction from its homeland in 1838 affect the Cherokee Nation of Native Americans?
Thesis statement	Disastrous as it was, the forced resettlement of the Cherokee did less to damage the tribe than did its allegiance to the Confederacy during the Civil War.
Psychology question	How common is violence between partners in dating relationships?
Thesis statement	The survey showed that violence may have occurred in a fifth of dating relationships among students at this college.
Biology question	Does the same physical exertion have the same or different effects on the blood pressure of men and women?
Thesis statement	After the same physical exertion, the average blood pressure of female participants increased significantly more than the average blood pressure of male participants.

Most of the thesis statements you write in college papers will be either argumentative or explanatory. The first two examples above are argumentative: the writers mainly want to convince readers of something. The last two examples are explanatory: the writers mainly want to explain something to readers.

ESL In some other cultures it is considered unnecessary or impolite for a writer to express an opinion or to state his or her main idea outright. When writing in American academic situations, you can assume that your readers expect a clear expression of what you think.

Organization

An effective paper has a recognizable shape—an arrangement of parts that guides readers, helping them see how ideas and details relate to each other and contribute to the thesis. Many academic papers divide into an **introduction,** which presents the subject and often the thesis; the **body,** which contains the substance of the paper; and a **conclusion,** which ties together the parts of the body.

Beyond this basic scheme, organization in academic writing varies widely depending on the discipline and the type of writing. Whatever framework you're using, develop your ideas as simply and directly as your purpose and content allow. And clearly relate sentences, paragraphs, and sections so that readers always know where they are in the paper's development.

1c Evidence and research

The thesis statement of your paper will be based on evidence, drawn sometimes from your own experience but more usually from research. Ask these questions to determine the kind of research you may have to do:

- **What kinds of evidence will best suit your writing and support your thesis?** Depending on the discipline you're writing in and the type of paper you're working on, you'll use a mix of facts, examples, and expert opinions to support your ideas. See pages 11–12 for more on evidence in argument papers and pages 17–20 for more on evidence in the disciplines.
- **Does your assignment require research?** Will you need to consult sources or conduct interviews, surveys, or experiments?
- **Even if research is not required, what information do you need to develop your subject?** How will you obtain it?
- **What documentation style should you use to cite your sources?** See pages 155–56 on source documentation in the academic disciplines.

ESL Research serves different purposes in some other cultures than it does in the United States. For instance, students in some cultures may be expected to consult only well-known sources and to adhere closely to the sources' ideas. In US colleges and universities, students are expected to look for relevant and reliable sources, whether well known or not, and to use sources mainly to support their own ideas.

1d Synthesis

Academic writing often requires you to read, analyze, and expand on the work of others. Using **synthesis,** you select and respond to others' ideas and information in order to support your own conclusions. The example below follows a pattern common in academic writing: it opens with the writer's own idea, gives and interprets evidence from a source, and ends with the writer's own conclusion.

> Thomas Sowell claims that government money goes to waste on student loans because many recipients do not need or deserve the help. But his portrait of recipients is questionable: it is based on averages, some statistical and some not, but averages are often deceptive. For example, Sowell cites college graduates' low average debt of $7,000 to $9,000 (131) without acknowledging the fact that many students' debt is much higher or giving the full range of statistics. Similarly, Sowell dismisses "heart-rending stories" of "the low-income student with a huge debt" as "not at all typical" (132), yet he invents his own exaggerated version of the typical loan recipient: an affluent slacker ("Rockefellers" and "Vanderbilts") for whom college is a "place to hang out for a few years" sponging off the government, while his or her parents clear a profit from making use of the loan program (132). Although such students (and parents) may well exist, are they really typical? Sowell does not offer any data one way or the other—for instance, how many loan recipients come from each income group, what percentage of loan funds go to each group, how many loan recipients receive significant help from their parents, and how many receive none. Together, Sowell's statements and omissions cast doubt on the argument that government loans are wasted on well-to-do and undeserving students.

Writer's idea

Evidence

Interpretation

Evidence

Evidence

Interpretation

Writer's conclusion

1e Source citation

Using the ideas and information in sources carries the responsibility to acknowledge those sources fully. Not acknowledging sources undermines the incremental construction of knowledge on which academic work depends. It also opens you to charges of plagiarism, which can be punishable. (See Chapter 39.)

Most disciplines have a preferred style of source citation. For lists of disciplines' style guides, see page 156. For documentation guidelines and samples, see pages 157–99 (MLA style), 200–19 (APA style), 219–31 (Chicago style), and 232–38 (CSE style).

ESL Cultures have varying definitions of a writer's responsibilities to sources. In some cultures, for instance, a writer need not cite sources that are well known. In the

United States, in contrast, a writer is obligated to cite all sources.

1f Language

American academic writing relies on a dialect called **standard American English.** The dialect is also used in business, the professions, the media, and other sites of social and economic power where people of diverse backgrounds must communicate with one another. It is "standard" not because it is better than other forms of English, but because it is accepted as the common language, much as the dollar bill is accepted as the common currency.

For academic writing, use these guidelines:

- **Follow the conventions of standard American English for grammar and usage.** These conventions are described in guides to the dialect, such as this handbook.
- **Use a standard vocabulary,** not one that only some groups understand, such as slang, an ethnic or regional dialect, or another language.
- **Create some distance between yourself and the reader.** Generally, prefer the third person (*he, she, it, they*), not the first (*I, we*) or the second (*you*).
- **Write authoritatively and neutrally.** Express yourself confidently, not timidly, and refrain from hostility and overt enthusiasm.

Checklist for academic language

Rapid communication by e-mail and text or instant messaging encourages some informalities that are inappropriate in academic writing. Check your academic papers especially for the following:

☑ **Complete sentences** Make sure every sentence has a subject and a verb. Avoid fragments such as *Observing the results* and *After the meeting*. For more on fragments, see pages 77–79.

☑ **Punctuation** Use standard punctuation between and within sentences. Check especially for missing commas and apostrophes. See pages 85–102.

☑ **Spelling** Use correct, standard spellings, avoiding spellings such as *enuf* for *enough, cuz* for *because, nite* for *night, u* for *you,* and *wl* for *will.* See pages 105–07.

☑ **Capital letters** Use capital letters at the beginnings of sentences, for proper nouns and adjectives, and in titles. See pages 108–10.

☑ **Standard abbreviations** Use only conventional abbreviations for the discipline you are writing in. Avoid short forms such as *2* for *to* or *too; b4* for *before; bc* for *because; ur* for *your, you are,* or *you're;* and + or & for *and.* See pages 112–13.

1g Revision

In revising, you adopt a critical eye toward your writing, examining it as readers will for ideas and evidence, their relationships and arrangement, and the degree to which they work or don't work for your thesis.

Whenever possible, let a draft rest for a while to get some distance from it and perhaps to gather comments from others, such as your classmates or instructor. Then revise the draft using the checklist on page 2, concentrating on the effectiveness of the whole. (Leave style, correctness, and other specific issues for the separate step of editing, discussed below.)

1h Editing and proofreading

Much of this book concerns editing—tightening or clarifying sentences, polishing words, repairing mistakes in grammar and punctuation. Leave this work until after revision so that your content and organization are set before you tinker with your expression. For editing guidelines, see the checklists on pages 30 (effective sentences), 50 (grammatical sentences), 84 (punctuation), and 104 (spelling and mechanics).

Most writers find that they spot errors better on paper than on a computer screen, so edit a printout if you can. And be sure to proofread your final draft before you submit it, even if you have used a spelling checker or similar aid (see below).

Spelling checkers

A spelling checker can be a great ally: it will flag words that are spelled incorrectly and will usually suggest alternative spellings that resemble what you've typed. However, this ally has limitations:

- **The checker may flag a word that you've spelled correctly,** just because the word does not appear in its dictionary.
- **The checker may suggest incorrect alternatives.** Before accepting any highlighted suggestion from the checker, you need to verify that the word is actually what you

intend. Consult an online or printed dictionary when you aren't sure of the checker's recommendations.

- **Most important, a spelling checker will not flag words that appear in its dictionary but you have misused.** The jingle in the following screen shot has circulated widely as a warning about spelling checkers. Can you spot the thirteen errors that a spelling checker failed to catch?

> I have a spelling checker,
> It came with my PC;
> It plainly marks four my revue
> Mistakes I cannot sea.
> I've run this poem threw it,
> I'm sure your please too no.
> Its letter perfect in it's weigh,
> My checker tolled me sew.

Grammar/style checkers

Grammar/style checkers can flag incorrect grammar or punctuation and wordy or awkward sentences. You may be able to customize a checker to suit your needs and habits as a writer—for instance, instructing it to look for problems with subject-verb agreement or for passive verbs.

Like spelling checkers, however, grammar/style checkers are limited:

- **They miss many errors** because they are not yet capable of analyzing language in all its complexity.
- **They often question passages that don't need editing,** such as an appropriate passive verb or a deliberate and emphatic use of repetition.

Each time a grammar/style checker questions something, you must determine whether a change is needed at all and what change will be most effective, and you must read your papers carefully on your own to find any errors the program missed.

2 Writing Arguments

Argument is writing that attempts to solve a problem, introduce and defend a particular interpretation, shape or change readers' opinions, or move readers to action. Many of the academic papers you write in college courses will be arguments.

2a Elements of argument

All arguments have four main elements: subject, claims, evidence, and assumptions.

Subject

A subject for argument should meet the following requirements:

- **It can be disputed:** reasonable people can disagree over it.
- **It *will* be disputed:** it is controversial.
- **It is narrow enough:** it can be researched and argued in the space and time available.

Claims

Claims are statements that require support. In an argument, the central claim is the thesis, asserted outright in the thesis statement. (See p. 5.) An argumentative thesis statement is always an opinion, a judgment you have made based on facts and arguable on the basis of facts. It may be one of the following:

- **A claim about past or present reality,** such as *Academic cheating increases with students' economic insecurity.*
- **A claim of value,** such as *The new room fees are unfair given the condition of the dorm.*
- **A recommendation for a course of action,** such as *The campus can relieve traffic congestion by improving bus service and rewarding bus riders.*

The backbone of the argument consists of specific claims that support the thesis statement. These claims may also state opinions, or they may state facts or beliefs.

Evidence

Evidence shows the validity of your claims. There are several kinds of evidence.

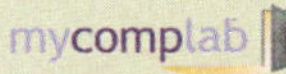

- **Facts:** statements whose truth can be verified.
- **Statistics:** facts expressed as numbers.
- **Examples:** specific instances of the point being made.
- **Expert opinions:** the judgments formed by authorities on the basis of their own analyses of the facts.

Evidence must be reliable to be convincing. Ask these questions about your evidence:

- **Is it accurate**—trustworthy, exact, undistorted?
- **Is it relevant**—authoritative, pertinent, and current?
- **Is it representative**—true to its context, neither under- nor overrepresenting any element of the sample it's drawn from?
- **Is it adequate**—plentiful and specific?

Assumptions

An **assumption** is an opinion, a principle, or a belief that ties evidence to claims: the assumption explains why a particular piece of evidence is relevant to a particular claim. For example:

Claim	The college needs a new chemistry lab.
Evidence (in part)	The testimony of chemistry professors.
Assumption	Chemistry professors are reliable evaluators of the present lab's quality.

Assumptions are always present in arguments, even when they are not stated. In writing an argument, you need to recognize your own assumptions. If you think that readers may not agree with an assumption, you should make it explicit and establish its validity.

2b Balance in argument

Balance is essential if an argument is to establish common ground between you and your readers. You need to make appropriate appeals to readers and treat opposing views fairly.

Appeals

In presenting your claims and evidence, you'll make three kinds of appeals to readers:

- **A *rational* appeal calls on readers' sense of logic.** It requires reasonable claims and sound evidence to support the claims.
- **An *emotional* appeal calls on readers' feelings.** You strengthen support for your claims by encouraging readers to feel empathy, pride, anger, or some other emotion.

- **An *ethical* appeal is the sense you give of being reasonable, fair, and competent.**

Appeals require balance. Emotional appeals in particular can be risky if they misjudge readers' feelings or are inappropriate to the argument (for example, creating fear to force agreement with a claim).

Opposing views

If your thesis is arguable, then others can provide their own evidence to support different views. Dealing with these views fairly, giving them their due, shows your responsibility and gives you a chance to deal with objections your readers may have. Find out what the opposing views are and what evidence supports them.

A common way to handle opposing views is to state them, refute those you can, grant the validity of others, and demonstrate why, despite their validity, the opposing views are less compelling than your own.

Another approach emphasizes the search for common ground. In a **Rogerian argument** you start by showing that you understand readers' views and by establishing points on which you and readers agree and disagree. Creating a connection in this way can be especially helpful when you expect readers to resist your argument.

2c Organization of argument

Argument papers all include the same parts:

- **Introduction:** Running a paragraph or two, the introduction establishes the significance of the subject, provides background, and generally includes the thesis statement. If readers are likely to resist the thesis statement, you may want to put it later in the paper, after the evidence.
- **Body:** In one or more paragraphs, the body develops each claim supporting the thesis with sound evidence.
- **Response to opposing views:** Depending on what you think readers need, this response may come early or late in the paper or may be covered point by point throughout.
- **Conclusion:** Usually one paragraph, the conclusion often restates the thesis, summarizes the supporting claims, and makes a final appeal to readers.

2d Visual arguments

A visual argument, such as an advertisement, uses an image to engage and convince viewers. The claims, evidence, and assumptions of written arguments also appear in visual arguments, as illustrated by the ad below featuring the tennis champion Serena Williams.

- **Claims:** The claims in an image can be made by composition as well as by content, with or without accompanying words. In the Williams ad, the image claims that strong, attractive winners drink milk, while the text claims that milk can help dieters reduce to a healthy weight.
- **Evidence:** In a visual argument, evidence may be strictly visual or may consist of facts, statistics, examples, or expert opinions that accompany the visual. In the ad's image, Williams's milk mustache and glass of milk say she's a milk drinker, while her strong, shapely body says that she's exceptionally healthy. In the ad's text, Williams says she drinks milk, and she gives research data that support the claim about milk consumption and weight loss.

Advertisement by the Milk Processor Education Program

- **Assumptions:** Like a written argument, a visual argument is based on assumptions that connect claims and evidence. In the ad, one assumption is that the endorsement of an accomplished and attractive athlete like Williams will sell viewers on the benefits of milk.

2e Sample argument

As you read the following essay by Craig Holbrook, a student, notice especially the structure, the relation of claims and supporting evidence, the kinds of appeals Holbrook makes, and the way he addresses opposing views.

TV Can Be Good for You

Television wastes time, pollutes minds, destroys brain cells, and turns some viewers into murderers. Thus runs the prevailing talk about the medium, supported by serious research as well as simple belief. However, television can have strong virtues, too: it can ease loneliness, spark healthful laughter, and even educate young children by providing voices that supplement those of real people.

Almost everyone who has lived alone understands the curse of silence, when the only sound is the buzz of unhappiness or anxiety inside one's own head. Although people of all ages who live alone can experience intense loneliness, the elderly are especially vulnerable to solitude. For example, they may suffer increased confusion or depression when left alone for long periods but then rebound when they have steady companionship (Bondevik and Skogstad 329-30).

A study of elderly men and women in New Zealand found that television can actually serve as a companion by assuming "the role of social contact with the wider world," reducing "feelings of isolation and loneliness because it directs viewers' attention away from themselves" ("Television Programming"). Thus television's voices can provide comfort because they distract from a focus on being alone.

The absence of real voices can be most damaging when it means a lack of laughter. Here, too, research shows that television can have a positive effect on health. Laughter is one of the most powerful calming forces available to human beings, proven in many studies to reduce heart rate, lower blood pressure, and ease other stress-related ailments (Burroughs, Mahoney, and Lippman 172; Griffiths 18). Television offers plenty of laughter: the recent listings for a single Friday night included more than twenty comedy programs running on the networks and on basic cable.

A study reported in a health magazine found that laughter inspired by television and video is as healthful as the laughter generated by live comedy. Volunteers laughing at a video comedy routine "showed significant improvements in several immune functions, such as natural killer-cell activity" (Laliberte 78). Further, the effects of the comedy were so profound that "merely anticipating watching a funny video improved mood, depression, and anger as much as two days beforehand" (Laliberte 79). Even for people with plenty of companionship, television's voices can have healthful effects by causing laughter.

Television also provides information about the world. This service can be helpful to everyone but especially to children, whose natural curiosity can exhaust the knowledge and patience of their parents and caretakers. While the TV may be baby-sitting children, it can also enrich them. For example, educational programs such as those on the Discovery Channel, the Disney Channel, and PBS offer a steady stream of information at various cognitive levels. Even many cartoons, which are generally dismissed as mindless or worse, familiarize children with the material of literature, including strong characters enacting classic narratives.

Three researchers conducting a review of studies involving children and television found that TV can inspire imaginative play, which psychologists describe as important for children's cognitive development (Thakkar, Garrison, and Christakis 2028). In the studies reviewed, children who watched *Mister Rogers' Neighborhood*, a show that emphasized make-believe, demonstrated significant increases in imaginative play (2029). Thus high-quality educational programming can both inform young viewers and improve their cognitive development.

The value of television voices should not be oversold. For one thing, almost everyone agrees that too much TV does no one any good and may cause much harm. Many studies show that excessive TV watching increases violent behavior, especially in children, and can cause, rather than ease, other antisocial behaviors (Reeks 114; Walsh 34). In addition, human beings require the give and take of actual interaction. Steven Pinker, an expert in children's language acquisition, warns that children cannot develop language properly by watching television. They need to interact with actual speakers who respond directly to their needs (282). Television voices are not real voices and in the end can do only limited good.

But even limited good is something, especially for those who are lonely or neglected. Television is not an entirely positive force, but neither is it an entirely negative one. Its voices stand by to provide company, laughter, and information whenever they're needed.

Works Cited

Bondevik, Margareth, and Anders Skogstad. "The Oldest Old, ADL, Social Network, and Loneliness." *Western Journal of Nursing Research* 20.3 (1998): 325-43. Print.

Burroughs, W. Jeffrey, Diana L. Mahoney, and Louis G. Lippman. "Attributes of Health-Promoting Laughter: Cross-Generational Comparison." *Journal of Psychology* 136.2 (2004): 171-81. Print.

Griffiths, Joan. "The Mirthful Brain." *Omni* Aug. 1996: 18-19. Print.

Laliberte, Richard W. "The Benefits of Laughter." *Shape* Sept. 2003: 78-79. Print.

Pinker, Steven. *The Language Instinct: How the Mind Creates Language*. New York: Harper, 1994. Print.

Reeks, Anne. "Kids and TV: A Guide." *Parenting* Apr. 2005: 110-15. Print.

"Television Programming for Older People: Summary Research Report." *NZ on Air*. NZ on Air, 25 July 2004. Web. 15 Oct. 2008.

Thakkar, Rupin R., Michelle M. Garrison, and Dimitri A. Christakis. "A Systematic Review for the Effects of Television Viewing by Infants and Preschoolers." *Pediatrics* 18.5 (2006): 2025-31. Web. 12 Oct. 2008.

Walsh, Teri. "Too Much TV Linked to Depression." *Prevention* Feb. 2001: 34-36. Print.

—Craig Holbrook (student)

3 Writing in the Disciplines

Chapters 1 and 2 discuss features of academic writing in any discipline. This chapter outlines key differences among the disciplines.

3a Literature

Works of literature include novels, short stories, poems, plays, and forms of creative nonfiction. Writing about a literary work requires close reading of the text and particular attention to the words in order to form an interpretation of meaning. In turn, the evidence for the interpretation is

Visit *mycomplab.com* for more help with writing in the disciplines.

mainly quotations from the work that support the ideas about it. Literary analysis also sometimes draws on secondary sources—that is, the comments of critics, biographers, and others on the work or its author.

Writing assignments

You may be asked to write one or more of the following types of papers. The first two are the most common.

- **Literary analysis paper:** your ideas about a work of literature, interpreting its meaning, context, or representations based on specific words, passages, characters, and events.
- **Literary research paper:** analysis of a literary work combined with research about the work and perhaps its author.
- **Personal response or reaction paper:** your thoughts or feelings about a literary work.
- **Book review:** a summary and evaluation of a book.
- **Theater review:** a summary and evaluation of a theatrical performance.

Source documentation

Unless your instructor specifies otherwise, follow the guidelines in the *MLA Handbook for Writers of Research Papers,* detailed on pages 157–96.

3b Other humanities

The humanities include literature, discussed above, as well as the visual arts, music, film, dance, history, philosophy, and religion. Writers in the humanities explain, analyze, and reconstruct human experience by drawing on written words, works of art, and other human creations. The evidence in humanities writing comes largely from primary sources, such as eyewitness accounts of events, news reporting, works of art, and religious texts. Evidence may also come from secondary sources, such as a historian's interpretation of events or a critic's review of a painting.

Writing assignments

Papers in the humanities generally perform one or more of the following operations, often in combination with one another:

- **Explanation:** for instance, showing how a painter developed a particular technique or clarifying a general's role in a battle.
- **Analysis:** examining the elements of a philosophical

argument or breaking down the causes of a historical event.

- **Interpretation:** inferring the meaning of a film from its images or the significance of a historical event from contemporary accounts of it.
- **Synthesis:** finding a pattern in a historical period or a composer's works.
- **Evaluation:** judging the quality of an architect's design or a historian's conclusions.

Source documentation

Writers in the humanities generally use the recommendations in either the *MLA Handbook for Writers of Research Papers* (pp. 157–96) or the *Chicago Manual of Style* (pp. 219–29). Ask your instructor whether you should use MLA or Chicago style.

3c Social sciences

The social sciences include anthropology, economics, education, management, political science, psychology, and sociology. Researchers in the social sciences examine the way human beings relate to themselves, to one another, and to their environment. Using the scientific method, they pose a question, formulate a hypothesis (a generalization that can be tested), collect and analyze data, and draw conclusions to support, refine, or disprove the hypothesis. The data may be numerical or more subjective, and they may come from firsthand observations, interviews, surveys, or controlled experiments. When writing, social scientists explain their research carefully and document their evidence so that readers can check the sources and replicate the research.

Writing assignments

Depending on the courses you take, you may be asked to write one or more of the following assignments:

- **Summary or review of research:** a report on the available research literature on a subject.
- **Case analysis:** an explanation of the components of a phenomenon, such as a factory closing.
- **Problem-solving analysis:** an explanation of the elements of a problem with suggestions for how to solve it.
- **Research paper:** an interpretation, analysis, or evaluation of the writings of experts on a subject.
- **Research report:** a description of your own original research or your attempt to replicate someone else's research.

Source documentation

The most widely used style guide in the social sciences is the *Publication Manual of the American Psychological Association*. See pages 200–15 for a description of this style. Other social science style guides are listed on page 156.

3d Natural and applied sciences

The natural and applied sciences include biology, chemistry, physics, mathematics, engineering, computer science, and their branches. Researchers in these fields strive to understand natural and technological phenomena and, often, to apply the knowledge to solving problems. Like social scientists, natural and applied scientists gather evidence using the scientific method, a process of continually testing and refining a hypothesis. Scientific evidence is almost always numerical data obtained from measurement in a controlled laboratory setting or in the natural world. In their writing, scientists, like social scientists, explain their research carefully and document their evidence so that readers can check the sources and replicate the research.

Writing assignments

Assignments in the natural and applied sciences include the following:

- **Summary:** a distillation of a research article in a brief, concise form.
- **Critique:** a summary and evaluation of a scientific report.
- **Lab report:** an explanation of the procedure and results of an experiment you conduct.
- **Research report:** a report on the research of other scientists and your own methods, findings, and conclusions.
- **Research proposal:** a report of relevant literature on a subject and a plan for further research.

Source documentation

The most widely used style guide in the natural and applied sciences is *Scientific Style and Format: The CSE Manual for Authors, Editors, and Publishers*. See pages 232–38 for a description of this style. Other science style guides are listed on page 156.

4 Designing Documents

Legible, consistent, and attractive papers serve your readers and reflect well on you. This chapter covers the basics of formatting any document clearly and effectively.

4a Formats for academic papers

Many academic disciplines prefer specific formats for students' papers. This book details three such formats:

- **MLA,** used in English, foreign languages, and some other humanities (pp. 196–99).
- **APA,** used in the social sciences and some natural sciences (pp. 215–19).
- **Chicago,** used in history, art history, religion, and some other humanities (pp. 229–31).

The design guidelines in this chapter extend the range of elements and options covered by most academic styles. Your instructors may want you to adhere strictly to a particular style or may allow some latitude in design. Ask them for their preferences.

4b Clear and effective documents

Your papers must of course be neat and legible. But you can do more to make your work accessible and attractive by taking care with margins, text, lists, and headings.

Margins

Provide minimum one-inch margins on all sides of a page to prevent unpleasant crowding. If your document will be presented in a binder, provide a larger left margin—say, $1^1/2$ inches.

Text

Line spacing

Double-space most academic documents, with an initial indention for paragraphs. Double- or triple-space to set off headings.

Type fonts and sizes

The readability of text derives partly from the type fonts (or faces) and their sizes. For academic documents,

Visit *mycomplab.com* for more help with document design.

choose a standard font and a type size of 10 or 12 points, as in the samples below.

10-point Times New Roman

12-point Times New Roman

Highlighting

Within a document's text, *italic,* **boldface,** underlined, or even color type can emphasize key words or sentences. Underlining is rarest these days, having been replaced by italics in most academic writing. Boldface can give strong emphasis—for instance, to a term being defined. Color can highlight headings and illustrations.

Lists

Lists visually reinforce the relations between like items—for example, the steps in a process or the elements of a proposal. A list is easier to read than a paragraph and adds white space to the page.

When wording a list, work for parallelism among items—for instance, all complete sentences or all phrases (see also p. 38). Set the list with space above and below and with numbering or bullets (centered dots or other devices, such as the small squares in the lists below and on the next page).

Headings

Headings are signposts. In a long or complex document, they direct the reader's attention by focusing the eye on a document's most significant content. Most academic documents use headings functionally, to divide text, orient readers, and create emphasis. Follow these guidelines:

- **Use one, two, or three levels of headings** depending on the needs of your material and the length of your document. Some level of heading every two or so pages will help keep readers on track.
- **Create an outline of your document** to plan where headings should go. Reserve the first level of heading for the main points (and sections) of your document. Use a second and perhaps a third level of heading to mark subsections of supporting information.
- **Keep headings as short as possible** while making them specific about the material that follows.
- **Word headings consistently**—for instance, all questions (*What Is the Scientific Method?*), all phrases with *-ing* words (*Understanding the Scientific Method*), or all phrases with nouns (*The Scientific Method*).

- **Indicate the relative importance of headings** with type size, positioning, and highlighting, such as capital letters, underlining, or boldface.

FIRST-LEVEL HEADING

Second-Level Heading

Third-Level Heading

- **Keep the appearance simple,** using the same type font and size for headings as for the text.
- **Don't break a page immediately after a heading.** Move the heading to the next page.

Note Document format in many social sciences requires a particular treatment of headings. See pages 216–17.

4c Illustrations

An illustration can often make a point more efficiently and effectively than words can. Tables present data. Figures (such as graphs or charts) usually recast data in visual form. Images (such as drawings and photographs) can explain processes, represent what something looks like, add emphasis, or convey a theme.

Follow these guidelines when using tables, figures, or images in academic writing:

- **Focus on a purpose for your illustration**—a reason for including it and a point you want it to make. Otherwise, readers may find it irrelevant or confusing.
- **Provide a source note for someone else's independent material,** whether it's data or a complete illustration (see pp. 152–53). Each discipline has a slightly different style for such source notes; those in the illustrations on the next two pages reflect MLA style for English and some other humanities.
- **Number and label figures, photographs, and images together:** Fig. 1, Fig. 2, and so on.
- **Number and label tables separately from figures:** Table 1, Table 2, and so on.
- **Refer to each illustration in your text**—for instance, "See fig. 2." Place the reference at the point(s) in the text where readers should consult the illustration.
- **Determine the placement of illustrations.** The social sciences and some other disciplines require each illustration to fall on a page by itself immediately after the text reference to it. You may want to follow this rule in other situations as well if you have a large number of illustrations. Otherwise, you can embed them in your text pages just after you refer to them.

Tables

Tables usually summarize raw data, displaying the data concisely and clearly to show how variables relate to one another, how variables change over time, or how two or more groups contrast.

- **Provide a self-explanatory title above the table.**
- **Provide self-explanatory headings for horizontal rows and vertical columns.** Use abbreviations only if you are certain readers will understand them.
- **Lay out rows and columns for maximum clarity.** In the sample below, for instance, lines divide the table into parts, headings align with their data, and numbers align vertically down columns.

Table 1

Public- and private-school enrollment of US students age five and older, 2008

	Number of students (in thousands)	Percentage in public school	Percentage in private school
All students	74,603	85	15
Kindergarten through grade 8	39,179	88	12
Grades 9-12	16,332	92	8
College	16,366	77	23
Graduate and professional school	2,737	50	50

Source: Data from *Digest of Education Statistics: 2009*; Natl. Center for Educ. Statistics, Apr. 2010; Web; 10 May 2010; table 2.

Figures

Figures represent data or show concepts graphically. They include charts, graphs, and diagrams.

Pie charts

Pie charts show the relations among the parts of a whole. The whole totals 100 percent, and each pie slice is proportional in size to its share of the whole. Use a pie chart to emphasize shares rather than underlying data.

- **Use color to mark segments of the chart.** Use distinct shades of gray, black, and white if your paper will not be read in color.
- **Clearly label every segment.**

- **Provide a self-explanatory caption below the chart.**

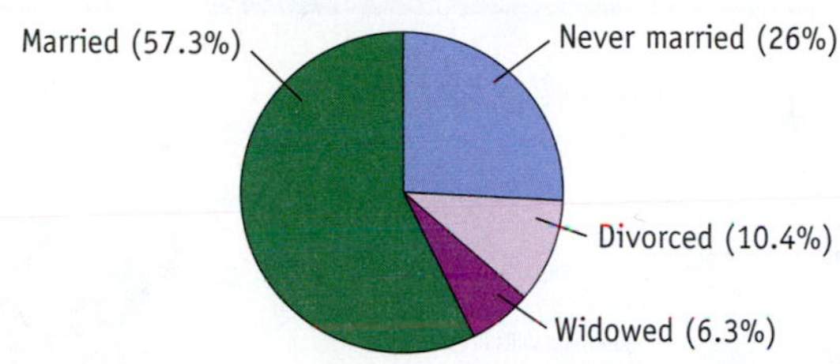

Fig. 1. Marital status in 2008 of adults age eighteen and over. Data from *2010 Statistical Abstract;* US Census Bureau, Jan. 2009; Web; 26 Feb. 2010.

Bar charts

Bar charts compare groups or time periods on a measure such as quantity or frequency.

- **Label the vertical scale and include a zero point** to clarify the values being measured.
- **Label the horizontal scale** to show the groups being compared.
- **Provide a self-explanatory caption below the chart.**

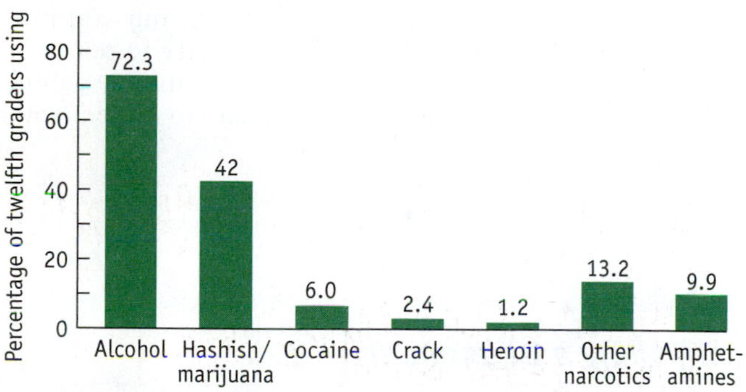

Fig. 2. Lifetime prevalence of use of alcohol, compared with other drugs, among twelfth graders in 2008. Data from *Monitoring the Future: A Continuing Study of American Youth*; U of Michigan, 14 Dec. 2009; Web; 16 Mar. 2010.

4d Web sites

When you create a Web site, be aware that readers generally alternate between skimming pages for highlights and focusing intently on sections of text.

4e

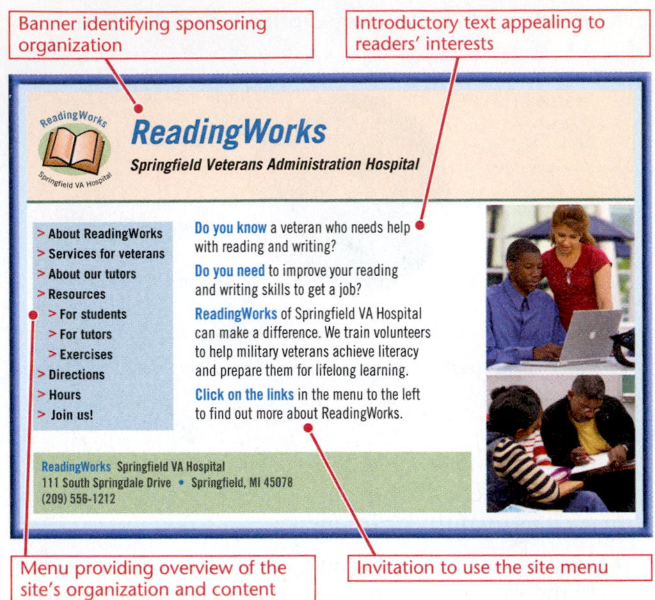

4e *PowerPoint* presentations

Many speakers use software such as *PowerPoint* to show summaries, images, or other aids during oral presentations. When using *PowerPoint,* don't try to put your entire presentation on screen. Instead, select the key points, words, and images that you want listeners to remember.

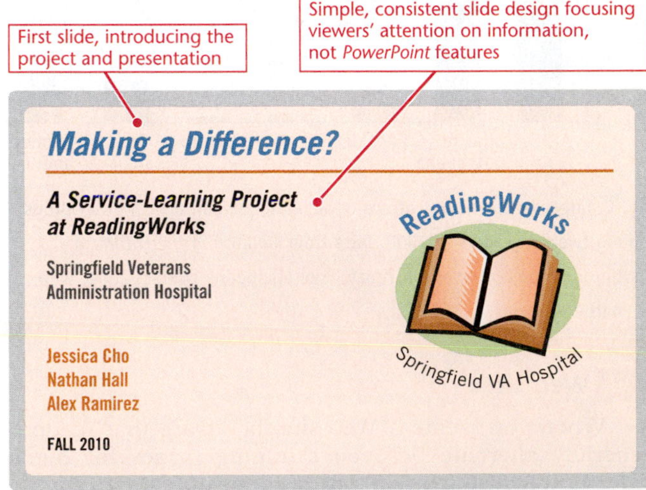

4f Readers with vision loss

Your audience may include readers who have low vision, problems with color perception, or difficulties processing visual information. If so, consider adapting your design to meet these readers' needs. Here are a few pointers:

- **Use large type fonts.** Most guidelines call for 14 points or larger.
- **Use standard type fonts.** Avoid decorative fonts with unusual flourishes, even in headings.
- **Avoid words in all-capital letters.**
- **Avoid relying on color alone to distinguish elements.** Label elements, and distinguish them by position or size.
- **Use contrasting colors.** To make colors distinct, choose them from opposite sides of the color spectrum—violet and yellow, for instance, or orange and blue.
- **Use red and green selectively.** To readers who are red-green colorblind, these colors will appear in shades of gray, yellow, or blue.
- **Use only light colors for tints behind type.** Make the type itself black or a very dark color.

PART 2

Effective Sentences

Checklist for effective sentences

Emphasis

- ☑ Make subjects and verbs of sentences focus on key actors and actions. (See opposite.)
- ☑ Stress main ideas by placing them first or last in a sentence. (See p. 32.)
- ☑ Link equally important ideas with coordination. (See p. 33.)
- ☑ De-emphasize less important ideas with subordination. (See p. 34.)

Conciseness

- ☑ Use the active voice to focus on key actors and actions. (See p. 35.)
- ☑ Cut empty words and unneeded repetition. (See pp. 35–36.)
- ☑ Avoid unneeded *there is* and *it is* constructions. (See p. 36.)
- ☑ Reduce word groups to their essence, and combine sentences where appropriate. (See pp. 36–37.)

Parallelism

- ☑ Use parallel constructions to show the equivalence of elements that are connected by *and, or, not only . . . but also,* and similar words. (See pp. 37–38.)

Variety and details

- ☑ Vary sentence lengths and structures to stress your main ideas and hold readers' attention. (See pp. 39–40.)
- ☑ Provide details that make your sentences clear and interesting. (See pp. 40–41.)

Appropriate words

- ☑ Use language appropriate for your writing situation. (See pp. 41–43.)
- ☑ Avoid sexist and other biased language. (See pp. 43–46.)

Exact words

- ☑ Choose words that are suited to your meaning and are concrete and specific. (See pp. 46–47.)
- ☑ Make words correct in idiom and also fresh, not clichéd. (See pp. 47–48.)

5 Emphasis

Emphatic writing leads readers to see your main ideas immediately, without having to puzzle out meanings or importance. Besides the following strategies for achieving emphasis, see also the discussions of conciseness (p. 34) and variety (p. 39).

5a Subjects and verbs

The heart of every sentence is its subject° and its verb.° The subject is the person or thing that acts, and the verb is what the subject does: *Children* [subject] *grow* [verb]. When these elements do not identify the key actor and action in the sentence, readers must find that information elsewhere and the sentence may be wordy and unemphatic. In the following sentences, the subjects and verbs are underlined:

Unemphatic — The intention of the company was to expand its workforce. A proposal was also made to diversify the backgrounds and abilities of employees.

These sentences are unemphatic because their key ideas do not appear in their subjects and verbs. Revised, the sentences are not only clearer but also more concise:

Revised — The company intended to expand its workforce. It also proposed to diversify the backgrounds and abilities of employees.

The unemphatic constructions shown below and on the next page usually drain meaning from the subject and verb of a sentence.

Nouns made from verbs

Nouns made from verbs can obscure the key actions of sentences and add words. These nouns include *intention* (from *intend*), *proposal* (from *propose*), *decision* (from *decide*), *expectation* (from *expect*), *persistence* (from *persist*), *argument* (from *argue*), and *inclusion* (from *include*).

Unemphatic — After the company made a decision to hire more workers with disabilities, its next step was the construction of wheelchair ramps and other facilities.

°See Glossary of Terms, page 249.

Revised	After the company decided to hire more workers with disabilities, it next constructed wheelchair ramps and other facilities.

Weak verbs

Weak verbs don't express much action. They include *made* and *was* in the second unemphatic example on the previous page. Such verbs tend to stall sentences just where they should be moving, and they often bury key actions:

Unemphatic	The company is now the leader among businesses in complying with the 1990 Americans with Disabilities Act. Its officers make speeches on the act to business groups.
Revised	The company now leads other businesses in complying with the 1990 Americans with Disabilities Act. Its officers speak on the act to business groups.

Passive voice

Verbs in the passive voice° state actions received by, not performed by, their subjects. Thus the passive de-emphasizes the true actor of the sentence, sometimes omitting it entirely. Generally, use the active voice,° in which the subject performs the verb's action. (See p. 59 for more on passive and active voice.)

Unemphatic	The 1990 law is seen by most businesses as fair, but the costs of complying have sometimes been objected to.
Revised	Most businesses see the 1990 law as fair, but some have objected to the costs of complying.

5b Sentence beginnings and endings

The beginning and ending of a sentence are the most emphatic positions, and the ending is usually more emphatic than the beginning. To emphasize information, place it first or last, reserving the middle for incidentals.

Unemphatic	Education remains the single best means of economic advancement, despite its shortcomings.
Revised	Education remains, despite its shortcomings, the single best means of economic advancement.

Generally, readers expect the beginning of a sentence to contain information that they already know or that you have already introduced. They then look to the ending for new information. In the unemphatic passage below, the

°See Glossary of Terms, page 249.

second and third sentences both begin with new topics (underlined), while the old topics from the first sentence (the controversy and education) appear at the end. The pattern of the passage is A→B. C→B. D→A.

Unemphatic Education often means controversy these days, with rising costs and constant complaints about its inadequacies. But the value of schooling should not be obscured by the controversy. The single best means of economic advancement, despite its shortcomings, remains education.

In the revision below, the underlined old information begins each sentence and new information ends the sentence. The passage follows the pattern A→B. B→C. A→D.

Revised Education often means controversy these days, with rising costs and constant complaints about its inadequacies. But the controversy should not obscure the value of schooling. Education remains, despite its shortcomings, the single best means of economic advancement.

5c

5c Coordination

Use **coordination** to show that two or more elements in a sentence are equally important in meaning:

- **Link two complete sentences (main clauses°) with a comma and a coordinating conjunction:°** *and, but, or, nor, for, so, yet.*

  Independence Hall in Philadelphia is now restored, but fifty years ago it was in bad shape.

- **Link two main clauses with a semicolon alone or a semicolon and a conjunctive adverb°** such as *however, indeed,* and *therefore.*

  The building was standing; however, it suffered from decay and vandalism.

- **Within clauses, link words and word groups with a coordinating conjunction** such as *and, but, or,* and *nor.*

  The people and officials of the nation were indifferent to Independence Hall or took it for granted.

- **Link main clauses, words, or phrases° with a correlative conjunction°** such as *not only . . . but also* and *either . . . or.*

  People not only took the building for granted but also neglected it.

°See Glossary of Terms, page 249.

Notes A string of main clauses connected by *and* implies that all ideas are equally important and creates a dull, plodding rhythm. Use subordination (see below) to revise such excessive coordination. See also page 39.

Two punctuation errors, the comma splice and the fused sentence, can occur when you link main clauses. See pages 79–81.

5d Subordination

Use **subordination** to indicate that some elements in a sentence are less important than others for your meaning. Usually, the main idea appears in the main clause° and supporting information appears in subordinate structures:

- **Use a subordinate clause° beginning with a subordinating word** such as *although, because, before, if, since, that, when, where, which,* and *who* (*whom*).

  Although production costs have declined, they are still high. [Stresses that costs are still high.]

  Costs, which include labor and facilities, are difficult to control. [Stresses that costs are difficult to control.]

- **Use a phrase.°**

  Despite some decline, production costs are still high.
  Costs, including labor and facilities, are difficult to control.

- **Use a single word.**

  Declining costs have not matched prices.
  Labor costs are difficult to control.

Generally, subordinate clauses give the most emphasis to secondary information, phrases give less, and single words give the least.

Note A subordinate clause or a phrase is not a complete sentence and should not be set off and punctuated as one. See pages 77–79 on sentence fragments.

6 Conciseness

Concise writing makes every word count. Conciseness is not the same as brevity: detail and originality should not

°See Glossary of Terms, page 249.

be cut along with needless words. Rather, the length of an expression should be appropriate to the thought.

6a Focusing on the subject and verb

Using the subjects° and verbs° of your sentences for the key actors and actions will tighten sentences. See page 31 under emphasis for help identifying the subject and verb and for a discussion of these ways of stressing them:

- **Avoid nouns made from verbs,** such as *intention* (from *intend*) and *decision* (from *decide*).
- **Strengthen weak verbs,** such as *is* and *make*.
- **Rewrite the passive voice as active**—for instance, changing *The star was seen by astronomers* to *Astronomers saw the star*.

6b Cutting empty words

Cutting words that contribute nothing to your meaning will make your writing move faster and work harder.

Wordy — In my opinion, the council's proposal to improve the city center is inadequate, all things considered.

Concise — The council's proposal to improve the city center is inadequate.

The underlining in the wordy example above highlights these kinds of empty words:

- **Phrases that add nothing to meaning:**

all things considered
a person by the name of
as far as I'm concerned
for all intents and purposes
in a manner of speaking
in my opinion
last but not least
more or less

- **Abstract or general words that pad sentences (and usually require additional words such as *of* and *the*):**

area, aspect, case, element, factor, field, kind, manner, nature, situation, thing, type

- **Word groups that mean the same thing as single words:**

For	Substitute
at all times	always
at the present time	now
at this point in time	now
for the purpose of	for
due to the fact that	because
because of the fact that	because
in the final analysis	finally

°See Glossary of Terms, page 249.

6c Cutting unneeded repetition

Repeating or restating key words from sentence to sentence can link the sentences and emphasize information the reader already knows (see p. 32). But unnecessary repetition weakens sentences and paragraphs.

Wordy — Many unskilled workers without training in a particular job are unemployed and do not have any work.

Concise — Many unskilled workers are unemployed.

Be especially alert to phrases that say the same thing twice. In the following examples, only the underlined words are needed:

circle around
consensus of opinion
continue on
cooperate together
few in number
final completion
the future to come
important essentials
repeat again
return again
square [round] in shape
surrounding circumstances

6d Reducing clauses and phrases

Modifiers° can be expanded or contracted depending on the emphasis you want to achieve. (Generally, the longer a construction, the more emphasis it has.) When editing your sentences, consider whether any modifiers can be reduced without loss of emphasis or clarity.

Wordy — The weight-loss industry faces new competition from lipolysis, which is a cosmetic procedure that is noninvasive.

Concise — The weight-loss industry faces new competition from lipolysis, a noninvasive cosmetic procedure.

6e Revising *there is* or *it is*

Sentences beginning *there is* or *it is* (called expletive constructions°) are sometimes useful to emphasize a change in direction, but usually they just add needless words.

Wordy — There is a noninvasive laser treatment that makes people thinner by rupturing fat cells and releasing the fat into the spaces between cells. It is the expectation of some doctors that the procedure will replace liposuction.

Concise — A noninvasive laser treatment makes people thinner by rupturing fat cells and releasing the fat into the spaces between cells. Some doctors expect that the procedure will replace liposuction.

°See Glossary of Terms, page 249.

6f Combining sentences

Often the information in two or more sentences can be combined into one tight sentence.

Wordy — People who receive fat-releasing laser treatments can lose inches from their waists. They can also lose inches from their hips and thighs. They do not lose weight. The released fat remains in their bodies.

Concise — People who receive fat-releasing laser treatments can lose inches from their waists, hips, and thighs; but they do not lose weight because the released fat remains in their bodies.

7 Parallelism

Parallelism matches the form of your sentence to its meaning: when your ideas are equally important, or parallel, you express them in similar, or parallel, grammatical form.

The air is dirtied by factories belching smoke and vehicles spewing exhaust.

Parallelism can work like glue to link the parts of a sentence and also the sentences of a paragraph:

Pulleys are ancient machines for transferring power. Unfortunately, they are also inefficient machines.

7a Parallelism with *and, but, or, nor, yet*

The coordinating conjunctions° *and, but, or, nor,* and *yet* signal a need for parallelism.

The industrial base was shifting and shrinking.

Politicians seldom acknowledged the problem or proposed alternatives.

Industrial workers were understandably disturbed that they were losing their jobs and that no one seemed to care.

Nonparallel — The reasons that steel companies kept losing money were that their plants were inefficient, high labor costs, and foreign competition was increasing.

Revised — The reasons that steel companies kept losing money were inefficient plants, high labor costs, and increasing foreign competition.

°See Glossary of Terms, page 249.

mycomplab

Visit *mycomplab.com* for more help with parallelism.

Notes Parallel elements match in structure, but they need not match word for word. In the preceding example, each element consists of at least one modifier° and a noun,° but two of the elements also include an additional modifier.

Be careful not to omit needed words in parallel structures.

Nonparallel Given training, workers can acquire the skills and interest in other jobs. [Idiom dictates different prepositions with *skills* and *interest.*]

Revised Given training, workers can acquire the skills for and interest in other jobs.

7b Parallelism with *both . . . and, either . . . or,* and so on

Correlative conjunctions° stress equality and balance between elements. The correlative conjunctions include *both . . . and, either . . . or, neither . . . nor, not only . . . but also,* and *whether . . . or.* Parallelism confirms the equality between elements: the words after the first and second connectors must match.

Nonparallel Huck Finn learns not only that human beings have an enormous capacity for folly but also enormous dignity. [The first element includes *that human beings have;* the second element does not.]

Revised Huck Finn learns that human beings have not only an enormous capacity for folly but also enormous dignity. [Repositioning *not only* makes the two elements parallel.]

7c Parallelism with lists, headings, and outlines

The items in a list or outline should be parallel. Parallelism is essential in the headings that divide a paper into sections (see pp. 22–23).

Nonparallel	Revised
Changes in Renaissance England	Changes in Renaissance England
1. Extension of trade routes	1. Extension of trade routes
2. Merchant class became more powerful	2. Increased power of the merchant class
3. The death of feudalism	3. Death of feudalism
4. Upsurging of the arts	4. Upsurge of the arts
5. Religious quarrels began	5. Rise of religious quarrels

°See Glossary of Terms, page 249.

8 Variety and Details

To make your writing interesting as well as clear, use varied sentences that are well textured with details.

8a Varied sentence lengths and structures

In most contemporary writing, sentences tend to vary from about ten to about forty words, with an average of fifteen to twenty-five words. If your sentences are all at one extreme or the other, your readers may have difficulty locating main ideas and seeing the relations among them.

- **Long sentences.** Break a sequence of long sentences into shorter, simpler ones that stress key ideas.
- **Short sentences.** Combine a sequence of short sentences with coordination (p. 33) and subordination (p. 34) to show relationships and stress main ideas.

A good way to focus and hold readers' attention is to vary the structure of sentences so that they do not all follow the same pattern.

Varied sentence structures

A long sequence of main clauses° can make all ideas seem equally important and create a plodding rhythm, as in the unvaried passage below. You want to emphasize your key subjects and verbs, moving in each sentence from old information to new (see pp. 32–33). Subordinating less important information (bracketed in the revised passage) can help you achieve this emphasis.

Unvaried

The moon is now drifting away from the earth. It moves away about one inch a year. This movement is lengthening our days, and they increase about a thousandth of a second every century. Forty-seven of our present days will someday make up a month. We might eventually lose the moon altogether. Such great planetary movement rightly concerns astronomers, but it need not worry us. It will take 50 million years.

Revised

The moon is now drifting away from the earth [about one inch a year.] [At a thousandth of a second every century,] this movement is lengthening our days. Forty-seven of our present days will someday make up a month, [if we don't

°See Glossary of Terms, page 249.

eventually lose the moon altogether.] Such great planetary movement rightly concerns astronomers, but it need not worry us. It will take 50 million years.

Varied sentence beginnings

An English sentence often begins with its subject, which generally captures old information from a preceding sentence (see pp. 32–33):

8b

The defendant's lawyer was determined to break the prosecution's witness. He relentlessly cross-examined the stubborn witness for a week.

However, an unbroken sequence of sentences beginning with the subject quickly becomes monotonous:

Monotonous

The defendant's lawyer was determined to break the prosecution's witness. He relentlessly cross-examined the witness for a week. The witness had expected to be dismissed in an hour and was visibly irritated. She did not cooperate. She was reprimanded by the judge.

Revised

The defendant's lawyer was determined to break the prosecution's witness. For a week he relentlessly cross-examined the witness. Expecting to be dismissed in an hour, the witness was visibly irritated. She did not cooperate. Indeed, she was reprimanded by the judge.

The underlined expressions represent the most common choices for varying sentence beginnings:

- **Adverb modifiers,** such as *For a week* (modifies the verb *cross-examined*).
- **Adjective modifiers,** such as *Expecting to be dismissed in an hour* (modifies *witness*).
- **Transitional expressions,** such as *Indeed*. (See *transitional expression*, p. 259, for a list.)

Varied word order

Occasionally, to achieve special emphasis, reverse the usual word order of a sentence.

A dozen witnesses testified, and the defense attorney barely questioned eleven of them. The twelfth, however, he grilled. [Compare normal word order: *He grilled the twelfth, however.*]

8b Details

Relevant details such as facts and examples create the texture and life that keep readers alert and help them grasp your meaning. For instance:

Flat

Constructed after World War II, Levittown, New York, comprised thousands of houses in two basic styles. Over the decades, residents have altered the houses so dramatically that the original styles are often unrecognizable.

Detailed

Constructed on potato fields after World War II, Levittown, New York, comprised more than 17,000 houses in Cape Cod and ranch styles. Over the decades, residents have added expansive columned porches, punched dormer windows through roofs, converted garages to sun porches, and otherwise altered the houses so dramatically that the original styles are often unrecognizable.

9 Appropriate Words

Appropriate language suits your writing situation—your subject, purpose, and audience. In most college and career writing you should rely on what's called **standard American English,** the dialect of English normally expected and used in school, business, the professions, government, and the communications media. (For more on its role in academic writing, see pp. 8–9.)

The vocabulary of standard American English is huge, allowing expression of an infinite range of ideas and feelings; but it does exclude words that only some groups of people use, understand, or find inoffensive. It also excludes words and expressions that are commonly spoken but are too imprecise for exact writing. Whenever you doubt a word's status, consult a dictionary. A label such as *nonstandard, slang*, or *colloquial* tells you that the word is not generally appropriate in academic or business writing.

9a Nonstandard dialect

Like many countries, the United States includes scores of regional, social, and ethnic groups with their own distinct **dialects,** or versions of English. Standard American English is one of those dialects, and so are African American English, Appalachian English, and Creole. All the dialects of English share many features, but each also has its own vocabulary, pronunciation, and grammar.

If you speak a dialect of English besides standard American English, be careful about using your dialect in situations where standard English is the norm, such as in academic or business writing. Dialects are not wrong in themselves, but forms imported from one dialect into another may still be perceived as unclear or incorrect. When you know standard English is expected in your writing, edit to eliminate expressions in your dialect that differ from standard English. These expressions may include *theirselves, hisn, them books,* and others labeled "nonstandard" by a dictionary. They may also include certain verb forms, as discussed on pages 51–52.

Your participation in the community of standard American English does not require you to abandon your own dialect. You may want to use it in writing you do for yourself, such as journals, notes, and drafts, which should be composed as freely as possible. You may want to quote it in an academic paper, as when analyzing or reporting conversation in dialect. And, of course, you will want to use it with others who speak it.

9b Slang

Slang is the insider language used by a group, such as musicians or football players, to reflect common experiences and to make technical references efficient. The following example is from an essay on the slang of "skaters" (skateboarders):

> Curtis slashed ultra-punk crunchers on his longboard, while the Rube-man flailed his usual Gumbyness on tweaked frontsides and lofty fakie ollies.
>
> —Miles Orkin, "Mucho Slingage by the Pool"

Though valuable within a group, slang is often too private or imprecise for academic or business writing.

9c Colloquial language

Colloquial language is the everyday spoken language, including expressions such as *go crazy, get along with, a lot, kids* (for *children*), and *stuff* (for possessions or other objects). Colloquial language suits informal writing, and an occasional colloquial word can help you achieve a desired emphasis in otherwise formal writing. But most colloquial language is not precise enough for academic or business writing.

9d Technical words

All disciplines and professions rely on specialized language that allows members to communicate precisely and efficiently with each other. Chemists, for instance, have their *phosphatides,* and literary critics have their *subtexts.* Use the terms of a discipline or profession when you are writing within it. However, when you are writing for a nonspecialist audience, avoid unnecessary technical terms and carefully define the terms you must use.

9e Indirect and pretentious writing

Small, plain, and direct words are usually preferable to big, showy, or evasive words. Take special care to avoid the following:

- **Euphemisms** are presumably inoffensive words that substitute for words deemed potentially offensive or too blunt, such as *passed away* for *died* or *misspeak* for *lie.* Use euphemisms only when you know that blunt, truthful words would needlessly hurt or offend members of your audience.
- **Double talk** (at times called **doublespeak** or **weasel words**) is language intended to confuse or to be misunderstood: the *revenue enhancement* that is really a tax, the *biodegradable* bags that still last decades. Double talk has no place in honest writing.
- **Pretentious writing** is fancy language that is more elaborate than its subject requires. Choose your words for their exactness and economy. The big, ornate word may be tempting, but pass it up. Your readers will be grateful.

Pretentious	To perpetuate our endeavor of providing funds for our elderly citizens as we do at the present moment, we will face the exigency of enhanced contributions from all our citizens.
Revised	We cannot continue to fund Social Security and Medicare for the elderly unless we raise taxes.

9f Sexist and other biased language

Even when we do not mean it to, our language can reflect and perpetuate hurtful prejudices toward groups of people. Such biased language can be obvious—words such as *nigger, honky, mick, kike, fag, dyke,* and *broad.* But it can also be subtle, generalizing about groups in ways that may be familiar but that are also inaccurate or unfair.

Biased language reflects poorly on the user, not on the person or persons whom it mischaracterizes or insults. Unbiased language does not submit to false generalizations. It treats people respectfully as individuals and labels groups as they wish to be labeled.

9f

Stereotypes of race, ethnicity, and other characteristics

A **stereotype** characterizes and judges people simply on the basis of their membership in a group: *Men are uncommunicative. Women are emotional. Liberals want to raise taxes. Conservatives are affluent.*

In your writing, avoid statements about the traits of whole groups that may be true of only some members. Be especially cautious about substituting such statements for the evidence you should be providing instead.

Stereotype: Elderly drivers should have their licenses limited to daytime driving only. [Asserts that all elderly people are poor night drivers.]

Revised: Drivers with impaired night vision should have their licenses limited to daytime driving only.

Some stereotypes have become part of the language, but they are still potentially offensive.

Stereotype: The administrators are too blind to see the need for a new gymnasium.

Revised: The administrators do not understand the need for a new gymnasium.

Sexist language

Sexist language distinguishes needlessly between men and women in matters such as occupation, ability, behavior, temperament, and maturity. It can wound or irritate readers and indicates the writer's thoughtlessness or unfairness. The following guidelines can help you eliminate sexist language from your writing.

- **Avoid demeaning and patronizing language**—for instance, identifying women and men differently or trivializing either gender.

Sexist: Dr. Keith Kim and Lydia Hawkins collaborated.

Revised: Dr. Keith Kim and Dr. Lydia Hawkins collaborated.

Revised: Keith Kim and Lydia Hawkins coauthored the article.

Sexist: Ladies are entering almost every occupation formerly filled by men.

Revised: Women are entering almost every occupation formerly filled by men.

- **Avoid occupational or social stereotypes that assume a role or profession is exclusively male or female.**

Sexist: A doctor should commend a nurse when she provides his patients with good care.

Revised A doctor should commend a nurse who provides good care for patients.

- **Avoid using *man* or words containing *man* to refer to all human beings.** Some alternatives:

businessman	businessperson
chairman	chair, chairperson
congressman	representative in Congress, legislator
craftsman	craftsperson, artisan
layman	layperson
mankind	humankind, humanity, human beings, people
manpower	personnel, human resources
policeman	police officer
salesman	salesperson

Sexist Man has not reached the limits of social justice.

Revised Humankind [or Humanity] has not reached the limits of social justice.

Sexist The furniture consists of manmade materials.

Revised The furniture consists of synthetic materials.

- **Avoid using *he* to refer to both genders.** (See also p. 67.)

Sexist The newborn child explores his world.

Revised Newborn children explore their world. [Use the plural for the pronoun and the word it refers to.]

Revised The newborn child explores the world. [Avoid the pronoun altogether.]

Revised The newborn child explores his or her world. [Substitute male and female pronouns.]

Use the last option sparingly—only once in a group of sentences and only to stress the singular individual.

Inappropriate labels

Labels for groups of people can be shorthand stereotypes and can be discourteous when they ignore readers' preferences. Although sometimes dismissed as "political correctness," sensitivity in applying labels hurts no one and helps gain your readers' trust and respect.

- **Avoid labels that (intentionally or not) insult the person or group you refer to.** A person with emotional problems is not a *mental patient.* A person using a wheelchair is not *wheelchair-bound.*
- **Use names for racial, ethnic, and other groups that reflect the preferences of each group's members,** or at least many of them. Examples of current preferences include *African American* or *black, latino/latina* (for Americans of Spanish-speaking descent), and *people*

with disabilities (rather than *the disabled* or *the handicapped*). But labels change often. To learn how a group's members wish to be labeled, ask them directly, attend to usage in reputable periodicals, or check a recent dictionary.

- **Identify a person's group only when it is relevant to the point you're making.** Consider the context of the label: Is it a necessary piece of information? If not, don't use it.

10 Exact Words

To write clearly and effectively, you will want to find the words that fit your meaning exactly and convey your attitude precisely.

10a The right word for your meaning

One key to helping readers understand you is to use words according to their established meanings.

- **Consult a dictionary whenever you are unsure of a word's meaning.**
- **Distinguish between similar-sounding words that have widely different meanings.**

  Inexact Older people often suffer infirmaries [places for the sick].

  Exact Older people often suffer infirmities [disabilities].

  Some words, called **homonyms,** sound exactly alike but differ in meaning: for example, *principal/principle* or *rain/reign/rein.* (Many homonyms and near-homonyms are listed in the Glossary of Usage, p. 239.)
- **Distinguish between words with related but distinct meanings.**

  Inexact Television commercials continuously [unceasingly] interrupt programming.

  Exact Television commercials continually [regularly] interrupt programming.
- **Distinguish between words that have similar basic meanings but different emotional associations, or *connotations*.**

  It is a daring plan. [The plan is bold and courageous.]
  It is a reckless plan. [The plan is thoughtless and risky.]

mycomplab

Visit *mycomplab.com* for more help with exact words.

Many dictionaries list and distinguish such **synonyms,** words with approximately, but often not exactly, the same meanings.

10b Concrete and specific words

Clear, exact writing balances abstract and general words, which outline ideas and objects, with concrete and specific words, which sharpen and solidify.

- **Abstract words** name qualities and ideas: *beautiful, management, culture, freedom, awesome.* **Concrete words** name things we can know by our five senses of sight, hearing, touch, taste, and smell: *sleek, humming, rough, bitter, musty.*
- **General words** name classes or groups of things, such as *buildings, weather,* or *birds,* and they include all the varieties of the class. **Specific words** limit a general class, such as *buildings,* by naming one of its varieties, such as *skyscraper, Victorian courthouse, ranch house,* or *hut.*

Abstract and general statements need development with concrete and specific details. For example:

Vague The size of his hands made his smallness real. [How big were his hands? How small was he?]

Exact Not until I saw his delicate, doll-like hands did I realize that he stood a full head shorter than most other men.

10c Idioms

Idioms are expressions in any language that do not fit the rules for meaning or grammar—for instance, *put up with, plug away at, make off with.*

Because they are not governed by rules, idioms usually cause particular difficulty for people learning to speak and write a new language. But even native speakers of English can confuse idioms involving prepositions,° such as *agree on a plan, agree to a proposal,* and *agree with a person* or *occupied by a person, occupied in study,* and *occupied with a thing.*

When in doubt about an idiom, consult your dictionary under the main word (*agree* and *occupy* in the examples). (See also p. 55 on verbs with particles.)

10d Clichés

Clichés, or **trite expressions,** are phrases so old and so often repeated that they have become stale. Examples include *better late than never, beyond the shadow of a*

°See Glossary of Terms, page 249.

doubt, face the music, green with envy, ladder of success, point with pride, sneaking suspicion, and *wise as an owl.*

Clichés may slide into your drafts. In editing, be wary of any expression you have heard or used before. Substitute fresh words of your own, or restate the idea in plain language.

PART 3

Grammatical Sentences

VERBS

PRONOUNS

MODIFIERS

SENTENCE FAULTS

Checklist for grammatical sentences

This checklist focuses on the most common grammatical errors and the ones that most often confuse or distract readers. See the contents inside the back cover for a more detailed guide to this part.

Verbs

- ☑ Use the correct forms of irregular verbs such as *has broken* [not *has broke*]. (See opposite.)
- ☑ Use helping verbs where required, as in *she has been* [not *she been*]. (See opposite.)
- ☑ Match verbs to their subjects, as in *The list of items is* [not *are*] *long*. (See p. 60.)

Pronouns

- ☑ Match pronouns to the words they refer to, as in *Each of the women had her* [not *their*] *say*. (See p. 66.)
- ☑ Make pronouns refer clearly to the words they substitute for, avoiding uncertainties such as *Jill thanked Tracy when she* [Jill or Tracy?] *arrived*. (See p. 68.)
- ☑ Use pronouns consistently, avoiding shifts such as *When one enters college, you encounter new ideas*. (See pp. 69–70.)

Modifiers

- ☑ Place modifiers close to the words they describe, as in *Trash cans without lids invite animals* [not *Trash cans invite animals without lids*]. (See p. 74.)
- ☑ Make each modifier clearly modify another word in the sentence, as in *Jogging, she pulled a muscle* [not *Jogging, a muscle was pulled*]. (See p. 76.)

Sentence faults

- ☑ Make every sentence complete, with its own subject and verb, and be sure none is a freestanding subordinate clause—for instance, *But first she called the police.* [Not *But first called the police.*] *New stores open weekly.* [Not *New stores weekly.*] *The new cow calved after the others did.* [Not *The new cow calved. After the others did.*]. (See p. 77.)
- ☑ Within sentences, link main clauses with a comma and a coordinating conjunction (*Cars jam the roadways, and they contribute to smog*), with a semicolon (*Many parents did not attend; they did not want to get involved*), or with a semicolon and a conjunctive adverb (*The snow fell heavily; however, it soon melted*). (See p. 79.)

VERBS

11 Verb Forms

Verb forms may give you trouble when the verb is irregular, when you omit certain endings, or when you need to use helping verbs.

11a *Sing/sang/sung* and other irregular verbs

Most verbs are **regular:** their past-tense form° and past participle° end in *-d* or *-ed*:

> Today the birds migrate. [Plain form° of verb.]
> Yesterday the birds migrated. [Past-tense form.]
> In the past the birds have migrated. [Past participle.]

About two hundred **irregular verbs** in English create their past-tense form and past participle in some way other than adding *-d* or *-ed.*

> Today the birds fly. They begin migration. [Plain form.]
>
> Yesterday the birds flew. They began migration. [Past-tense form.]
>
> In the past the birds have flown. They have begun migration. [Past participle.]

You can find a verb's forms by looking up the plain form in a dictionary. For a regular verb, the dictionary will give the *-d* or *-ed* form. For an irregular verb, the dictionary will give the past-tense form and then the past participle. If the dictionary gives only one irregular form after the plain form, then the past-tense form and past participle are the same (*think, thought, thought*).

11b Helping verbs

Helping verbs combine with some verb forms to indicate time and other kinds of meaning, as in *can run, might suppose, will open, was sleeping, had been eaten.* The main verb° in these phrases is the one that carries the main meaning (*run, suppose, open, sleeping, eaten*).

Required helping verbs

Standard American English requires helping verbs in the situations listed on the next page.

°See Glossary of Terms, page 249.

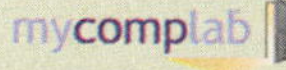

Visit *mycomplab.com* for more help with verb forms.

- **The main verb ends in *-ing*:**

  Archaeologists are conducting fieldwork all over the world. [Not *Archaeologists conducting. . . .*]

- **The main verb is *been* or *be*:**

  Many have been fortunate in their discoveries. [Not *Many been. . . .*]

  Some could be real-life Indiana Joneses. [Not *Some be. . . .*]

- **The main verb is a past participle,°** such as *given, talked, begun,* or *thrown*:

  The researchers have given interviews on radio and TV. [Not *The researchers given. . . .*]

In these examples, omitting the helping verb would create an incomplete sentence, or **sentence fragment** (p. 77).

Combinations of helping and main verbs ESL

Helping verbs and main verbs combine in specific ways.

Note The main verb in a verb phrase (the one carrying the main meaning) does not change to show a change in subject or time: *she has sung, you had sung.* Only the helping verb may change, as in these examples.

Form of *be* + present participle

Create the progressive tenses° with *be, am, is, are, was, were,* or *been* followed by the main verb's present participle° (ending in *-ing*).

Faulty She is work on a new book.
Revised She is working on a new book.

Faulty She has been work on it several months.
Revised She has been working on it several months.

Note Verbs that express mental states or activities rather than physical actions do not usually appear in the progressive tenses. These verbs include *adore, appear, believe, belong, have, hear, know, like, love, need, see, taste, think, understand,* and *want.*

Faulty She is wanting to understand contemporary ethics.
Revised She wants to understand contemporary ethics.

Form of *be* + past participle

Create the passive voice° with *be, am, is, are, was, were, being,* or *been* followed by the main verb's past participle° (usually ending in *-d* or *-ed* or, for irregular verbs, in *-t* or *-n*).

°See Glossary of Terms, page 249.

Faulty Her last book was complete in four months.
Revised Her last book was completed in four months.

Faulty It was bring to the President's attention.
Revised It was brought to the President's attention.

Note Only transitive verbs° may form the passive voice.

Faulty A philosophy conference was occurred that week. [*Occur* is not a transitive verb.]
Revised A philosophy conference occurred that week.

Form of *have* + past participle

To create one of the perfect tenses,° use the main verb's past participle preceded by a form of *have,* such as *has, had, have been,* or *will have had.*

Faulty Some students have complain about the lab.
Revised Some students have complained about the lab.

Faulty Money has not been spend on the lab in years.
Revised Money has not been spent on the lab in years.

Form of *do* + plain form

Always with the plain form° of the main verb, three forms of *do* serve as helping verbs: *do, does, did.*

Faulty Safety concerns do exists.
Revised Safety concerns do exist.

Faulty Didn't the lab closed briefly last year?
Revised Didn't the lab close briefly last year?

Modal + plain form

Most **modal** helping verbs combine with the plain form of the main verb to convey ability, possibility, necessity, and other meanings. The modals include *be able to, be supposed to, can, could, had better, have to, may, might, must, ought to, shall, should, used to, will,* and *would.*

Faulty The lab equipment may causes injury.
Revised The lab equipment may cause injury.

Faulty The school ought to replaced it.
Revised The school ought to replace it.

Note When a modal combines with another helping verb, the main verb generally changes from the plain form to a past participle:

Faulty The equipment could have fail.
Revised The equipment could have failed.

°See Glossary of Terms, page 249.

11b

11c Verb + gerund or infinitive ESL

A **gerund** is the *-ing* form of a verb used as a noun (*Smoking kills*). An **infinitive** is the plain form° of the verb plus *to* (*Try to quit*). Gerunds and infinitives may follow certain verbs but not others. And sometimes the use of a gerund or infinitive with the same verb changes the meaning of the verb.

Either gerund or infinitive

A gerund or an infinitive may follow certain verbs with no significant difference in meaning: *begin, can't bear, can't stand, continue, hate, hesitate, like, love, prefer, start.*

The pump began working. The pump began to work.

Meaning change with gerund or infinitive

A gerund and an infinitive have quite different meanings when they follow four verbs: *forget, remember, stop,* and *try*.

The engineer stopped watching the pump. [She no longer watched.]

The engineer stopped to watch the pump. [She stopped in order to watch.]

Gerund, not infinitive

Do not use an infinitive after these verbs: *admit, adore, appreciate, avoid, consider, deny, detest, discuss, dislike, enjoy, escape, finish, imagine, keep, mind, miss, practice, put off, quit, recall, resent, resist, risk, suggest, tolerate, understand.*

Faulty She suggested to check the pump.
Revised She suggested checking the pump.

Infinitive, not gerund

Do not use a gerund after these verbs: *agree, ask, assent, beg, claim, decide, expect, have, hope, manage, mean, offer, plan, pretend, promise, refuse, say, wait, want, wish.*

Faulty She decided checking the pump.
Revised She decided to check the pump.

Noun or pronoun + infinitive

Some verbs may be followed by an infinitive alone or by a noun° or pronoun° and an infinitive: *ask, beg, choose, dare, expect, help, need, promise, want, wish, would like.* A noun or pronoun changes the meaning.

°See Glossary of Terms, page 249.

She expected to watch.
She expected her workers to watch.

Some verbs *must* be followed by a noun or pronoun before an infinitive: *advise, allow, cause, challenge, command, convince, encourage, forbid, force, hire, instruct, order, permit, persuade, remind, require, teach, tell, warn.*

She instructed her workers to watch.

Do not use *to* before the infinitive when it comes after one of the following verbs and a noun or pronoun: *feel, have, hear, let, make* ("force"), *see, watch.*

She let her workers learn by observation.

11d Verb + particle ESL

Some verbs consist of two words: the verb itself and a **particle**, a preposition° or adverb° that affects the meaning of the verb, as in *Look up the answer* (research the answer) or *Look over the answer* (check the answer). Many of these two-word verbs, also called idioms, are defined in dictionaries. (For more on idioms, see p. 47.)

Some two-word verbs may be separated in a sentence; others may not.

Inseparable two-word verbs

Verbs and particles that may not be separated by any other words include the following: *catch on, get along, give in, go out, grow up, keep on, look into, run into, run out of, speak up, stay away, take care of.*

Faulty Children grow quickly up.
Revised Children grow up quickly.

Separable two-word verbs

Most two-word verbs that take direct objects° may be separated by the object.

Parents help out their children.
Parents help their children out.

If the direct object is a pronoun,° the pronoun *must* separate the verb from the particle.

Faulty Parents help out them.
Revised Parents help them out.

The separable two-word verbs include the following: *call off, call up, fill out, fill up, give away, give back, hand in, help out, look over, look up, pick up, point out, put away, put back, put off, take out, take over, try on, try out, turn down.*

°See Glossary of Terms, page 249.

12 Verb Tenses

The **tense** of a verb expresses the time its action occurred. Definitions and examples of the verb tenses appear on pages 258–59. The following are the most common trouble spots.

12c

12a Uses of the present tense (*sing*)

The present tense has several distinctive uses:

Action occurring now

We define the problem differently.

Habitual or recurring action

Banks regularly undergo audits.

A general truth

The earth is round.

Discussion of literature, film, and so on

Huckleberry Finn has adventures we all envy.

Future time

Funding ends in less than a year.

12b Uses of the perfect tenses (*have/had/will have sung*)

The perfect tenses° generally indicate an action completed before another specific time or action. The present perfect tense° also indicates action begun in the past and continued into the present.

The dancer has performed (present perfect) here only once.

The dancer had trained (past perfect) in Asia before his performance here ten years ago.

He will have danced (future perfect) here again by the end of the year.

12c Consistency in tense

Within a sentence, the tenses of verbs and verb forms need not be identical as long as they reflect actual changes in time: *Ramon will graduate from college twenty years after his father arrived in America.* In speech we often shift tenses even when they don't reflect changes in

mycomplab

Visit *mycomplab.com* for more help with verb tenses.

°See Glossary of Terms, page 249.

time. But in writing such needless shifts in tense will confuse or distract readers.

Inconsistent Immediately after Booth shot Lincoln, Major Rathbone threw himself upon the assassin. But Booth pulls a knife and plunges it into the major's arm.

Revised Immediately after Booth shot Lincoln, Major Rathbone threw himself upon the assassin. But Booth pulled a knife and plunged it into the major's arm.

12d Sequence of tenses

When the tenses in a sentence are in **sequence**, the verbs in the main clause° and the subordinate clause° relate appropriately for meaning. Problems with tense sequence often occur with the past tense and past perfect tense.°

Faulty When researchers tried [past] to review the study, many of the original participants died [past].

Revised When researchers tried [past] to review the study, many of the original participants had died [past perfect]. [The deaths had occurred before the review.]

Faulty Because other participants refused [past] interviews, the review had been terminated [past perfect].

Revised Because other participants refused [past] interviews, the review was terminated [past]. [The refusal occurred before the termination.]

Other tense-sequence problems occur with the distinctive verb forms of **conditional sentences**, in which a subordinate clause begins *if, when,* or *unless* and the main clause states the result.

Faulty If voters have [present] more confidence, they would vote [*would* + verb] more often.

Revised If voters had [past] more confidence, they would vote [*would* + verb] more often.

See the next page for more on conditional sentences.

°See Glossary of Terms, page 249.

13 Verb Mood

The **mood** of a verb indicates whether a sentence is a statement or a question (*The theater needs help. Can you help the theater?*), a command (*Help the theater*), or a suggestion, desire, or other nonfactual expression (*I wish I were an actor*).

13a Subjunctive mood: *I wish I were*

13b

The **subjunctive mood** expresses a suggestion, requirement, or desire, or it states a condition that is contrary to fact (that is, imaginary or hypothetical).

- **Suggestion or requirement with the verb *ask, insist, urge, require, recommend,* or *suggest*:** use the verb's plain form° with all subjects.

  Rules require that every donation be mailed.

- **Desire or present condition contrary to fact:** use the verb's past-tense form;° for *be,* use the past-tense form *were* with all subjects.

  If the theater were in better shape and had more money, its future would be guaranteed.

  I wish I were able to donate money.

- **Past condition contrary to fact:** use the verb's past perfect form° (*had* + past participle°).

  The theater would be better funded if it had been better managed.

Note In a sentence expressing a condition contrary to fact, (1) use *have,* not *of,* after *would* or *could* in the main clause; and (2) do not use *would* or *could* in the subordinate clause:

Faulty People would of helped if they would have known.

Revised People would have helped if they had known.

13b Consistency in mood

Shifts in mood within a sentence or among related sentences can be confusing. Such shifts occur most frequently in directions.

mycomplab

Visit *mycomplab.com* for more help with verb mood.

°See Glossary of Terms, page 249.

Inconsistent	Dissolve the crystals in the liquid. Then you should heat the solution to 120°C. [The first sentence is a command, the second a statement.]
Revised	Dissolve the crystals in the liquid. Then heat the solution to 120°C. [Consistent commands.]

14 Verb Voice

14a

The **voice** of a verb tells whether the subject° of the sentence performs the action (**active voice**) or is acted upon (**passive voice**).

Active voice	The administration increased the library's budget.
Passive voice	The library's budget was increased by the administration.

14a Active voice vs. passive voice

The active voice always names the actor in a sentence (whoever performs the verb's action), whereas the passive voice puts the actor in a phrase after the verb or even omits the actor altogether. Thus the active voice is usually more clear, emphatic, and concise than the passive voice.

Weak passive	The library is used by both students and teachers for studying and research, and the plan to expand it has been praised by many.
Strong active	Both students and teachers use the library for studying and research, and many have praised the plan to expand it.

The passive voice is useful in two situations: when the actor is unknown and when the actor is unimportant or less important than the object of the action.

> The Internet was established in 1969 by the Department of Defense. The network has been extended both nationally and internationally. [In the first sentence the writer wishes to stress the Internet. In the second sentence the actor is unknown or too complicated to name.]
>
> After the solution had been cooled to 10°C, the acid was added. [The person who cooled and added, perhaps the

°See Glossary of Terms, page 249.

writer, is less important than the actions. Passive sentences are common in scientific writing.]

14b Consistency in voice

A shift in voice (and subject) within or between sentences can be awkward or even confusing.

Inconsistent	Internet blogs cover an enormous range of topics. Opportunities for people to discuss pet issues are provided on these sites.
Revised	Internet blogs cover an enormous range of topics and provide opportunities for people to discuss pet issues.

15 Agreement of Subject and Verb

A subject° and its verb° should agree in number°—singular with singular, plural with plural.

Many Japanese Americans live in Hawaii and California.
subject verb

Daniel Inouye was the first Japanese American in Congress.
subject verb

15a *-s* ending for noun *or* verb, but not both

An *-s* or *-es* ending does opposite things to nouns and verbs: it usually makes a noun *plural*, but it always makes a present-tense verb *singular*. Thus if the subject noun is plural, it will probably end in *-s* or *-es* and the verb will not. If the subject is singular, it will not end in *-s* and the verb will.

Singular noun	Plural noun
The boy plays.	The boys play.
The bird soars.	The birds soar.
The street is busy.	The streets are busy.
The town has a traffic problem.	The towns have a traffic problem.
The new light does not [or doesn't] help.	The new lights do not [or don't] help.

mycomplab

Visit *mycomplab.com* for more help with subject-verb agreement.

°See Glossary of Terms, page 249.

ESL Most noncount nouns—those that do not form plurals—take singular verbs: *That information is helpful.* (See pp. 73–74 for more on noncount nouns.)

15b Words between subject and verb

The survival of hibernating frogs in freezing temperatures is [not are] fascinating.

A chemical reaction inside the cells of the frogs stops [not stop] the formation of ice crystals.

Phrases beginning with *as well as, together with, along with,* and *in addition to* do not change the number of the subject.

The president, together with the deans, has [not have] agreed to improve the computer labs.

15c Subjects with *and*

Frost and Roethke were American poets who died in the same year.

Note When *each* or *every* precedes the compound subject, the verb is usually singular.

Each man, woman, and child has a right to be heard.

15d Subjects with *or* or *nor*

When parts of a subject are joined by *or* or *nor,* the verb agrees with the nearer part.

Either the painter or the carpenter knows the cost.

The cabinets or the bookcases are too costly.

When one part of the subject is singular and the other is plural, the sentence will be awkward unless you put the plural part second.

Awkward Neither the owners nor the builder agrees.

Improved Neither the builder nor the owners agree.

15e *Everyone* and other indefinite pronouns

Indefinite pronouns° include *anybody, anyone, each, everybody, everyone, neither, no one, one,* and *somebody.* Most are singular in meaning and take singular verbs.

Something smells. Neither is right.

°See Glossary of Terms, page 249.

A few indefinite pronouns such as *all, any, none,* and *some* may take a singular or plural verb depending on whether the word they refer to is singular or plural.

All of the money is reserved for emergencies.

All of the funds are reserved for emergencies.

15f *Team* and other collective nouns

A collective noun° such as *team* or *family* takes a singular verb when the group acts as a unit.

The team has won five of the last six meets.

But when the group's members act separately, use a plural verb.

The old team have gone their separate ways.

If the sentence above seems awkward, reword it: *The members of the old team have gone their separate ways.*

15g *Who, which,* and *that*

When used as subjects, *who, which,* and *that* refer to another word in the sentence. The verb agrees with this other word.

Mayor Garber ought to listen to the people who work for her.

Bardini is the only aide who has her ear.

Bardini is one of the aides who work unpaid. [Of the aides who work unpaid, Bardini is one.]

Bardini is the only one of the aides who knows the community. [Of the aides, only one, Bardini, knows the community.]

15h *News* and other singular nouns ending in *-s*

Singular nouns° ending in *-s* include *athletics, economics, mathematics, measles, mumps, news, physics, politics,* and *statistics.* They take singular verbs.

After so long a wait, the news has to be good.

Statistics is required of psychology majors.

These words take plural verbs when they describe individual items rather than bodies of activity or knowledge.

The statistics prove him wrong.

°See Glossary of Terms, page 249.

15i Verb preceding subject

Is voting a right or a privilege?

Are a right and a privilege the same thing?

There are differences between them.

Here are some possible solutions.

15j *Is, are,* and other linking verbs

Make a linking verb° agree with its subject, usually the first element in the sentence, not with other words referring to the subject.

The child's sole support is her court-appointed guardians.

Her court-appointed guardians are the child's sole support.

PRONOUNS

16 Pronoun Forms

A noun° or pronoun° changes form to show the reader how it functions in a sentence. These forms—called **cases**—are **subjective** (such as *I, she, they, man*), **objective** (such as *me, her, them, man*), and **possessive** (such as *my, her, their, man's*). A list of the case forms appears on pages 249–50.

16a Compound subjects and objects: *she and I* vs. *her and me*

Subjects° and objects° consisting of two or more nouns and pronouns have the same case forms as they would if one pronoun stood alone.

compound subject
She and Ming discussed the proposal.

compound object
The proposal disappointed her and him.

°See Glossary of Terms, page 249.

mycomplab

Visit *mycomplab.com* for more help with pronoun forms.

To test for the correct form, try one pronoun alone in the sentence. The case form that sounds correct is probably correct for all parts of the compound.

> The prize went to [he, him] and [I, me].
> The prize went to him.
> The prize went to him and me.

16b Subject complements: *it was she*

Both a subject and a subject complement° appear in the same form—the subjective case.

> subject complement
> The one who cares most is she.

If this construction sounds stilted to you, use the more natural order: *She is the one who cares most.*

16c *Who* vs. *whom*

The choice between *who* and *whom* depends on the use of the word.

Questions

At the beginning of a question, use *who* for a subject and *whom* for an object.

> subject → object ←
> Who wrote the policy? Whom does it affect?

Test for the correct form by answering the question with the form of *he* or *she* that sounds correct. Then use the same form in the question.

> [Who, Whom] does one ask?
> One asks her.
> Whom does one ask?

Subordinate clauses

In a subordinate clause,° use *who* or *whoever* for a subject, *whom* or *whomever* for an object.

> subject →
> Give old clothes to whoever needs them.
>
> object ←
> I don't know whom the mayor appointed.

Test for the correct form by rewriting the subordinate clause as a sentence. Replace *who* or *whom* with the form of *he* or *she* that sounds correct. Then use the same form in the original subordinate clause.

> Few people know [who, whom] they should ask.
> They should ask her.
> Few people know whom they should ask.

°See Glossary of Terms, page 249.

Note Don't let expressions such as *I think* and *she says* confuse you when they come between the subject *who* and its verb.

> subject
> He is the one who I think is best qualified.

16d Other constructions

We or *us* with a noun

The choice of *we* or *us* before a noun depends on the use of the noun.

> object of preposition
> Freezing weather is welcomed by us skaters.
>
> subject
> We skaters welcome freezing weather.

Pronoun in an appositive

An **appositive** is a word or word group that renames a noun or pronoun. Within an appositive the form of a pronoun depends on the function of the word the appositive renames.

> object of verb
> The class elected two representatives, DeShawn and me.
>
> subject
> Two representatives, DeShawn and I, were elected.

Pronoun after *than* or *as*

After *than* or *as* in a comparison, the form of a pronoun indicates what words may have been omitted. A subjective pronoun is the subject of the omitted verb:

> subject
> Some critics like Glass more than she [does].

An objective pronoun is the object of the omitted verb:

> object
> Some critics like Glass more than [they like] her.

Subject and object of an infinitive

An **infinitive** is the plain form° of the verb plus *to* (*to swim*). Both its object and its subject are in the objective form.

> subject of infinitive
> The school asked him to speak.
>
> object of infinitive
> Students chose to invite him.

Form before a gerund

A **gerund** is the *-ing* form of a verb used as a noun (*a runner's breathing*). Generally, use the possessive form of a pronoun or noun immediately before a gerund.

°See Glossary of Terms, page 249.

16d

The coach disapproved of their lifting weights.

The coach's disapproving was a surprise.

17 Agreement of Pronoun and Antecedent

The word a pronoun refers to is its **antecedent.**

Successful students complete their homework.
antecedent pronoun

For clarity, a pronoun should agree with its antecedent in person° (first, second, third), number° (singular, plural), and gender° (masculine, feminine, neuter).

17a Antecedents with *and*

The dean and my adviser have offered their help.

Note When *each* or *every* precedes the compound antecedent, the pronoun is singular.

Every girl and woman took her seat.

17b Antecedents with *or* or *nor*

When parts of an antecedent are joined by *or* or *nor,* the pronoun agrees with the nearer part.

Tenants or owners must present their grievances.

Either the tenant or the owner will have her way.

When one subject is plural and the other singular, put the plural subject second to avoid awkwardness.

Neither the owner nor the tenants have made their case.

17c *Everyone, person,* and other indefinite words

Indefinite words do not refer to any specific person or thing. They include indefinite pronouns° (such as *anyone, everybody, everything, none, no one, somebody*) and generic nouns° (such as *person, individual, child, student*).

mycomplab

Visit *mycomplab.com* for more help with pronoun-antecedent agreement.

°See Glossary of Terms, page 249.

Most indefinite words are singular in meaning and take singular pronouns.

> Everyone on the women's team now has her own locker.
>
> Each of the men still has his own locker.

Though they are singular, indefinite words often seem to mean "many" or "all" rather than "one" and are mistakenly referred to with plural pronouns, as in *Everyone deserves their privacy.* Often, too, we mean indefinite words to include both masculine and feminine genders and thus resort to *they* instead of the **generic** *he*—the masculine pronoun referring to both genders, which is generally regarded as sexist: *Everyone deserves his privacy*.

To achieve nonsexist agreement in such cases, you have several options:

- **Change the indefinite word to a plural, and use a plural pronoun to match.**

  Faulty Each athlete is entitled to his own locker.

  Revised All athletes are entitled to their own lockers. [*Is* changes to *are*, and *locker* changes to *lockers*.]

- **Rewrite the sentence to omit the pronoun.**

  Revised Each athlete is entitled to a locker.

- **Use *he or she* (*him or her, his or her*) to refer to the indefinite word.**

  Revised Each athlete is entitled to his or her own locker.

  He or she can be awkward, so avoid using it more than once in several sentences. Also avoid the combination *he/she,* which many readers do not accept.

17d *Team* and other collective nouns

Use a singular pronoun with *team, family, group,* or another collective noun° when referring to the group as a unit.

> The committee voted to disband itself.

When referring to the individual members of the group, use a plural pronoun.

> The old team have gone their separate ways.

If the sentence above sounds awkward to you, you can reword it: *The members of the old team have gone their separate ways.*

°See Glossary of Terms, page 249.

18 Reference of Pronoun to Antecedent

If a pronoun° does not refer clearly to the word it substitutes for (its **antecedent**), readers will have difficulty grasping the pronoun's meaning.

18a Single antecedent

When either of two nouns can be a pronoun's antecedent, the reference will not be clear.

18c

Confusing Emily Dickinson is sometimes compared with Jane Austen, but she was quite different.

Revise such a sentence in one of two ways:

- **Replace the pronoun with the appropriate noun.**

Clear Emily Dickinson is sometimes compared with Jane Austen, but Dickinson [or Austen] was quite different.

- **Avoid repetition by rewriting the sentence.** If you use the pronoun, make sure it has only one possible antecedent.

Clear Despite occasional comparison, Emily Dickinson and Jane Austen were quite different.

Clear Though sometimes compared with her, Emily Dickinson was quite different from Jane Austen.

18b Close antecedent

A clause° beginning *who, which,* or *that* should generally fall immediately after the word it refers to.

Confusing Jody found a dress in the attic that her aunt had worn.

Clear In the attic Jody found a dress that her aunt had worn.

18c Specific antecedent

A pronoun should refer to a specific noun° or other pronoun. Readers can only guess at the meaning of a pronoun when its antecedent is not stated outright.

mycomplab

Visit *mycomplab.com* for more help with pronoun reference.

°See Glossary of Terms, page 249.

Vague *this, that, which,* or *it*

This, that, which, or *it* should refer to a specific noun, not to a whole word group expressing an idea or situation.

Confusing — The British knew little of the American countryside, and they had no experience with the colonists' guerrilla tactics. This gave the colonists an advantage.

Clear — The British knew little of the American countryside, and they had no experience with the colonists' guerrilla tactics. This ignorance and inexperience gave the colonists an advantage.

Implied nouns

A pronoun cannot refer clearly to a noun that is merely implied by some other word or phrase, such as *news* in *newspaper* or *happiness* in *happy.*

Confusing — Cohen's report brought her a lawsuit.

Clear — Cohen was sued over her report.

Confusing — Her reports on psychological development generally go unnoticed outside it.

Clear — Her reports on psychological development generally go unnoticed outside the field.

Indefinite *it, they,* or *you*

It and *they* should have definite antecedents.

Confusing — In the average television drama they present a false picture of life.

Clear — The average television drama presents a false picture of life.

You should clearly mean "you, the reader," and the context must support such a meaning.

Inappropriate — In the fourteenth century you had to struggle to survive.

Revised — In the fourteenth century one [or a person or people] had to struggle to survive.

18d Consistency in pronouns

Within a sentence or a group of related sentences, pronouns should be consistent. You may shift pronouns unconsciously when you start with *one* and soon find it too stiff.

Inconsistent — One will find when reading that your concentration improves with practice, so that you comprehend more in less time.

Revised — You will find when reading that your concentration improves with practice, so that you comprehend more in less time.

Inconsistent pronouns also occur when singular shifts to plural: *Everyone who reads regularly will improve his or her* [not *their*] *speed.* See pages 66–67.

MODIFIERS

19 Adjectives and Adverbs

Adjectives modify nouns° (*good child*) and pronouns° (*special someone*). **Adverbs** modify verbs° (*see well*), adjectives (*very happy*), other adverbs (*not very*), and whole word groups (*Otherwise, the room was empty*). The only way to tell if a modifier should be an adjective or an adverb is to determine its function in the sentence.

19a Adjective vs. adverb

Use only adverbs, not adjectives, to modify verbs, adverbs, or other adjectives.

Not — They took each other serious. They related good.

But — They took each other seriously. They related well.

19b Adjective with linking verb: *felt bad*

A modifier after a verb should be an adverb only if it describes the verb. If the modifier follows a linking verb° and describes the subject, it should be an adjective.

Two word pairs are especially tricky. One is *bad* and *badly*:

The weather grew bad. (grew: linking verb; bad: adjective)

She felt bad. (felt: linking verb; bad: adjective)

°See Glossary of Terms, page 249.

Flowers grow badly in such soil.
verb adverb

The other word pair is *good* and *well*. *Good* serves only as an adjective. *Well* may serve as an adverb with a host of meanings or as an adjective meaning only "fit" or "healthy."

Decker trained well.
verb adverb

She felt well.
linking verb adjective

Her health was good.
linking verb adjective

19c Comparison of adjectives and adverbs

Comparison° allows adjectives and adverbs to show degrees of quality or amount by changing form: *red, redder, reddest; awful, more awful, most awful; quickly, less quickly, least quickly.* A dictionary will list the *-er* and *-est* endings if they can be used. Otherwise, use *more* and *most* or *less* and *least.*

Some modifiers are irregular, changing their spelling for comparison: for example, *good, better, best; many, more, most; badly, worse, worst.*

Comparisons of two or more than two

Use the *-er* form, *more,* or *less* when comparing two items. Use the *-est* form, *most,* or *least* when comparing three or more items.

Of the two tests, the litmus is better.
Of all six tests, the litmus is best.

Double comparisons

A double comparison combines the *-er* or *-est* ending with the word *more* or *most.* It is redundant.

Chang was the wisest [not most wisest] person in town.
He was smarter [not more smarter] than anyone else.

Complete comparisons

A comparison should be complete.

- **The comparison should state a relation fully enough to ensure clarity.**

Unclear Car makers worry about their industry more than environmentalists.

Clear Car makers worry about their industry more than environmentalists do.

Clear Car makers worry about their industry more than they worry about environmentalists.

°See Glossary of Terms, page 249.

- **The items being compared should in fact be comparable.**

Illogical The cost of a hybrid car can be greater than a gasoline-powered car. [Illogically compares a cost and a car.]

Revised The cost of a hybrid car can be greater than the cost of [or that of] a gasoline-powered car.

19d Double negatives

In a **double negative** two negative words cancel each other out. Some double negatives are intentional, as *She was not unhappy* indicates with understatement that she was indeed happy. But most double negatives say the opposite of what is intended: *Jenny did not feel nothing* asserts that Jenny felt other than nothing, or something.

Faulty The IRS cannot hardly audit all tax returns. None of its audits never touch many cheaters.

Revised The IRS cannot audit all tax returns. Its audits never touch many cheaters.

19e Present and past participles as adjectives ESL

Both present participles° and past participles° may serve as adjectives: *a burning house, a burned house.* As in the examples, the two participles usually differ in the time they indicate.

But some present and past participles—those derived from verbs expressing feeling—can have altogether different meanings. The present participle refers to something that causes the feeling: *That was a frightening storm.* The past participle refers to something that experiences the feeling: *They quieted the frightened horses.* Similar pairs include the following:

annoying/annoyed
boring/bored
confusing/confused
exciting/excited
exhausting/exhausted
interesting/interested
pleasing/pleased
satisfying/satisfied
surprising/surprised
tiring/tired
troubling/troubled
worrying/worried

19f Articles: *a, an, the* ESL

Articles° usually trouble native English speakers only in the choice of *a* versus *an*: *a* for words beginning with consonant sounds (*a bridge*), *an* for words beginning with vowel sounds, including a silent *h* (*an apple, an hour*).

For nonnative speakers, *a, an,* and *the* can be difficult because many other languages use such words quite differently or not at all. In English, their uses depend on their context and the kinds of nouns they precede.

°See Glossary of Terms, page 249.

Singular count nouns

A **count noun** names something countable and can form a plural: *glass/glasses, mountain/mountains, child/children, woman/women.*

- ***A* or *an* precedes a singular count noun when your reader does not already know its identity,** usually because you have not mentioned it before.

  A scientist in our chemistry department developed a process to strengthen metals. [*Scientist* and *process* are being introduced for the first time.]

- ***The* precedes a singular count noun that has a specific identity for your reader,** usually because (1) you have mentioned it before, (2) you identify it immediately before or after you state it, (3) it is unique (the only one in existence), or (4) it refers to an institution or facility that is shared by the community.

  A scientist in our chemistry department developed a process to strengthen metals. The scientist patented the process. [*Scientist* and *process* were identified before.]

  The most productive laboratory is the research center in the chemistry department. [*Most productive* identifies *laboratory. In the chemistry department* identifies *research center.* And *chemistry department* is a shared facility.]

  The sun rises in the east. [*Sun* and *east* are unique.]

  Many men and women aspire to the presidency. [*Presidency* is a shared institution.]

Plural count nouns

A or *an* never precedes a plural noun. *The* does not precede a plural noun that names a general category. *The* does precede a plural noun that names specific representatives of a category.

> Men and women are different. [*Men* and *women* name general categories.]
>
> The women joined a team. [*Women* refers to specific people.]

Noncount nouns

A **noncount noun** names something that is not usually considered countable in English, and so it does not form a plural. Examples include the following:

> **Abstractions:** confidence, democracy, education, equality, evidence, health, information, intelligence, knowledge, luxury, peace, pollution, research, success, supervision, truth, wealth, work
>
> **Emotions:** anger, courage, happiness, hate, love, respect, satisfaction

Food and drink: bread, flour, meat, milk, salt, water, wine

Natural events and substances: air, blood, dirt, gasoline, gold, hair, heat, ice, oil, oxygen, rain, smoke, wood

Groups: clergy, clothing, equipment, furniture, garbage, jewelry, junk, legislation, mail, military, money, police

Fields of study: architecture, accounting, biology, business, chemistry, engineering, literature, psychology, science

A or *an* never precedes a noncount noun. *The* does precede a noncount noun that names specific representatives of a general category.

Vegetation suffers from drought. [*Vegetation* names a general category.]

The vegetation in the park withered or died. [*Vegetation* refers to specific plants.]

Note Many nouns are sometimes count nouns and sometimes noncount nouns.

The library has a room for readers. [*Room* is a count noun meaning "walled area."]

The library has room for reading. [*Room* is a noncount noun meaning "space."]

Proper nouns

A **proper noun** names a particular person, place, or thing and begins with a capital letter: *February, Joe Allen. A* or *an* never precedes a proper noun. *The* does occasionally, as with oceans (*the Pacific*), regions (*the Middle East*), rivers (*the Snake*), some countries (*the United States*), and some universities (*the University of Texas*).

Garcia lives in Boulder and attends the University of Colorado.

20 Misplaced and Dangling Modifiers

For clarity, modifiers generally must fall close to the words they modify.

20a Misplaced modifiers

A **misplaced modifier** falls in the wrong place in a sentence. It may be awkward, confusing, or even unintentionally funny.

Visit *mycomplab.com* for more help with misplaced and dangling modifiers.

Clear placement

Confusing He served steak to the men on paper plates.

Revised He served the men steak on paper plates.

Confusing Many dogs are killed by autos and trucks roaming unleashed.

Revised Many dogs roaming unleashed are killed by autos and trucks.

Only and other limiting modifiers

Limiting modifiers include *almost, even, exactly, hardly, just, merely, nearly, only, scarcely,* and *simply.* They should fall immediately before the word or word group they modify.

Unclear They only saw each other during meals.

Revised They saw only each other during meals.

Revised They saw each other only during meals.

Infinitives and other grammatical units

Some grammatical units should generally not be split by long modifiers. For example, a long adverb° between subject° and verb° can be awkward and confusing.

Awkward The city, after the hurricane, began massive rebuilding. (subject: The city; adverb: after the hurricane; verb: began)

Revised After the hurricane, the city began massive rebuilding. (adverb: After the hurricane; subject: the city; verb: began)

A **split infinitive**—a modifier placed between *to* and the verb—can be especially awkward and will annoy many readers.

Awkward Farmers expected temperatures to not rise. (infinitive: to rise)

Revised Farmers expected temperatures not to rise. (infinitive: to rise)

A split infinitive may sometimes be unavoidable without rewriting, though it may still bother some readers.

Several US industries expect to more than triple their use of robots. (infinitive: to triple)

Order of adjectives ESL

English follows distinctive rules for arranging two or three adjectives before a noun. (A string of more than

°See Glossary of Terms, page 249.

three adjectives before a noun is rare.) The adjectives follow this order:

Determiner	Opinion	Size or shape	Color	Origin	Material	Noun used as adjective	Noun
many						state	**laws**
	lovely		green	Thai			**birds**
a		square			wooden		**table**
all						business	**reports**
the			blue		litmus		**paper**

20b

20b Dangling modifiers

A **dangling modifier** does not sensibly modify anything in its sentence.

Dangling Passing the building, the vandalism became visible.

Like most dangling modifiers, this one introduces a sentence, contains a verb form (*passing*), and implies but does not name a subject (whoever is passing). Readers assume that this implied subject is the same as the subject of the sentence (*vandalism*). When it is not, the modifier "dangles" unconnected to the rest of the sentence.

Revise dangling modifiers to achieve the emphasis you want.

- **Rewrite the dangling modifier as a complete clause with its own stated subject and verb.** Readers can accept different subjects when they are both stated.

Dangling Passing the building, the vandalism became visible.

Revised As we passed the building, the vandalism became visible.

- **Change the subject of the sentence to a word the modifier properly describes.**

Dangling Trying to understand the causes, vandalism has been extensively studied.

Revised Trying to understand the causes, researchers have extensively studied vandalism.

SENTENCE FAULTS

21 Sentence Fragments

A **sentence fragment** is part of a sentence that is set off as if it were a whole sentence by an initial capital letter and a final period or other end punctuation. Although writers occasionally use fragments deliberately and effectively, readers perceive most fragments as serious errors in standard English. Use the tests below to ensure that you have linked or separated your ideas both appropriately for your meaning and correctly, without creating sentence fragments.

ESL Some languages other than English allow the omission of the subject° or the verb.° Except in commands (*Close the door*), English always requires you to state the subject and verb.

21a

21a Tests for fragments

A word group punctuated as a sentence should pass *all three* of the following tests. If it does not, it is a fragment and needs to be revised.

Test 1: Find the verb.

Some sentence fragments lack any verb form:°

Fragment	Uncountable numbers of sites on the Web.
Revised	Uncountable numbers of sites make up the Web.

The verb in a complete sentence must be able to change form as on the left of the following chart. A verb form that cannot change this way (as on the right) cannot serve as a sentence verb.

	Complete sentences	Sentence fragments
Singular	The network grows.	The network growing.
Plural	Networks grow.	Networks growing.
Present	The network grows.	The network growing.
Past	The network grew.	
Future	The network will grow.	

(See also pp. 51–52 on the use of helping verbs° to prevent sentence fragments.)

°See Glossary of Terms, page 249.

mycomplab

Visit *mycomplab.com* for more help with sentence fragments.

Test 2: Find the subject.

The subject of the sentence will usually come before the verb. If there is no subject, the word group is probably a fragment.

Fragment And has enormous popular appeal.

Revised And the Web has enormous popular appeal.

Note Commands, in which the subject *you* is understood, are not sentence fragments: [*You*] *Close the door.*

Test 3: Make sure the clause is not subordinate.

A **subordinate clause** begins with either a subordinating conjunction° (such as *because, if, when*) or a relative pronoun° (*who, which, that*). Subordinate clauses serve as parts of sentences, not as whole sentences.

21b

Fragment The Internet was greatly improved by Web technology. Which allows users to move easily between sites.

Revised The Internet was greatly improved by Web technology, which allows users to move easily between sites. [The subordinate clause joins a main clause in a complete sentence.]

Revised The Internet was greatly improved by Web technology. It allows users to move easily between sites. [Substituting *It* for *Which* makes the subordinate clause into a complete sentence.]

Note Questions beginning *who, whom,* or *which* are not sentence fragments: *Who rattled the cage?*

21b Revision of fragments

Correct sentence fragments in one of two ways, depending on the importance of the information in the fragment:

- **Rewrite the fragment as a complete sentence.** The information in the fragment will then have the same importance as that in other complete sentences.

  Fragment The Internet was a true innovation. Because no expansive computer network existed before it.

  Revised The Internet was a true innovation. No expansive computer network existed before it. [Deleting *Because* makes the fragment into a complete sentence.]

- **Combine the fragment with the appropriate main clause.** The information in the fragment will then be subordinated to that in the main clause.

°See Glossary of Terms, page 249.

Fragment The Web is easy to use. Loaded with links and graphics.

Revised The Web, loaded with links and graphics, is easy to use.

22 Comma Splices and Fused Sentences

When you combine two complete sentences (main clauses°) in one sentence, you need to give readers a clear signal that one clause is ending and the other beginning. Two common errors fail to give this signal. In a **comma splice** two main clauses are joined (or spliced) only by a comma, which is usually too weak to signal the link between main clauses.

Comma splice The ship was huge, its mast stood eighty feet high.

In a **fused sentence** (or **run-on sentence**) the clauses are not separated at all.

Fused sentence The ship was huge its mast stood eighty feet high.

You can repair comma splices and fused sentences with coordination or subordination (pp. 33–34) and at the same time clarify the relations between the clauses.

22a

22a Main clauses without *and, but, or, nor, for, so, yet*

Two main clauses in a sentence are usually separated with a comma and a coordinating conjunction° such as *and* or *but*. These signals tell readers to expect another main clause. When one or both signals are missing, the sentence may be confusing and may require rereading. Revise it in one of the following ways:

- **Insert a coordinating conjunction when the ideas in the main clauses are closely related and equally important.**

Comma splice Some laboratory-grown foods taste good, they are nutritious.

Revised Some laboratory-grown foods taste good, and they are nutritious.

°See Glossary of Terms, page 249.

mycomplab

Visit *mycomplab.com* for more help with comma splices and fused sentences.

In a fused sentence insert a comma and a coordinating conjunction.

Fused sentence — Chemists have made much progress they still have a way to go.

Revised — Chemists have made much progress, but they still have a way to go.

- **Insert a semicolon between clauses if the relation between the ideas is very close and obvious without a conjunction.**

Comma splice — Good taste is rare in laboratory-grown vegetables, they are usually bland.

Revised — Good taste is rare in laboratory-grown vegetables; they are usually bland.

- **Make the clauses into separate sentences when the ideas expressed are only loosely related.**

Comma splice — Chemistry has contributed to our understanding of foods, many foods such as wheat and beans can be produced in the laboratory.

Revised — Chemistry has contributed to our understanding of foods. Many foods such as wheat and beans can be produced in the laboratory.

- **Subordinate one clause to the other when one idea is less important than the other.** The subordinate clause will modify something in the main clause.

Comma splice — The vitamins are adequate, the flavor and color are deficient.

Revised — Even though the vitamins are adequate, the flavor and color are deficient.

22b Main clauses related by *however, for example,* and so on

Two kinds of words can describe how one main clause relates to another: conjunctive adverbs,° such as *however, instead, meanwhile,* and *thus*; and other transitional expressions,° such as *even so, for example, in fact,* and *of course.* Two main clauses related by any conjunctive adverb and most transitional expressions must be separated by a period or by a semicolon. The connecting word or phrase is also generally set off by a comma or commas.

Comma splice — Healthcare costs are higher in the United States than in many other countries, consequently health insurance is also more costly.

Revised — Healthcare costs are higher in the United States than in many other countries. Consequently, health insurance is also more costly.

°See Glossary of Terms, page 249.

Revised Healthcare costs are higher in the United States than in many other countries; consequently, health insurance is also more costly.

To test whether a word or phrase is a conjunctive adverb or transitional expression, try moving it around in its clause. Either kind of word can move, whereas other kinds (such as *and* or *because*) cannot.

Healthcare costs are higher in the United States than in many other countries; health insurance, consequently, is also more costly.

PART 4

Punctuation

Checklist for punctuation

This checklist focuses on the most troublesome punctuation marks and uses, showing correctly punctuated sentences with brief explanations. For the other marks and other uses covered in this part, see the contents inside the back cover.

Comma

☑ Subways are convenient, but they are costly to build.

Subways are convenient but costly.

[With *and, but,* etc., only between main clauses. See opposite.]

☑ Because of their cost, new subways are rarely built.

[With an introductory element. See opposite.]

☑ Light rail, which is less costly, is often more feasible.

Those who favor mass transit often propose light rail.

[With a nonessential element, not with an essential element. See p. 86.]

☑ In a few older cities, commuters can choose from subways, buses, light rail, and railroads.

[Separating items in a series. See p. 88.]

Semicolon

☑ She chose carpentry; she wanted manual work.

She had a law degree; however, she became a carpenter.

[Between main clauses not joined by *and, but,* etc., and those joined by *however, for example,* etc. See p. 90.]

Colon

☑ The school has one goal: to train businesspeople.

[With a main clause to introduce information. See p. 91.]

Apostrophe

☑ Bill Smith's dog saved the life of the Smiths' grandchild.

[Showing possession: with *-'s* for singular nouns; with *-'* alone for plural nouns ending in *-s*. See pp. 92–93.]

☑ Its [for The dog's] bark warned the family.

It's [for It is] an intelligent dog.

[Not with possessive pronouns, only with contractions. See pp. 93–94.]

23 The Comma

The comma helps to separate sentence elements and to prevent misreading. Its main uses (and misuses) appear in this chapter.

23a Comma with *and, but, or, nor, for, so, yet*

Comma between main clauses

Use a comma before *and, but, or, nor, for, so,* and *yet* (the coordinating conjunctions°) when they link main clauses.°

Banks offer many services, but they could do more.

Many banks offer investment advice, and they may help small businesses establish credit.

Note The comma goes before, not after, the coordinating conjunction.

No comma between words, phrases, or subordinate clauses

Generally, do not use a comma before *and, but, or,* and *nor* when they link pairs of words, phrases,° or subordinate clauses°—that is, elements other than main clauses.

Not One bank established special accounts for older depositors, and counseled them on investments.

But One bank established special accounts for older depositors and counseled them on investments.

23b Comma with introductory elements

Use a comma after most elements that begin sentences and are distinct from the main clause.

When a new century nears, futurists multiply.

Fortunately, some news is good.

You may omit the comma after a short introductory element if there's no risk that the reader will run the introductory element and main clause together: *By 2010 we may have reduced pollution.*

Note The subject° of a sentence is not an introductory element but a part of the main clause. Thus, do not use a comma to separate the subject and its verb.

mycomplab

Visit *mycomplab.com* for more help with the comma.

°See Glossary of Terms, page 249.

Not Some pessimists, may be disappointed.
But Some pessimists may be disappointed.

23c Comma or commas with interrupting and concluding elements

Use a comma or commas to set off information that could be deleted without altering the basic meaning of the sentence.

Note When such optional information falls in the middle of the sentence, be sure to use one comma *before* and one *after* it.

Commas around nonessential elements

A **nonessential** (or **nonrestrictive**) **element** adds information about a word in the sentence but does not limit (or restrict) the word to a particular individual or group. Omitting the underlined element from any sentence below would remove incidental details but would not affect the sentence's basic meaning.

Nonessential modifiers

Hai Nguyen, who emigrated from Vietnam, lives in Denver.

His company, which is ten years old, studies air and water pollution.

Nguyen's family lives in Baton Rouge and Chicago, even though he lives in Denver.

Nonessential appositives

Appositives are words or word groups that rename nouns.

Hai Nguyen's work, advanced research into air pollution, keeps him in Denver.

His wife, Tina Nguyen, reports for a newspaper in Chicago. [Nguyen has only one wife, so her name merely adds nonessential information about her.]

No commas around essential elements

Do not use commas to set off **essential** (or **restrictive**) **elements:** modifiers and appositives that contain information essential to the meaning of the sentence. Omitting the underlined element from any of the following sentences would alter the meaning substantially, leaving the sentence unclear or too general.

Essential modifiers

People who join recycling programs rarely complain about the extra work.

The programs that succeed are often staffed by volunteers.

Most people recycle because they believe they have a responsibility to the earth.

Essential appositives

The label "Recycle" on products becomes a command.

The activist Susan Bower urges recycling.

The book *Efficient Recycling* provides helpful tips.

Commas around absolute phrases

An **absolute phrase** usually consists of the *-ing* form of a verb plus a subject for the verb. The phrase modifies the whole main clause of the sentence.

Health insurance, its cost always rising, is a concern for many students.

Commas around transitional or parenthetical expressions

A transitional expression° such as *however, for example,* or *of course* forms a link between ideas. It is nonessential and is usually set off with a comma or commas.

Most students at the city colleges, for example, have no health insurance.

23c

A parenthetical expression° provides supplementary information not essential for meaning. Examples are *fortunately, to be frank,* and *all things considered.* Such an expression may be enclosed in parentheses (see p. 99) or, for more emphasis, in commas.

Some schools, it seems, do not offer group insurance.

Note Do not add a comma after a coordinating conjunction° (*and, but,* and so on) or a subordinating conjunction° (*although, because,* and so on). To distinguish between these words and transitional or parenthetical expressions, try moving the word or expression around in its clause. Transitional or parenthetical expressions can be moved; coordinating and subordinating conjunctions cannot.

Commas around phrases of contrast

Students may focus on the cost of health care, not their health.

Commas around *yes* and *no*

All schools should agree that, yes, they will provide at least minimal insurance at low cost.

Commas around words of direct address

Heed this lesson, readers.

°See Glossary of Terms, page 249.

23d Commas with series

Commas between series items

Use commas to separate the items in lists or series.

The names Belia, Beelzebub, and Lucifer sound ominous.

The comma before the last item in a series (before *and*) is optional, but it is never wrong and it is usually clearer.

No commas around series

Do not use a comma *before* or *after* a series.

Not The skills of, agriculture, herding, and hunting, sustained the Native Americans.

But The skills of agriculture, herding, and hunting sustained the Native Americans.

23e Comma with adjectives

23f

Comma between equal adjectives

Use a comma between two or more adjectives° when each one modifies the same word equally. As a test, such adjectives could be joined by *and*.

The book had a worn, cracked binding.

No comma between unequal adjectives

Do not use a comma between adjectives when one forms a unit with the modified word. As a test, the two adjectives could not sensibly be joined by *and*.

The study examined the eye movements of healthy young men.

The researchers watched for one specific movement.

23f Commas with dates, addresses, place names, numbers

When they appear within sentences, elements punctuated with commas are also ended with commas.

Dates

July 4, 1776, was the day the Declaration was signed. [Note that commas appear before *and* after the year.]

The United States entered World War II in December 1941. [No comma is needed between a month or season and a year.]

Addresses and place names

Use the address 806 Ogden Avenue, Swarthmore, Pennsylvania 19081, for all correspondence. [No comma is needed between the state name and zip code.]

°See Glossary of Terms, page 249.

Numbers

The new assembly plant cost $7,525,000.

A kilometer is 3,281 feet [*or* 3281 feet].

23g Commas with quotations

A comma or commas usually separate a quotation from a signal phrase that identifies the source, such as *she said* or *he replied.*

Eleanor Roosevelt said, "You must do the thing you think you cannot do."

"Knowledge is power," wrote Francis Bacon.

"You don't need a weatherman," sings Bob Dylan, "to know which way the wind blows."

Exceptions Do not use commas with signal phrases in the following situations:

- **Use a semicolon or a period after a signal phrase that interrupts a quotation between main clauses.** The choice depends on the punctuation of the original:

  "That part of my life was over," she wrote; "his words had sealed it shut."

  "That part of my life was over," she wrote. "His words had sealed it shut."

- **Use a colon when a complete sentence introduces a quotation:**

  Her statement was clear: "I will not resign."

- **Omit commas when a quotation is integrated into your sentence structure,** including a quotation introduced by *that*:

  James Baldwin insists that "one must never, in one's life, accept . . . injustices as commonplace."

  Baldwin thought that the violence of a riot "had been devised as a corrective" to his own violence.

24

24 The Semicolon

The semicolon separates equal and balanced sentence elements, usually main clauses.°

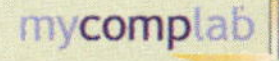

Visit *mycomplab.com* for more help with the semicolon.

°See Glossary of Terms, page 249.

24a Semicolon between main clauses not joined by *and, but, or, nor,* etc.

Semicolon between main clauses

Use a semicolon between main clauses° that are not connected by *and, but, or, nor, for, so,* or *yet* (the coordinating conjunctions°).

> Increased taxes are only one way to pay for programs; cost cutting also frees up money.

> A new ulcer drug arrived on the market with a mixed reputation; doctors find that the drug works but worry about its side effects.

No semicolon between main clauses and subordinate elements

Do not use a semicolon between a main clause and a subordinate element, such as a subordinate clause° or a phrase.°

24b

Not According to African authorities; Pygmies today number only about 35,000.

But According to African authorities, Pygmies today number only about 35,000.

Not Anthropologists have campaigned; for the protection of the Pygmies' habitat.

But Anthropologists have campaigned for the protection of the Pygmies' habitat.

24b Semicolon with *however, for example,* and so on

Use a semicolon between main clauses° that are related by two kinds of words: conjunctive adverbs,° such as *however, indeed, therefore,* and *thus*; and other transitional expressions,° such as *after all, for example, in fact,* and *of course.*

> Blue jeans have become fashionable all over the world; however, the American originators still wear more jeans than anyone else.

A conjunctive adverb or transitional expression may move around within its clause, so the semicolon will not always come just before the adverb or expression. The adverb or expression itself is usually set off with a comma or commas.

> Blue jeans have become fashionable all over the world; the American originators, however, still wear more jeans than anyone else.

°See Glossary of Terms, page 249.

24c Semicolons with series

Semicolons between series items

Use semicolons (rather than commas) to separate items in a series when the items contain commas.

> The custody case involved Amy Dalton, the child; Ellen and Mark Dalton, the parents; and Ruth and Hal Blum, the grandparents.

No semicolon before a series

Do not use a semicolon to introduce a series. (Use a colon or a dash instead.)

> Not Teachers have heard all sorts of reasons why students do poorly; psychological problems, family illness, too much work, too little time.
>
> But Teachers have heard all sorts of reasons why students do poorly: psychological problems, family illness, too much work, too little time.

25 The Colon

The colon is mainly a mark of introduction, but it has a few other conventional uses as well.

25a Colon for introduction

Colon at the end of a main clause

The colon ends a main clause° and introduces various additions:

> *Soul food* has a deceptively simple definition: the ethnic cooking of African Americans. [Introduces an explanation.]
>
> At least three soul food dishes are familiar to most Americans: fried chicken, barbecued spareribs, and sweet potatoes. [Introduces a series.]
>
> Soul food has one disadvantage: fat. [Introduces an appositive.°]
>
> One soul food chef has a solution: "Instead of using ham hocks to flavor beans, I use smoked turkey wings. The soulful, smoky taste remains, but without all the fat of pork." [Introduces a long quotation.]

°See Glossary of Terms, page 249.

mycomplab

Visit *mycomplab.com* for more help with the colon.

No colon inside a main clause

Do not use a colon inside a main clause, especially after *such as* or a verb.

Not The best-known soul food dish is: fried chicken. Many Americans have not tasted delicacies such as: chitlins and black-eyed peas.

But The best-known soul food dish is fried chicken. Many Americans have not tasted delicacies such as chitlins and black-eyed peas.

25b Colon with salutation of business letter, title and subtitle, and divisions of time

Salutation of a business letter

Dear Ms. Burak:

Title and subtitle

Anna Freud: Her Life and Work

Time

12:26 6:00

26 The Apostrophe

The apostrophe (') appears as part of a word to indicate possession, the omission of one or more letters, or (in a few cases) plural number.

26a Apostrophe with possessives

The **possessive** form of a word indicates that it owns or is the source of another word: *the dog's hair, everyone's hope*. For nouns° and indefinite pronouns,° such as *everyone*, the possessive form always includes an apostrophe and often an *-s*. (Only personal pronouns such as *hers* and *its* do not use apostrophes for possession.)

Note The apostrophe or apostrophe-plus-*s* is an *addition*. Before this addition, always spell the name of the owner or owners without dropping or adding letters.

Singular words: Add *-'s.*

Some of the earth's forests are regenerating.

Everyone's fitness can be improved through daily exercise.

mycomplab

Visit *mycomplab.com* for more help with the apostrophe.

°See Glossary of Terms, page 249.

The *-'s* ending for singular words usually pertains to singular words ending in *-s*.

Sandra Cisneros's work is highly regarded.

The business's customers filed suit.

However, some writers add only the apostrophe to singular words ending in *-s*, especially when the additional *s* would make the word difficult to pronounce (*Moses'*) or when the name sounds like a plural (*Rivers'*).

Plural words ending in *-s*: Add *-'* only.

Workers' incomes have fallen slightly over the past year.

Many students take several years' leave after high school.

The Murphys' son lives at home.

Plural words not ending in *-s*: Add *-'s*.

Children's educations are at stake.

We need to attract the media's attention.

Compound words: Add *-'s* only to the last word.

The brother-in-law's business failed.

Taxes are always somebody else's fault.

Two or more owners: Add *-'s* depending on possession.

Zimbale's and Mason's comedy techniques are similar. [Each comedian has his own technique.]

The child recovered despite her mother and father's neglect. [The mother and father were jointly neglectful.]

26b Misuses of the apostrophe

No apostrophe with plural nouns°

Not The unleashed dog's belonged to the Jones'.

But The unleashed dogs belonged to the Joneses.

No apostrophe with singular verbs°

Not The subway break's down less often now.

But The subway breaks down less often now.

No apostrophe with possessives of personal pronouns°

Not The frog is her's, not their's. It's skin is speckled.

But The frog is hers, not theirs. Its skin is speckled.

Note Don't confuse possessive pronouns and contractions: *its, your, their,* and *whose* are possessives. *It's, you're, they're,* and *who's* are contractions. See the next page.

°See Glossary of Terms, page 249.

26c Apostrophe with contractions

A **contraction** replaces one or more letters, numbers, or words with an apostrophe.

it is	it's	cannot	can't
you are	you're	does not	doesn't
they are	they're	were not	weren't
who is	who's	class of 1997	class of '97

Note The contractions *it's, you're, they're,* and *who's* are easily confused with the possessive pronouns° *its, your, their,* and *whose.* To avoid misusing any of these words, search for all of them in your drafts and test for correctness:

- **Do you intend the word to contain the sentence verb *is* or *are*,** as in *It is a shame, They are to blame, You are right, Who is coming?* Then use an apostrophe: *it's, they're, you're, who's.*
- **Do you intend the word to indicate possession,** as in *Its tail was wagging, Their car broke down, Your eyes are blue, Whose book is that?* Then don't use an apostrophe.

27

26d Apostrophe with plural abbreviations, dates, and words or characters named as words

You'll sometimes see apostrophes used to form the plurals of abbreviations (*BA's*), dates (*1900's*), and words or characters used as words (*but*'s). However, current style guides recommend against the apostrophe in these cases.

BAs PhDs 1990s 2000s

The sentence has too many *buts*.
Two *3*s end the zip code.

Note Italicize or underline a word or character named as a word (see p. 111), but not the added -*s*.

27 Quotation Marks

Quotation marks—either double (" ") or single (' ')—mainly enclose direct quotations from speech and from writing.

mycomplab

Visit *mycomplab.com* for more help with quotation marks.

°See Glossary of Terms, page 249.

This chapter treats the main uses of quotation marks. Additional issues with quotations are discussed elsewhere in this book:

- **Using commas with signal phrases introducing quotations.** See page 89.
- **Using brackets and the ellipsis mark to indicate changes in quotations.** See pages 99–101.
- **Quoting sources versus paraphrasing or summarizing them.** See pages 142–44.
- **Integrating quotations into your text.** See pages 144–49.
- **Avoiding plagiarism with quotations.** See pages 153–54.
- **Formatting long prose quotations and poetry quotations.** See pages 197 (MLA style), 217 (APA style), and 229 (Chicago style).

Note Always use quotation marks in pairs, one at the beginning of a quotation and one at the end.

27a Quotation marks with direct quotations

Double quotation marks

A **direct quotation** reports what someone said or wrote, in the exact words of the original.

> "Life," said the psychoanalyst Karen Horney, "remains a very efficient therapist."

Note Do not use quotation marks with an **indirect quotation,** which reports what someone said or wrote but not in the exact words of the original: *Karen Horney remarked that life is a good therapist.*

Single quotation marks

Use single quotation marks to enclose a quotation within a quotation.

> "In formulating any philosophy," Woody Allen writes, "the first consideration must always be: What can we know? Descartes hinted at the problem when he wrote, 'My mind can never know my body, although it has become quite friendly with my leg.'"

Dialog

When quoting a conversation, use double quotation marks and begin a new paragraph for each speaker.

> "What shall I call you? Your name?" Andrews whispered rapidly, as with a high squeak the latch of the door rose.
>
> "Elizabeth," she said. "Elizabeth."
>
> —Graham Greene, *The Man Within*

27a

27b Quotation marks for titles of works

Do not use quotation marks for the titles of your own papers. Within your text, however, use quotation marks to enclose the titles of works that are published or released within larger works. Use underlining or italics for all other titles (see pp. 110–11).

Short story
"The Gift of the Magi"

Short poem
"Her Kind"

Article in a periodical
"Does 'Scaring' Work?"

Page or document on a Web site
"Reader's Page" (on the site *Friends of Prufrock*)

Essay
"Joey: A 'Mechanical Boy'"

Song
"Satisfaction"

Episode of a television or radio program
"The Mexican Connection" (on *60 Minutes*)

Subdivision of a book
"The Mast Head" (Chapter 35 of *Moby-Dick*)

27d

Note APA and CSE styles do not use quotation marks for titles within source citations. See pages 203 and 233.

27c Quotation marks with words used in a special sense

On movie sets movable "wild walls" make a one-walled room seem four-walled on film.

Avoid using quotation marks to excuse slang or to express irony—that is, to indicate that you are using a word with a different or even opposite meaning than usual.

Not Americans "justified" their treatment of the Indians.

But Americans attempted to justify their treatment of the Indians.

Note Use italics or underlining to highlight words you are defining. (See p. 111.)

27d Quotation marks with other punctuation

Commas and periods: Inside quotation marks

Jonathan Swift wrote a famous satire, "A Modest Proposal," in 1729.

"Swift's 'A Modest Proposal,'" wrote one critic, "is so outrageous that it cannot be believed."

Exception When a parenthetical source citation immediately follows a quotation, place any comma or period *after* the citation:

One critic calls the essay "outrageous" (Olms 26).

Colons and semicolons: Outside quotation marks

A few years ago the slogan in elementary education was "learning by playing"; now educators stress basic skills.

We all know the meaning of "basic skills": reading, writing, and arithmetic.

Dashes, question marks, and exclamation points: Inside quotation marks only if part of the quotation

When a dash, exclamation point, or question mark is part of the quotation, place it *inside* quotation marks. Don't use any other punctuation, such as a period or comma.

"But must you—" Marcia hesitated, afraid of the answer.

"Go away!" I yelled.

Did you say, "Who is she?" [When both your sentence and the quotation would end in a question mark or exclamation point, use only the mark in the quotation.]

When a dash, question mark, or exclamation point applies only to the larger sentence, not to the quotation, place it *outside* quotation marks—again, with no other punctuation.

Betty Friedan's question in 1963—"Who knows what women can be?"—encouraged others to seek answers.

Who said, "Now cracks a noble heart"?

28 End Punctuation

End a sentence with one of three punctuation marks: a period, a question mark, or an exclamation point.

28a Period for most sentences and some abbreviations

Statement
The airline went bankrupt.

Mild command
Think of the possibilities.

Indirect question°
The article asks how we can improve math education. It asks what cost we are willing to pay.

°See Glossary of Terms, page 249.

mycomplab
Visit *mycomplab.com* for more help with end punctuation.

Abbreviations

Use periods with abbreviations that end in small letters. Otherwise, omit periods from abbreviations.

Dr.	Mr., Mrs.	e.g.	Feb.	ft.
St.	Ms.	i.e.	p.	a.m., p.m.
PhD	BC, AD	USA	IBM	JFK
BA	AM, PM	US	USMC	AIDS

Note When a sentence ends in an abbreviation with a period, don't add a second period: *My first class is at 8 a.m.*

28b Question mark for direct questions°

What is the result?
What is the difference between those proposals?

28c Exclamation point for strong statements and commands

No! We must not lose this election!
Stop the car!

Note Use exclamation points sparingly to avoid seeming overly dramatic.

29 Other Marks

The other marks of punctuation are the dash, parentheses, the ellipsis mark, brackets, and the slash.

29a Dash or dashes: Shifts and interruptions

The dash (—) punctuates sentences, while the hyphen (-) punctuates words. Form a dash using two hyphens (--), with no extra space before, after, or between the hyphens. Or use the character called an em-dash on your word processor.

Note Be sure to use a pair of dashes when a shift or interruption falls in the middle of a sentence.

Shift in tone or thought

The novel—if one can call it that—appeared in 1994.

mycomplab

Visit *mycomplab.com* for more help with the dash, parentheses, the ellipsis mark, brackets, and the slash.

°See Glossary of Terms, page 249.

Nonessential element

The qualities Monet painted—sunlight, shadows, deep colors—typified the rivers and gardens he used as subjects. [Commas may also set off nonessential elements. See p. 86.]

Introductory series

Shortness of breath, skin discoloration, persistent indigestion—all these may signify cancer.

Concluding series or explanation

The patient undergoes a battery of tests—CAT scan, ultrasound, and biopsy. [A colon may also set off a concluding series. See p. 91.]

29b Parentheses: Nonessential elements

Parentheses always come in pairs, one before and one after the punctuated material.

Parenthetical expressions

Parentheses de-emphasize explanatory or supplemental words or phrases. (Commas emphasize these expressions more and dashes still more.)

The population of Philadelphia (now about 1.5 million) has declined since 1950.

Don't put a comma before an opening parenthesis. After a parenthetical expression, place any punctuation *outside* the closing parenthesis.

Not The population of Philadelphia compares with that of Phoenix, (just over 1.6 million.)

But The population of Philadelphia compares with that of Phoenix (just over 1.6 million).

If a complete sentence falls within parentheses, place the period *inside* the closing parenthesis.

The population of Philadelphia has been dropping. (See p. 77 for population data since 1950.)

Labels for lists within text

Outside the Middle East, the countries with the largest oil reserves are (1) Venezuela (63 billion barrels), (2) Russia (57 billion barrels), and (3) Mexico (51 billion barrels).

Do not use parentheses for such labels when you set a list off from your text.

29c Ellipsis mark: Omissions from quotations

The ellipsis mark, consisting of periods separated by space (. . .), generally indicates an omission from a quotation. The following examples quote from or refer to the passage below about environmentalism:

Original quotation

"At the heart of the environmentalist world view is the conviction that human physical and spiritual health depends on sustaining the planet in a relatively unaltered state. Earth is our home in the full, genetic sense, where humanity and its ancestors existed for all the millions of years of their evolution. Natural ecosystems—forests, coral reefs, marine blue waters—maintain the world exactly as we would wish it to be maintained. When we debase the global environment and extinguish the variety of life, we are dismantling a support system that is too complex to understand, let alone replace, in the foreseeable future."

—Edward O. Wilson, "Is Humanity Suicidal?"

1. Omission of the middle of a sentence

Wilson observes, "Natural ecosystems . . . maintain the world exactly as we would wish it to be maintained."

2. Omission of the end of a sentence, without source citation

Wilson writes, "Earth is our home. . . ." [The sentence period, closed up to the last word, precedes the ellipsis mark.]

3. Omission of the end of a sentence, with source citation

Wilson writes, "Earth is our home . . ." (27). [The sentence period follows the source citation.]

4. Omission of parts of two or more sentences

Wilson writes, "At the heart of the environmentalist world view is the conviction that human physical and spiritual health depends on sustaining the planet . . . where humanity and its ancestors existed for all the millions of years of their evolution."

5. Omission of one or more sentences

As Wilson puts it, "At the heart of the environmentalist world view is the conviction that human physical and spiritual health depends on sustaining the planet in a relatively unaltered state. . . . When we debase the global environment and extinguish the variety of life, we are dismantling a support system that is too complex to understand, let alone replace, in the foreseeable future."

6. Omission from the middle of a sentence through the end of another sentence

"Earth is our home. . . . When we debase the global environment and extinguish the variety of life, we are dismantling a support system that is too complex to understand, let alone replace, in the foreseeable future."

7. Omission of the beginning of a sentence, leaving a complete sentence

a. Bracketed capital letter

"[H]uman physical and spiritual health," Wilson writes, "depends on sustaining the planet in a relatively unaltered state." [No ellipsis mark is needed because the brackets around the *H* indicate that the letter was not capitalized originally and thus that the beginning of the sentence has been omitted.]

b. Small letter

According to Wilson, "human physical and spiritual health depends on sustaining the planet in a relatively unaltered state." [No ellipsis mark is needed because the small *h* indicates that the beginning of the sentence has been omitted.]

c. Capital letter from the original

Hami comments, ". . . Wilson argues eloquently for the environmentalist world view." [An ellipsis mark *is* needed because the quoted part of the sentence begins with a capital letter and it's otherwise not clear that the beginning of the original sentence has been omitted.]

8. Use of a word or phrase

Wilson describes the earth as "our home." [No ellipsis mark needed.]

Note these features of the examples:

- **Use an ellipsis mark when it is not otherwise clear that you have left out material from the source,** as when you omit one or more sentences (examples 5 and 6) or when the words you quote form a complete sentence that is different in the original (examples 1–4 and 7c).
- **You don't need an ellipsis mark when it is obvious that you have omitted something,** such as when a bracketed capital letter or a small letter indicates omission (examples 7a and 7b) or when a phrase clearly comes from a larger sentence (example 8).
- **Place an ellipsis mark after the sentence period *except* when a parenthetical source citation follows the quotation,** as in example 3. Then the sentence period falls after the citation.

If your quotation omits one or more lines of poetry or paragraphs of prose, show the omission with an entire line of ellipsis marks across the full width of the quotation.

29d Brackets: Changes in quotations

Though they have specialized uses in mathematical equations, brackets mainly indicate that you have altered a quotation to fit it into your sentence.

Jackson praised the report, saying that "[t]he study's findings give researchers new insights into [Alzheimer's] disease."

29e Slash: Options and breaks in poetry lines

Option

Some teachers oppose pass/fail courses.

Break in poetry lines that run into your text

Many readers have sensed a reluctant turn away from death in Frost's lines "The woods are lovely, dark and deep, / But I have promises to keep."

PART 5

Spelling and Mechanics

Checklist for spelling and mechanics

This checklist covers the main conventions of spelling and mechanics. For a detailed guide to this part, see the contents inside the back cover.

Spelling

☑ Proofread for correct spelling. Don't rely on your spelling checker. (See pp. 105–07.)

Capital letters

☑ Use capital letters appropriately for proper nouns and adjectives and for the titles of works and persons. (See pp. 108–10.)

Italics or underlining

☑ Use italics or underlining primarily for the titles of works published separately from other works. Ensure that italics or underlining in source citations conforms to your discipline's or instructor's requirements. (See pp. 110–11.)

Abbreviations

☑ Use abbreviations appropriately for the discipline or field you are writing in. (See pp. 112–13.)

Numbers

☑ Express numbers in numerals or words appropriately for the discipline or field you are writing in. (See pp. 113–14.)

30 Spelling and the Hyphen

Spelling, including using the hyphen, is a skill you can acquire by paying attention to words and by developing three habits:

- **Carefully proofread your writing.**
- **Cultivate a healthy suspicion of your spellings.**
- **Check a dictionary *every* time you doubt a spelling.**

30a Spelling checkers

A spelling checker can help you find and track spelling errors in your papers. But its usefulness is limited, mainly because it can't spot the confusion of words with similar spellings, such as *their/they're/there*. A grammar/style checker may flag such words, but only the ones listed in its dictionary, and you still must select the correct spelling. Proofread your papers to catch spelling errors.

See pages 9–10 for more on spelling checkers.

30b Spelling rules

We often misspell syllables rather than whole words. The following rules focus on troublesome syllables.

ie and *ei*

Follow the familiar jingle: *i* before *e* except after *c* or when pronounced "ay" as in *neighbor* and *weigh*.

i before *e*	believe	thief
e before *i*	receive	ceiling
ei pronounced "ay"	freight	vein

Exceptions Remember common exceptions with this sentence: *The weird foreigner neither seizes leisure nor forfeits height.*

Silent final *e*

Drop a silent *e* when adding an ending that begins with a vowel. Keep the *e* if the ending begins with a consonant.

advise + able = advisable care + ful = careful

Exceptions Keep the final *e* before a vowel to prevent confusion or mispronunciation: *dyeing, changeable.* Drop the *e* before a consonant when another vowel comes before the *e: argument, truly.*

mycomplab

Visit *mycomplab.com* for more help with spelling and the hyphen.

Final *y*

When adding to a word ending in *y*, change *y* to *i* when it follows a consonant. Keep the *y* when it follows a vowel, precedes *-ing*, or ends a proper name.

beauty, beauties	day, days
worry, worried	study, studying
supply, supplier	Minsky, Minskys

Consonants

When adding an ending to a one-syllable word that ends in a consonant, double the consonant if it follows a single vowel. Otherwise, don't double the consonant.

slap, slapping	pair, paired

For words of more than one syllable, double the final consonant when it follows a single vowel and ends a stressed syllable once the new ending is added. Otherwise, don't double the consonant.

submit, submitted	despair, despairing
refer, referred	refer, reference

Plurals

Most nouns form plurals by adding *s* to the singular form. Nouns ending in *s, sh, ch,* or *x* add *es* to the singular.

boy, boys	kiss, kisses
table, tables	lurch, lurches
Murphy, Murphys	tax, taxes

Nouns ending in a vowel plus *o* add *s*. Nouns ending in a consonant plus *o* add *es*.

ratio, ratios	hero, heroes

Form the plural of a compound noun by adding *s* to the main word in the compound. The main word may not fall at the end.

passersby	breakthroughs
fathers-in-law	city-states

Some English nouns that come from other languages form the plural according to their original language.

analysis, analyses	medium, media
crisis, crises	phenomenon, phenomena
criterion, criteria	piano, pianos

ESL Noncount nouns do not form plurals, either regularly (with an added *s*) or irregularly. Examples of noncount nouns include *equipment*, *intelligence*, and *wealth*. See pages 73–74.

American vs. British or Canadian spellings ESL

American and British or Canadian spellings differ in ways such as the following:

American	British or Canadian
color, humor	colour, humour
theater, center	theatre, centre
canceled, traveled	cancelled, travelled
judgment	judgement
realize, analyze	realise, analyse
defense, offense	defence, offence

30c The hyphen

Use the hyphen to form compound words and to divide words at the ends of lines.

Compound words

Compound words may be written as a single word (*breakthrough*), as two words (*decision makers*), or as a hyphenated word (*cross-reference*). Check a dictionary for the spelling of a compound word. Except as explained below, any compound not listed in the dictionary should be written as two words.

Sometimes a compound word comes from combining two or more words into a single adjective.° When such a compound adjective precedes a noun, a hyphen forms the words clearly into a unit.

She is a well-known actor.
Some Spanish-speaking students work as translators.

When a compound adjective follows the noun, the hyphen is unnecessary.

The actor is well known.
Many students are Spanish speaking.

The hyphen is also unnecessary in a compound modifier containing an *-ly* adverb, even before the noun: *clearly defined terms*.

Fractions and compound numbers

Hyphens join the parts of fractions: *three-fourths, one-half*. And the whole numbers *twenty-one* to *ninety-nine* are always hyphenated.

Prefixes and suffixes

Do not use hyphens with prefixes except as follows:

- **With the prefixes *self-*, *all-*, and *ex-*:** *self-control, all-inclusive, ex-student.*

°See Glossary of Terms, page 249.

30c

- **With a prefix before a capitalized word:** *un-American.*
- **With a capital letter before a word:** *T-shirt.*
- **To prevent misreading:** *de-emphasize, re-create a story.*

The only suffix that regularly requires a hyphen is *-elect*, as in *president-elect*.

Word division at the end of a line

You can avoid short lines in your documents by setting your word processor to divide words automatically. To divide words manually, follow these guidelines:

- **Divide words only between syllables**—for instance, *windows,* not *wi-ndows*. Check a dictionary for correct syllable breaks.
- **Never divide a one-syllable word.**
- **Leave at least two letters on the first line and three on the second line.** If a word cannot be divided to follow this rule (for instance, *a-bus-er*), don't divide it.

If you must break an electronic address or URL—for instance, in a source citation—do not hyphenate, because readers may perceive any added hyphen as part of the address. The documentation styles differ in where they allow breaks in URLs. For example, MLA style allows a break only after a slash, while APA style allows a break before most punctuation marks.

31 Capital Letters

As a rule, capitalize a word only when a dictionary or conventional use says you must. Consult one of the style guides listed on page 156 for special uses of capitals in the social, natural, and applied sciences.

31a First word of a sentence

No one expected the outcome.

31b Proper nouns° and proper adjectives°

Specific persons and things

Stephen King | Boulder Dam

mycomplab

Visit *mycomplab.com* for more help with capital letters.

°See Glossary of Terms, page 249.

Specific places and geographical regions

New York City	the Northeast, the South

But: northeast of the city, going south

Days of the week, months, holidays

Monday	Yom Kippur
May	Christmas

But: winter, spring, summer, fall

Historical events, documents, periods, movements

the Vietnam War	the Renaissance
the Constitution	the Romantic Movement

Government offices, departments, and institutions

Polk Municipal Court	House of Representatives
El Camino Hospital	Department of Defense

But: the court, the department, the hospital

Academic institutions and departments

University of Kansas	Department of Nursing
Santa Monica College	Haven High School

But: the university, college course, high school diploma

Organizations, associations, and their members

B'nai B'rith	Democratic Party, Democrats
Rotary Club	League of Women Voters
Atlanta Falcons	Chicago Symphony Orchestra

Races, nationalities, and their languages

Native American	Germans
African American	Swahili
Caucasian	Italian

But: blacks, whites

Religions, their followers, and terms for the sacred

Christianity, Christians	God
Judaism, Orthodox Jew	the Bible (*but* biblical)
Islam, Muslims	the Koran, the Qur'an

Common nouns as parts of proper nouns

Uncle Dan	Lake Superior
Professor Allen	Pacific Ocean
Main Street	Ford Motor Company

But: my uncle, the professor, the ocean, the company

31c

31c Titles and subtitles of works

Capitalize all the words in a title and subtitle *except* articles (*a, an, the*), *to* in infinitives,° coordinating conjunctions° (*and, but,* etc.), and prepositions° (*with, between,* etc.). Capitalize even these words when they are the first

°See Glossary of Terms, page 249.

or last word in the title or when they fall after a colon or semicolon.

"Once More to the Lake" | *Management: A New Theory*
Learning from Las Vegas | "The Truth about AIDS"
"Knowing Whom to Ask" | *An End to Live For*

Note The preceding guidelines reflect MLA style for English and some other humanities. Other disciplines' style guides have different rules for capitals within source citations. See pages 203 (APA style) and 233 (CSE style).

31d Titles of persons

Title before name Professor Jane Covington
Title after name Jane Covington, a professor

31e Online communication

Online messages written in all-capital letters or with no capitals are difficult to read, and those in all-capitals are often considered rude. Use capital letters according to the rules in 31a–31d in all your online communication.

32 Italics or Underlining

32a

Italic type and underlining indicate the same thing: the word or words are being distinguished or emphasized. Italic type is now used almost universally in academic writing. Some instructors do recommend underlining, so ask your instructor for his or her preference.

Use either italics or underlining consistently throughout a document. For instance, if you are using italics in source citations, use italics in the body of your paper as well. If you are using underlining and you underline two or more words in a row, underline the space between the words, too: Criminal Statistics: Misuses of Numbers.

32a Titles of works

Do not italicize or underline the title of your own paper unless it contains an element (such as a book title) that requires highlighting.

Within your text, italicize or underline the titles of works that are published, released, or produced separately from other works. Use quotation marks for all other titles (see p. 96).

Book
War and Peace

Play
Hamlet

Web site
Friends of Prufrock
Google

Computer software
Microsoft Internet Explorer

Long musical work
The Beatles' *Revolver*
But: Symphony in C

Work of visual art
Michelangelo's *David*

Long poem
Paradise Lost

Periodical
Philadelphia Inquirer

Television or radio program
60 Minutes

Movie
Psycho

Pamphlet
The Truth about Alcoholism

Published speech
Lincoln's *Gettysburg Address*

Exceptions Legal documents, the Bible, and parts of them are generally not italicized or underlined.

We studied the Book of Revelation in the Bible.

32b Ships, aircraft, spacecraft, trains

Challenger *Orient Express* *Queen Mary 2*
Apollo XI *Montrealer* *Spirit of St. Louis*

32c Foreign words and phrases

The scientific name for the brown trout is *Salmo trutta*. [The Latin names for plants and animals are always highlighted.]

The Latin *De gustibus non est disputandum* translates roughly as "There's no accounting for taste."

32d Words or characters named as words

Italicize or underline words or characters (letters or numbers) that are referred to as themselves rather than used for their meanings, including terms you are defining.

Some children pronounce *th*, as in *thought*, with an *f* sound.

The word *syzygy* refers to a straight line formed by three celestial bodies, as in the alignment of the earth, sun, and moon.

32e Online alternatives

Some forms of online communication do not allow highlighting with italics or underlining for the purposes described in this chapter. If you can't use italics or underlining to distinguish book titles and other elements, type an underscore before and after the element: *Measurements coincide with those in _Joule's Handbook_*. You can also emphasize words with asterisks before and after: *I *will not* be able to attend.*

Don't use all-capital letters for emphasis; they yell too loudly. (See also p. 110.)

33 Abbreviations

The following guidelines on abbreviations pertain to the text of a nontechnical document. For any special requirements of the discipline you are writing in, consult one of the style guides listed on page 151. In all disciplines, writers increasingly omit periods from abbreviations that end in capital letters. (See p. 156.)

If a name or term (such as *operating room*) appears often in a piece of writing, then its abbreviation (*OR*) can cut down on extra words. Spell out the full term at its first appearance, give the abbreviation in parentheses, and use the abbreviation thereafter.

33a Familiar abbreviations

Titles before names	Dr., Mr., Mrs., Ms., Rev., Gen.
Titles after names	MD, DDS, DVM, PhD, Sr., Jr.
Institutions	LSU, UCLA, TCU, NASA
Organizations	CIA, FBI, YMCA, AFL-CIO
Corporations	IBM, CBS, ITT, GM
People	JFK, LBJ, FDR
Countries	USA, UK
Specific numbers	no. 36 *or* No. 36
Specific amounts	$7.41, $1 million
Specific times	11:26 AM, 8:04 a.m., 2:00 PM, 8:05 p.m.
Specific dates	44 BC, AD 1492, 44 BCE, 1492 CE

Note The abbreviations BC ("before Christ"), BCE ("before the common era"), and CE ("common era") always follow the date. In contrast, AD (*anno domini*, "in the year of the Lord") always precedes the date.

mycomplab

Visit *mycomplab.com* for more help with abbreviations.

33b Latin abbreviations

Generally, use the common Latin abbreviations (without italics or underlining) only in source citations and comments in parentheses.

i.e.	*id est*: that is
cf.	*confer*: compare
e.g.	*exempli gratia*: for example
et al.	*et alii*: and others
etc.	*et cetera*: and so forth
NB	*nota bene*: note well

He said he would be gone a fortnight (i.e., two weeks).
Bloom et al., editors, *Anthology of Light Verse*

33c Words usually spelled out

Generally spell out certain kinds of words in the text of academic, general, and business writing. (In technical writing, however, abbreviate units of measurement.)

Units of measurement

Mount Everest is 29,028 feet high.

Geographical names

Lincoln was born in Illinois.

Names of days, months, and holidays

The truce was signed on Tuesday, April 16, and was ratified by Christmas.

Names of people

Robert Frost wrote accessible poems.

Courses of instruction

The writer teaches psychology and composition.

And

The new rules affect New York City and environs. [Use the ampersand, &, only in the names of business firms: *Lee & Sons*.]

34 Numbers

This chapter addresses the use of numbers (numerals versus words) in the text of a nontechnical document. Usage does vary, so consult one of the style guides listed on

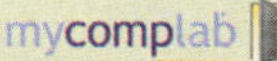

Visit *mycomplab.com* for more help with numbers.

page 156 for the requirements of the discipline you are writing in.

34a Numerals, not words

Numbers requiring three or more words
366 36,500

Round numbers over a million
26 million 2.45 billion

Exact amounts of money
$3.5 million $4.50

Days and years
June 18, 1985 AD 12
456 BC 12 CE

The time of day
9:00 AM 3:45 PM

Addresses
355 Heckler Avenue
Washington, DC 20036

Decimals, percentages, and fractions
22.5 3 1/2
48% (*or* 48 percent)

Scores and statistics
a ratio of 8 to 1 21 to 7
a mean of 26

Pages, chapters, volumes, acts, scenes, lines
Chapter 9, page 123
Hamlet, act 5, scene 3

34b Words, not numerals

Numbers of one or two words
sixty days, forty-two laps, one hundred people

In business and technical writing, use words only for numbers under 11 (*ten reasons, four laps*).

Beginnings of sentences
Seventy-five riders entered the race.

If a number beginning a sentence requires more than two words to spell out, reword the sentence so that the number falls later.

Faulty 103 visitors returned.
Awkward One hundred three visitors returned.
Revised Of the visitors, 103 returned.

Note Two numbers in a row can be confusing. Rewrite to separate the numbers:

Confusing Out of 530 101 children caught the virus.
Clear Out of 530 children 101 caught the virus.

PART 6

Research and Documentation

Checklist for research and documentation

This checklist covers the main considerations in using and documenting sources. For a detailed guide to this part, see the contents inside the back cover.

Developing a research strategy

☑ Formulate a question about your subject that can guide your research. (See opposite.)

☑ Set goals for your sources: library vs. Internet, primary vs. secondary, and so on. (See opposite.)

☑ Prepare a working, annotated bibliography to keep track of sources. (See p. 120.)

Finding sources

☑ Develop keywords that describe your subject for searches of electronic sources. (See p. 123.)

☑ Consult appropriate sources to answer your research question. (See p. 124.)

Evaluating and synthesizing sources

☑ Evaluate both print and online sources for their relevance and reliability. (See p. 132.)

☑ Synthesize sources to find their relationships and to support your own ideas. (See p. 141.)

Integrating sources into your text

☑ Summarize, paraphrase, or quote sources depending on the significance of the source's ideas or wording. (See p. 142.)

☑ Work source material smoothly and informatively into your own text. (See p. 144.)

Avoiding plagiarism and documenting sources

☑ Do not plagiarize, either deliberately or accidentally, by presenting the words or ideas of others as your own. (See p. 150.)

☑ Using the style guide appropriate for your discipline, document your sources and format your paper. (See p. 156 for a list of style guides and Chapters 40 for MLA style, 41 for APA style, 42 for Chicago style, and 43 for CSE style.)

35 Developing a Research Strategy

Research writing gives you a chance to work like a detective solving a case. The mystery is the answer to a question you care about. The search for the answer leads you to consider what others think about your subject, to build on that information, and ultimately to become an expert in your own right.

35a Subject, question, and thesis

Seek a research subject that you care about and want to know more about. Starting with such an interest and with your own views will motivate you and will make you a participant in a dialog when you begin examining sources.

Asking a question about your subject can give direction to your research by focusing your thinking on a particular approach. To discover your question, consider what about your subject intrigues or perplexes you, what you'd like to know more about. (See the next page for suggestions on using your own knowledge.)

Try to narrow your research question so that you can answer it in the time and space you have available. The question *How does human activity affect the environment?* is very broad, encompassing issues as diverse as pollution, climate change, population growth, land use, and biodiversity. In contrast, the question *How can buying environmentally friendly products help the environment?* or *How, if at all, should carbon emissions be taxed?* is much narrower. Each question also requires more than a simple yes-or-no answer, so that answering it, even tentatively, demands thought about pros and cons, causes and effects.

As you read and write, your question will probably evolve to reflect your increasing knowledge of the subject. Eventually its answer will become the **thesis** of your paper, the main idea that all the paper's evidence supports. (See also p. 5.)

35b Goals for sources

Before you start looking for sources, consider what you already know about your subject and where you are likely to find information on it.

mycomplab

Visit *mycomplab.com* for more help with research strategy.

Your own knowledge

Discovering what you already know about your topic will guide you in discovering what you don't know and thus need to research. Take some time to spell out facts you have learned, opinions you have heard or read elsewhere, and of course your own opinions.

When you've explored your thoughts, make a list of questions for which you don't have answers, whether factual (*How much do Americans spend on environmentally friendly products?*) or more open-ended (*Are green products worth the higher prices?*). These questions will give you clues about the sources you need to look for first.

Kinds of sources

For many research projects, you'll want to consult a mix of sources, as described below. You may start by seeking the outlines of your subject—the range and depth of opinions about it—in reference works and articles in popular periodicals or through a search of the Web. Then, as you refine your views and your research question, you'll move on to more specialized sources, such as scholarly books and periodicals and your own interviews or surveys. (See pp. 124–31 for more on each kind of source.)

Library and Internet sources

The sources available at your library or through its Web site—mainly reference works, periodicals, and books—have two big advantages over most of what you'll find on the open Web: they are cataloged and indexed for easy retrieval; and they are generally reliable, having been screened first by their publishers and then by the library's staff. In contrast, the Internet's retrieval systems are more difficult to use effectively, and Web sources can be less reliable because many do not pass through any screening before being posted. (There are many exceptions, such as online scholarly journals and reference works. But these sources are generally available through your library's Web site as well.)

Most instructors expect research writers to consult library sources. But they'll accept online sources, too, if you have used them judiciously. Even with its disadvantages, the Internet can be a valuable resource for primary sources, scholarly work, current information, and diverse views. For guidelines on evaluating both print and online sources, see pages 132–41.

Primary and secondary sources

Use **primary sources** when they are available or are required by your assignment. These sources are firsthand accounts, such as historical documents (letters, speeches, and so on), eyewitness reports, works of literature, reports on experiments or surveys conducted by the writer, and your own interviews, experiments, observations, or correspondence.

Many assignments will allow you to use **secondary sources,** which report and analyze information drawn from other sources, often primary ones. Examples include a reporter's summary of a controversial issue, a historian's account of a battle, a critic's reading of a poem, and a psychologist's evaluation of several studies. Secondary sources may contain helpful summaries and interpretations that direct, support, and extend your own thinking. However, most research-writing assignments expect your own ideas to go beyond those in such sources.

Scholarly and popular sources

The scholarship of acknowledged experts is essential for depth, authority, and specificity. The general-interest views and information of popular sources can help you apply more scholarly approaches to daily life.

When looking for sources, you can gauge how scholarly or popular they are from bibliographic information:

- **Check the title.** Is it technical, or does it use a general vocabulary?
- **Check the publisher.** Is it a scholarly journal (such as *Education Forum*) or a publisher of scholarly books (such as Harvard University Press), or is it a popular magazine (such as *Time* or *Newsweek*) or a publisher of popular books (such as Little, Brown)?
- **Check the length of periodical articles.** Scholarly articles are generally much longer than magazine and newspaper articles.
- **Check the author.** Have you seen the name elsewhere, which might suggest that the author is an expert?
- **Check the URL.** A Web site's URL, or electronic address, includes an abbreviation that tells you something about the origin of the source: scholarly sources usually end in *edu, org,* or *gov,* while popular sources usually end in *com*. See pages 128–30 for more on types of online sources.

Older and newer sources

For most subjects a combination of older, established sources (such as books) and current sources (such as newspaper articles or interviews) will provide both background and up-to-date information. Only historical subjects or very current subjects require an emphasis on one extreme or another.

Impartial and biased sources

Seek a range of viewpoints. Sources that attempt to be impartial can offer an overview of your subject and trustworthy facts. Sources with clear biases can offer a diversity of opinion. Of course, to discover bias, you may have to read the source carefully (see p. 133); but you can infer quite a bit just from a bibliographical listing:

- **Check the author.** You may have heard of the author as a respected researcher (thus more likely to be objective) or as a leading proponent of a certain view (less likely to be objective).
- **Check the title.** It may reveal something about point of view. (Consider these contrasting titles: "Go for the Green" and "Where the Green Is: Examining the Paradox of Environmentally Conscious Consumption.")

Note Internet sources must be approached with particular care. See pages 133 and 136–41.

Sources with helpful features

Depending on your topic and how far along your research is, you may want to look for sources with features such as illustrations (which can clarify important concepts), bibliographies (which can direct you to other sources), and indexes (which can help you develop keywords for electronic searches; see pp. 123–24).

35c Working, annotated bibliography

To track where sources are, compile a **working bibliography** of possibilities. When you have a substantial file—say, ten to thirty sources—you can decide which ones seem most promising and look them up first.

Source information

Use the following lists to track sources. For source samples that show where you can find the required information, see pages 168–69, 172–73, 182–83, and 190–91.

For a book

Library call number
Name(s) of author(s), editor(s), translator(s), or others listed
Title and subtitle
Publication data: (1) place of publication; (2) publisher's name; (3) date of publication
Other important data, such as edition or volume number
Medium (print, Web, etc.)

For a periodical article

Name(s) of author(s)

Title and subtitle of article
Title of periodical
Publication data: (1) volume number and issue number (if any) in which the article appears; (2) date of issue; (3) page numbers on which article appears
Medium (print, Web, etc.)

For electronic sources

Name(s) of author(s)
Title and subtitle of source
Title of Web site, periodical, or other larger work
Publication data, such as preceding data for a book or article; the publisher or sponsor of a Web site; and the date of release, revision, or online posting
Any publication data for the source in another medium (print, film, etc.)
Format of online source (Web site or page, podcast, e-mail, etc.)
Date you consulted the source
Title of any database used to reach the source
Complete URL (but see the note below)
Digital Object Identifier, if any (for APA and Chicago style)
Medium (Web, CD-ROM, etc.)

For other sources

Name(s) of author(s) or others listed, such as a government department or a recording artist
Title of the work
Format, such as unpublished letter or live performance
Publication or production data: (1) publisher's or producer's name; (2) date of publication, release, or production; (3) identifying numbers (if any)
Medium (print, typescript, etc.)

Note Documentation styles vary in requiring URLs for citations of electronic sources. For instance, MLA style generally does not require URLs, APA style generally requires just home page URLs, and some other styles always require complete URLs. Even if you don't need the complete URL in your final citation of a source, record it anyway so that you'll be able to track the source down if you want to consult it again. The exception is a source you reach through a library database, because most database URLs can't be used to locate a source.

Annotations

Creating annotations for a working bibliography converts it from a simple list into a tool for assessing sources. The annotations can help you discover gaps that may remain in your sources and will later help you decide which sources to pursue in depth. When you discover a possible source, record not only its publication information but also the following:

- **What you know about the content of the source.** Periodical databases and book catalogs generally include abstracts, or summaries, of sources that can help with this part of the annotation.
- **How you think the source may be helpful in your research.** Does it offer expert opinion, statistics, an important example, or a range of views? Does it place your subject in a historical, social, or economic context?

As you become more familiar with your sources, you can use your initial annotated bibliography to record your evaluation of them and more detailed thoughts on how they fit into your research. One student annotated a bibliography entry with a summary, a note on the source features he thought would be most useful to him, and an assessment.

Entry for an annotated bibliography

Gore, Al. *An Inconvenient Truth: The Planetary Emergency of Global Warming and What We Can Do about It*. Emmaus: Rodale, 2006. Print.

Book version of the documentary movie supporting Gore's argument that global warming is a serious threat to the planet. Includes summaries of scientific studies, short essays on various subjects, and dozens of images, tables, charts, and graphs. Last chapter offers several suggestions for ways to solve the problem, with an emphasis on changing individual buying habits.

Urgent and alarming argument, with lots of data that seem thorough and convincing. But book is aimed at a general audience and doesn't have formal source citations. Can use book for broad concepts, but for data I'd have to track down Gore's scholarly sources.

36 Finding Sources

This chapter discusses both using keywords to conduct electronic searches and taking advantage of the range of sources, both print and electronic, that you have access to:

reference works, books, periodicals, the Web, other online sources, government publications, images, and your own sources.

36a Electronic searches

The library's Web site

As you conduct research, the Web will be your gateway to ideas and information. Always begin your academic research on your library's Web site, not with a search engine such as *Google*. (*Google Scholar,* a tool that searches for scholarly articles, is discussed on p. 127.) The library site will lead you to vast resources that aren't available on the open Web. More important, its resources have passed through editors and librarians to ensure their value. *Google* and other search engines may seem more user-friendly than the library site, but many more of its sources will be unreliable.

Keyword searches

Keywords, or **descriptors,** name your subject for computer searches. As you develop keywords, be aware of an important difference between databases and Web search engines:

- **A database indexes sources under its own subject headings,** which are assigned by people who have read the indexed sources. Your search will be more productive if you use these headings as your keywords. To find them, use your own keywords until you locate a promising source and its list of the database's headings for that source. The listing will include the database's headings for the source.
- **A Web search engine seeks your keywords in the titles and texts of sites.** Since the process is entirely electronic, your results will depend on how well your keywords describe your subject and anticipate the words used in sources.

Every database and search engine provides a system that you can use to expand or limit your keywords and thus your search. The basic operators appear in the following list, but resources do differ. Use the Help or Advanced Search information to learn the system of a particular database or search engine.

- **Use *AND* or + to narrow the search** by including only sources that use all the given words. The keywords *green AND products* request only the sources that contain both words.

- **Use *NOT* or – ("minus") to narrow the search** by excluding irrelevant words. *Green AND products NOT guide* excludes sources that use the word *guide*.
- **Use *OR* to broaden the search** by giving alternative keywords. *Green AND products OR goods* allows for sources that use a synonym for *products*.
- **Use parentheses to form search phrases.** For instance, *(green products)* requests the exact phrase, not the separate words. (Some systems use quotation marks instead of parentheses for this purpose.)
- **Use wild cards to permit different versions of the same word.** In *consum**, for instance, the wild card * indicates that sources may include *consume, consumer, consumerism,* and *consumption* as well as *consumptive, consumedly*, and *consummate*. If a wild card opens up your search too much, you may be better off using *OR*: *consumption OR consumerism.* (Some systems use ?, :, or + for a wild card instead of *.)
- **Be sure to spell your keywords correctly.** Some search tools will look for close matches or approximations, but correct spelling gives you the best chance of finding relevant sources.

36b Reference works

Reference works, often available online, include encyclopedias, dictionaries, digests, bibliographies, indexes, handbooks, atlases, and almanacs. Your research *must* go beyond these sources, but they can help you decide whether your subject really interests you, can help you develop your keywords for electronic searches, and can direct you to more detailed sources.

You'll find many reference works through your library and directly on the Web. The following list gives general Web references for academic research.

BUBL Information Service (bubl.ac.uk/link)
EDSITEment (edsitement.neh.gov)
Google Directory (directory.google.com)
INFOMINE (infomine.ucr.edu)
Internet Public Library (ipl.org)
Library of Congress (lcweb.loc.gov)
LSU Libraries (www.lib.lsu.edu/weblio.html)
Voice of the Shuttle (vos.ucsb.edu)
WWW Virtual Library (vlib.org)

Note The Web-based encyclopedia *Wikipedia* (found at *wikipedia.org*) is one of the largest reference sites on the Internet. Like any encyclopedia, *Wikipedia* can provide background information for research on a topic. But unlike other encyclopedias, *Wikipedia* is a **wiki,** a kind of

Web site that can be contributed to or edited by anyone. Ask your instructor whether *Wikipedia* or any other wiki is an acceptable source before you use it. If you do use it, you must carefully evaluate any information you find, using the guidelines on pages 133 and 136–41.

36c Books

Depending on your subject, you may find some direction and information in so-called general or trade books, which include personal or popular views of culture, nonspecialist explanations of scholarly work, and how-to guides. But usually the books you consult for academic research will be scholarly, intended for specialists, and will include detailed statements of theory or surveys of research.

You can search your library's online catalog by authors' names, titles, or keywords. Using the tips on pages 123–24, experiment with your own keywords until you locate a source that seems relevant to your subject. The book's detailed record will show Library of Congress subject headings that you can use to find similar books.

36d Periodicals

Periodicals include newspapers, academic journals, and magazines, either printed or online. Newspapers are useful for detailed accounts of past and current events. Journals and magazines can be harder to distinguish, but their differences are important. Most college instructors expect students' research to rely more on journals than on magazines.

	Journals	Magazines
Examples	*American Anthropologist, Journal of Black Studies, Journal of Chemical Education*	*The New Yorker, Time, Rolling Stone, People*
Availability	Mainly through college and university libraries, either on library shelves or in online databases	Public libraries, newsstands, bookstores, the open Web, and online databases
Purpose	Advance knowledge in a particular field	Express opinion, inform, or entertain
Authors	Specialists in the field	May or may not be specialists in their subjects

Journals	Magazines
Readers	
Often specialists in the field	Members of the general public or a subgroup with a particular interest
Source citations	
Source citations always included	Source citations rarely included
Length of articles	
Usually long, ten pages or more	Usually short, fewer than ten pages
Frequency of publication	
Quarterly or less often	Weekly, biweekly, or monthly

Periodical databases

Periodical databases index the articles in journals, magazines, and newspapers. Often these databases include abstracts, or summaries, of the articles, and they may offer the full text of the articles as well. Your library subscribes to many databases, and you can search most of them through the library's Web site. They vary widely in what they index. To decide which ones to use, consider what you're looking for:

- **Does your research subject span more than one discipline?** Then start with a broad database such as *Academic Search Complete, JSTOR, Lexis Nexis Academic Universe,* or *CQ Researcher.* A broad database covers many subjects and disciplines but does not index the full range of periodicals in each subject.
- **Does your research subject focus on a single discipline?** Then start with a discipline-specific database such as *Historical Abstracts, MLA International Bibliography, Biological Abstracts,* or *Education Search Complete*. A specific database covers few subjects but includes most of the available periodicals in each subject. If you don't know the name of an appropriate database, the library's Web site probably lists possibilities by discipline.
- **Which databases most likely include the kinds of resources you need?** You can discover the focus of each database by checking its description (sometimes labeled "Help" or "Guide") or its list of indexed resources (sometimes labeled "Publications" or "Index"). The description will also tell you the time period the database covers, so you'll know whether you also need to consult older print indexes at the library.

Note The search engine *Google* has developed *Google Scholar,* a search engine at *scholar.google.com* that seeks out scholarly articles. It is particularly useful for subjects that range across disciplines, for which discipline-specific databases can be too limited. *Google Scholar* can connect to your library's holdings if you tell it to do so under Scholar Preferences. Keep in mind, however, that your library probably subscribes to most of the periodicals searched by *Google Scholar,* so begin there.

Database searches

The screen shot below shows partial results from a search of *EBSCOhost Academic Complete*. Clicking on either of these items would lead to a more detailed record containing two important kinds of information: a list of the subject headings the database uses for the source, which you can use to refine your search; and an abstract, or summary, of the article, which can tell you whether you want to pursue the article further. An abstract is not the article, however, and should not be used or cited as if it were.

Partial keyword search results

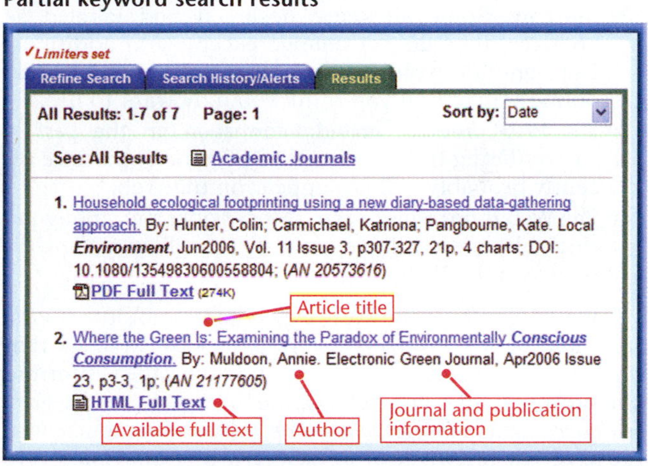

Note Many databases allow you to limit your search to so-called peer-reviewed or refereed journals—that is, scholarly journals whose articles have been reviewed before publication by experts in the field and then revised by the author. Limiting your search to peer-reviewed journals can help you navigate huge databases that might otherwise return scores of unusable articles.

36e The Web

As an academic researcher, you enter the Web in two ways: through your library's Web site, and through public search engines such as *Bing* and *Google*. The library entrance, covered in the preceding sections, is your main path to the books and periodicals that, for most subjects, should make up most of your sources. The public entrance, discussed here, can lead to a wealth of information and ideas, but it also has disadvantages that limit its usefulness for academic research:

- **The Web is a wide-open network.** Anyone with the right hardware and software can place information on the Internet, and even a carefully conceived search can turn up sources with widely varying reliability: journal articles, government documents, scholarly data, term papers written by high school students, sales pitches masked as objective reports, wild theories. You must be especially diligent about evaluating Internet sources (see pp. 133–41).
- **The Web changes constantly.** No search engine can keep up with the Web's daily additions and deletions, and a source you find today may be different or gone tomorrow. Some sites are designed and labeled as archives: they do not change except with additions. But generally you should not put off consulting an online source that you think you may want to use.
- **The Web provides limited information on the past.** A source dating from before the 1980s or even more recently probably will not appear on the Web.
- **The Web is not all-inclusive.** Most books and many periodicals are available only via the library, not directly via the Web.

When searching the Web, expect to use not just *Google* but three or four other search engines as well, so that you cover the range of sources. (For the latest information on Web search engines, see the links collected by *Easy Searcher* at *www.easysearcher.com.*) Also expect to use trial and error to minimize the irrelevant hits and maximize the relevant ones. For example, a student researching consumption of environmentally friendly products first used the keywords *green consumption* and turned up 3.4 million items. Revising his terms to *"green consumption" "environmental issues,"* he cut the results to 2400 items. Finally, he added *site:.org* to the end of his keywords, limiting the results to nonprofit organizations, and got just 387 results.

36f Other online sources

Several online sources can connect you with experts and others whose ideas and information may inform your research. Because these sources, like Web sites, are unfiltered, you must always evaluate them carefully. (See pp. 140–41.)

- **E-mail** allows you to communicate with others who may be interested in your subject, such as a teacher at your school or an expert in another state.
- **Blogs** (Web logs) are personal sites on which an author posts time-stamped comments, generally centering on a common theme, in a format that allows readers to respond to the author and to each other. You can find directories of blogs at *blogcatalog.com*.
- **Discussion lists** (or listservs) use e-mail to connect subscribers who are interested in a common subject. Many have a scholarly or technical purpose. For an index of discussion lists, see *tile.net/lists*.
- **Newsgroups and Web forums** are more open than discussion lists. For an index to Web forums, see *delphiforums.com*. For a newsgroup index, see *groups .google.com*.

36g Government publications

Government publications provide a vast array of data, compilations, reports, policy statements, public records, and other historical and contemporary information. For US government publications, consult the Government Printing Office's *GPO Access* at *www.gpoaccess.gov*. Also helpful is *Google US Government Search* (*google.com/unclesam*) because it returns *.gov* (government) and *.mil* (military) documents and its ranking system emphasizes the most useful documents. Many federal, state, and local government agencies post important publications—legislation, reports, press releases—on their own Web sites. You can find lists of sites for various federal agencies by using the keywords *United States federal government* with a search engine. Use the name of a state, city, or town with *government* for state and local information.

36h Images, video, and audio

Images, video, and audio can be used as both primary and secondary sources in academic writing. A painting, an advertisement, or a video of a speech might be the subject of a paper and thus a primary source. A podcast of a radio interview or a college lecture might serve as a secondary source. Because many Web sources for multimedia are unfiltered—they can be posted by anyone—you must always evaluate them as carefully as you would any source on the open Web.

- **Images** such as charts, graphs, and photographs can be found in print or online. Online sources for images include public image databases such as *American Memory* (Library of Congress) and *Digital Gallery* (New York Public Library); public image directories such as *Museum Link's Museum of Museums*; search engines such as *Google, AltaVista,* and *AlltheWeb*; and databases available through your library gateway.
- **Video files** capture performances, public presentations and speeches, and news events, among other activities. They are available through the Web and through your library. Online sources of video include *American Memory;* search engines such as *Google*; and *YouTube,* which includes commercials, historical footage, current events, and much more.
- **Audio files** such as podcasts, Webcasts, and CDs record radio programs, interviews, speeches, and music. They are available on the Web and through your library. Online sources of audio include *American Memory* and podcasts at *podcastdirectory.com.*

36i Your own sources

Academic writing will often require you to conduct primary research for information of your own.

Observation

Observation can be an effective way to gather fresh information on your subject. You may observe in a controlled setting—for instance, watching the behavior of children playing in a child-development lab. Or you may observe in a more open setting—for instance, watching the interactions among students at a cafeteria on your campus. Be sure your observation has a well-defined purpose that relates to your research project. Throughout the observation, take careful notes, and always record the date, time, and location for each session.

Personal interviews

An interview can be especially helpful for a research project because it allows you to ask questions precisely geared to your subject. You can conduct an interview in person, over the telephone, or online. A personal interview is preferable because you can hear the person's tone and see his or her expressions and gestures.

Here are a few guidelines for interviews:

- **Prepare a list of open-ended questions to ask**—perhaps ten or twelve for a one-hour interview. Do some research for these questions to discover background on the issues.
- **Take care in interpreting answers,** especially if you are online and thus can't depend on facial expressions, gestures, and tone of voice to convey the subject's attitudes.
- **Keep thorough notes.** Take notes during an in-person or telephone interview, or record the interview if your subject agrees. For online interviews, save the discussion in a file of its own.
- **Verify quotations.** Before you quote your subject in your paper, check with him or her to ensure that the quotations are accurate.

Surveys

Asking questions of a defined group of people can provide information about respondents' attitudes, behavior, backgrounds, and expectations. Use the following tips to plan and conduct a survey:

- **Decide what you want to find out.** The questions you ask should be dictated by your purpose. Formulating a **hypothesis** about your subject—a generalization that can be tested—will help you refine your purpose.
- **Define your population.** Think about the kinds of people your hypothesis is about—for instance, college men or preschool children—and sample this population.
- **Write your questions.** Surveys may contain closed questions (checklists and multiple-choice, true/false, or yes/no questions) or open-ended questions that allow brief, descriptive answers.
- **Test your questions on a few respondents.** Eliminate or recast questions that they find unclear, discomforting, or unanswerable.
- **Tally the results.** Count the actual numbers of answers, including any nonanswers.
- **Seek patterns in the raw data.** Such patterns may confirm or contradict your hypothesis. Revise the hypothesis or conduct additional research if necessary.

37 Evaluating and Synthesizing Sources

Research writing is much more than finding sources and reporting their contents. The challenge and interest come from selecting appropriate sources and then interacting with and synthesizing them through **critical reading.** To read critically, you analyze a text, identifying its main ideas, evidence, bias, and other relevant elements; you evaluate its usefulness and quality; and you relate it to other texts and to your own ideas.

37a Evaluation of sources

Not all the sources you find will prove worthwhile: some may be irrelevant to your subject, and others may be unreliable. Gauging the relevance and reliability of sources is the essential task of evaluating them.

Note In evaluating sources you need to consider how they come to you. The sources you find through the library, both print and online, have been previewed for you by their publishers and by the library's staff. They still require your critical reading, but you can have some confidence in the information they contain. With online sources, however, you can't assume similar previewing, so your critical reading must be especially rigorous.

Library sources

To evaluate sources you find through the library, look at dates, titles, summaries, introductions, headings, author biographies, bibliographies, and any source citations. Try to answer the following questions about each source.

Evaluate relevance

- **Does the source devote some attention to your subject?** Check whether the source focuses on your subject or covers it marginally, and compare the source's coverage to that in other sources.
- **Is the source appropriately specialized for your needs?** Check the source's treatment of a topic you know something about, to ensure that it is neither too superficial nor too technical.
- **Is the source up to date enough for your subject?** Check the publication date. If your subject is current, your sources should be, too.

mycomplab

Visit *mycomplab.com* for more help with evaluating and synthesizing sources.

Evaluate reliability

- **Where does the source come from?** It matters whether you found the source through your library or directly on the Internet. (If on the Internet, see below and pp. 136–41.) Check whether a library source is popular or scholarly. Scholarly sources, such as refereed journals and university press books, are generally deeper and more reliable.
- **Is the author an expert in the field?** The authors of scholarly publications tend to be experts. To verify expertise, check an author's credentials in a biography (if the source includes one), in a biographical reference, or by using the author's name in a keyword search of the Web.
- **What is the author's bias?** Every author has a point of view that influences the selection and interpretation of evidence. How do the author's ideas relate to those in other sources? What areas does the author emphasize, ignore, or dismiss? When you're aware of sources' biases, you can attempt to balance them.
- **Is the source fair and reasonable?** Even a strongly biased work should present sound reasoning, adequate evidence, and a fair picture of opposing views—all in an objective, calm tone. The absence of any of these qualities should raise a warning flag.
- **Is the source well written?** A coherent organization and clear, error-free sentences indicate a careful author.

See the next two pages for an example of how a student applied these criteria to two library sources.

Web sites

To a great extent, the same critical reading that serves you with library sources will help you evaluate Web sites. But most Web sites have not undergone prior screening by editors and librarians. On your own, you must distinguish scholarship from corporate promotion, valid data from invented statistics, well-founded opinion from clever propaganda.

To evaluate a Web site, add the following questions to those opposite and above.

- **What type of site are you viewing?** What does the type lead you to expect about the site's purpose and content?
- **Who is the author or sponsor?** How credible is the person or group responsible for the site?
- **What is the purpose of the site?** What does the site's author or sponsor intend to achieve?

(continued on p. 136)

Evaluating library sources

Below are a student's evaluations of the two library sources on the facing page. The student was researching consumption of environmentally friendly products.

	Makower	Jackson
Origin	Interview with Joel Makower published in *Vegetarian Times,* a popular magazine.	Article by Tim Jackson published in the *Journal of Industrial Ecology*, a scholarly journal sponsored by two reputable universities: MIT and Yale.
Author	Gives Makower's credentials at the beginning of the interview: the author of a book on green products and of a monthly newsletter on green businesses.	Includes a biography at the end of the article that describes Jackson as a professor at the University of Surrey (UK) and lists his professional activities related to the environment.
Bias	Describes and promotes green products. Concludes with an endorsement of a for-profit Web site that tracks and sells green products.	Gives multiple views of green consumerism. Argues that environmental solutions will involve green products and less consumption but differently than proposed by others.
Reasonableness and writing	Presents Makower's data and perspective on distinguishing good from bad green products, using conversational writing in an informal presentation.	Presents and cites opposing views objectively, using formal academic writing.
Source citations	Lacks citations for claims and data.	Lists scholarly and government sources in dozens of citations.
Assessment	**Probably unreliable:** The article comes from a nonscholarly source, takes a one-sided approach to consumption, and depends on statistics credited only to Makower.	**Probably reliable:** The article comes from a scholarly journal, discusses many views and concedes some, and includes evidence from and citations of reliable sources.

First and last pages of an interview with Joel Makower, published in *Vegetarian Times*

STATE OF THE DEBATE

Live Better by Consuming Less?

Is There a "Double Dividend" in Sustainable Consumption?

Tim Jackson

Keywords

consumer behavior
consumer choice
consumer culture
evolutionary psychology
industrial ecology
symbolic interactionism

Summar

Industrial ...
the efficie...
tion is also ...
ment. The...
this. But th...
really be u...
debates ab...
self. This article explores some of these wider debates. In particular, it draws attention to a fundamental disagreement that runs through the literature on consumption and haunts the debate on sustainable consumption: the question of whether, or to what extent, consumption can be taken as "good for us." Some approaches assume that increasing consumption is more or less synonymous with improved well-being the more we consume the better off we are. Others argue, just as vehemently, that the scale of consumption in modern society is both environmentally and psychologically damaging and that we could reduce consumption significantly without threatening the quality of our lives. This second viewpoint suggests that a kind of "double dividend" is inherent in sustainable consumption: the ability to live better by consuming less and reduce our impact on the environment in the process. In the final analysis, this article argues, such "win-win" solutions may exist but will require a concerted societal effort to realize.

... *for fundamental change.* ...penter Publishing.

UNDP (United Nations Development Programme) 1998. *Human development report 1998.* Oxford, UK: Oxford University Press.

UNEP (United Nations Environment Programme) 2001. Consumption opportunities: Strategies for change. Paris: UNEP.

Van den Bergh, J. C. J. M., A. Ferrer-i-Carbonell, and G. Munda. 2000. Alternative models of individual behaviour and implications for environmental policy. *Ecological Economics* 32(1): 43–61.

About the Author

Tim Jackson is Professor of Sustainable Development at the Centre for Environmental Strategy (CES) in the University of Surrey, Guildford, United Kingdom. He currently holds a research fellowship in sustainable consumption funded by the Economic and Social Research Council and leads the Ecological Economics Research Group at CES. He is also chair of the Economics Steering Group of the U.K. Sustainable Development Commission and sits on the U.K. Round Table on Sustainable Consumption.

First and last pages of an article by Tim Jackson, published in the *Journal of Industrial Ecology*

(continued from p. 133)

- **What does context tell you?** What do you already know about the site's subject that can inform your evaluation? What kinds of support or other information do the site's links provide?
- **What does presentation tell you?** Is the site's design well thought out and effective? Is the writing clear and error-free?
- **How worthwhile is the content?** Are the site's claims well supported by evidence? Is the evidence from reliable sources?

The following discussion elaborates on each of these questions. Pages 138–39 illustrate how a student applied the questions to two Web sites.

Note To evaluate a Web document, you'll often need to travel to the site's home page to discover the author or sponsor, date of publication, and other relevant information. The page you're reading may include a link to the home page. If it doesn't, you can find it by editing the URL in the Address or Location field of your browser.

Determine the type of site.

When you search the Web, you're likely to encounter various types of sites:

- **Scholarly sites:** These sites have a knowledge-building interest and include research reports with supporting data and extensive documentation of scholarly sources. The URLs of the sites generally end in *edu* (originating from an educational institution), *org* (a nonprofit organization), or *gov* (a government department or agency). Such sites are more likely to be reliable than the following types.
- **Informational sites:** Individuals, nonprofit organizations, schools, corporations, and government bodies all produce sites intended to centralize information on particular subjects. The sites' URLs may end in *edu, org, gov,* or *com* (originating from a commercial organization). Such sites generally do not have the knowledge-building focus of scholarly sites and may omit supporting data and documentation, but they can provide useful information and often include links to scholarly sources.
- **Advocacy sites:** Many sites present the views of individuals or organizations that promote certain policies or actions. Their URLs usually end in *org,* but they may end in *edu* or *com*. Some advocacy sites include serious, well-documented research to support their positions, but others select or distort evidence.

- **Commercial sites:** Corporations and other businesses maintain Web sites to explain or promote themselves or to sell goods and services. The URLs of commercial sites end in *com*. The information on such a site furthers the sponsor's profitmaking purpose, but it can include reliable data.
- **Personal sites:** Sites maintained by individuals range from diaries of a family's travels to opinions on political issues to reports on evolving scholarship. The sites' URLs usually end in *com* or *edu*. Personal sites are only as reliable as their authors, but some do provide valuable eyewitness accounts, links to worthy sources, and other usable information. A particular kind of personal site, the blog, is discussed on pages 140–41.

Identify the author or sponsor.

A reputable site will list the author or group responsible for the site and will provide information or a link for contacting the author or group. If none of this information is provided, you should not use the source. If you have only the author or group name, you may be able to discover more in a biographical dictionary or through a keyword search. You should also look for mentions of the author or group in your other sources. Make sure the author or sponsor has expertise in the subject.

Gauge purpose.

A Web site's purpose determines what ideas and information it offers. Inferring that purpose tells you how to interpret what you see on the site. If a site is intended to sell a product or an opinion, it will likely emphasize favorable ideas and information while ignoring or even distorting what is unfavorable. In contrast, if a site is intended to build knowledge—for instance, a scholarly project or journal—it will likely acknowledge diverse views and evidence.

Consider context.

Look outside the site itself. What do you already know about the site's subject and the prevailing views of it? Do the site's links support the site's credibility? Are they relevant to the site and reliable in themselves?

Look at presentation.

Considering both the look of a site and the way it's written can illuminate its intentions and reliability. Does the design reflect the apparent purpose of the site, or does it undercut or conceal that purpose in some way? Is the text clearly written, or is it difficult to understand?

(continued on p. 140)

Evaluating Web sites

Below are a student's evaluations of two Web sources he consulted during his research of environmentally friendly products.

	Allianz Knowledge Partnersite	*Nature Reports: Climate Change*
Author and sponsor	Site sponsor is the Allianz Group, a global insurance company. Author of article is identified as an editor, not a scientist.	Listed authors are scientists, experts on climate change. Site sponsor is the Nature Publishing Group, which also publishes the reputable science journal *Nature*.
Purpose and bias	Educational page on a corporate-sponsored Web site with self-stated purpose of gathering information about global issues and making it available to an international audience.	Informational site with self-stated purpose of providing reliable, scholarly reporting on climate change and its effects. Article expresses bias toward stopping climate change.
Context	One of many sites publishing current information on climate issues.	One of many sites publishing current research on climate issues.
Presentation	Clean, professionally designed site with mostly error-free writing.	Clean, professionally designed site with error-free writing.
Content	Article gives basic information about climate change and provides links to other pages that expand on its claims. The pages do not include citations of scholarly research.	Article is current and explains the science of climate change with references and links to scholarly sources and to articles elsewhere on the site about climate-related topics.
Assessment	**Probably unreliable:** Despite the wealth of information in the article and its links, the material lacks the scholarly source citations necessary for its use as evidence in an academic paper.	**Probably reliable:** The article has an explicit bias toward stopping climate change, but the authors are climate-change experts and the references cite many scholarly and government sources.

37a

Allianz Knowledge Partnersite

Climate Change | Energy | Microfinance | Demographics | Safety & Health | Media Section

Impacts | Climate Agenda | Solutions | Politics | Climate and Business

What is Global Warming?

Global Warming is defined as the increase of the average temperature on Earth. As the Earth is getting hotter, disasters like hurricanes, droughts and floods are getting more frequent.

Picture Gallery (click the image to start)

Over the last 100 years, the average temperature of the air near the Earth's surface has risen a little less than 1° Celsius (0.74 ± 0.18°C, or 1.3 ± 0.32° Fahrenheit). Does not seem all that much? It is responsible for the conspicuous increase in storms, floods and raging forest fires we have seen in the last ten years, though, say scientists.

Their data show that an increase of one degree Celsius makes the Earth warmer now than it has been for at least a thousand years. Out of the 20 warmest years on record, 19 have occurred since 1980. The three hottest years ever observed have all occurred in the last eight years, even.

Article published on the Web site *Allianz Knowledge Partnersite*

nature REPORTS climate change

the news behind the science, the science behind the news

home | current issue | journal club | archive | blogs | podcast | about

this issue

article navigation

article tools

Squaring up to reality

Both emissions reduction and adaptation will need to be much stronger than currently planned if dangerous global impacts of climate change are to be avoided. June's UN talks in Bonn and July's G8 summit present opportunities for world leaders to face this challenge.

We are now probably witnessing the first genuinely global effects of greenhouse gas warming. The steep increases in food prices around the world are the result of rising costs and demand aggravated by drought in food-producing regions — in the case of Australia, probably due in part to global warming — and by a poorly conceived experiment in climate policy that has converted cropland to biofuel plantations. This should serve as a wake-up call: impacts of climate change can surprise us, especially when they act in combination with other pressures.

We must use this as an opportunity to clarify climate policies, in particular the amount of emissions reductions needed globally to avoid dangerous climate change, generally defined as more than a 2 °C increase on pre-industrial temperatures[1]. Two forthcoming meetings — the UN climate change talks to take place in June in Bonn, Germany, and July's G8 summit in Hokkaido, Japan — provide yet another chance for world leaders to boldly declare their commitment to dramatically reducing greenhouse gases. Both will represent important milestones[3] in the lead-up to the UN climate change conference in Copenhagen in 2009, where an international deal will be agreed that will tackle carbon emissions beyond 2012 after the present pledges in the Kyoto Protocol run out.

Last year's G8 summit in Heiligendamm, Germany, resulted in a joint statement from international delegations that acknowledged a preference for global greenhouse gas emissions

Article published on the Web site *Nature Reports: Climate Change*

37a

(continued from p. 137)

Analyze content.

With information about a site's author, purpose, and context, you're in a position to evaluate its content. Are the ideas and information slanted and, if so, in what direction? Are they up to date? Are the views and data authoritative, or do you need to balance them—or even reject them? Answering these questions requires close reading of the text and its sources.

Other online sources

Blogs, online discussions, and online images, video, and audio require the same critical scrutiny as Web sites do. Blogs and discussion groups can be sources of reliable data and opinions, but you will also encounter wrong or misleading data and skewed opinions. One podcast may provide an interview with a recognized expert, while another claims authority that it doesn't deserve. A *YouTube* search using "I have a dream" brings up videos of Martin Luther King, Jr., delivering his famous speech as well as videos of people speaking hatefully about King and the speech.

Use the following questions for evaluating blogs, discussion groups, and multimedia:

- **Who is the author or creator?** How credible is that person? If the author/creator uses a screen name, write directly to him or her requesting full name and credentials. Do not use the source if he or she fails to respond.
- **What is the author's or creator's purpose?** What can you tell about *why* the author/creator is publishing this work? Look for cues in the work—claims, use (or not) of evidence, and treatment of opposing views—to figure out how to position the source among your other sources.
- **What does the context reveal?** What do others' responses to the work indicate about the source's balance and reliability? Comments on a blog posting or the other messages in a discussion thread will give you a sense of how the author/creator is regarded.
- **How worthwhile is the content?** Are the claims made by the author/creator supported by evidence from reliable sources? If you don't see supporting information, ask the author/creator for it. Then verify the sources with your own research: are they reputable?
- **How does the source compare with other sources?** Do the claims seem accurate and fair given what you've seen in sources you know to be reliable? Always consider blogs, messages, and multimedia in comparison

to other sources so that you can distinguish singular, untested views from more mainstream views that have been subject to verification.

37b Synthesis of sources

Evaluating sources moves you into the most significant part of research writing: forging relationships for your own purpose. This **synthesis** is an essential step in reading sources critically and in creating new knowledge.

Respond to sources.

Write down what your sources make you think. Do you agree or disagree with the author? Do you find his or her views narrow, or do they open up new approaches for you? Is there anything in the source that you need to research further before you can understand it? Does the source prompt questions that you should keep in mind while reading other sources?

Connect sources.

When you notice a link between sources, jot it down. Do two sources differ in their theories or their interpretations of facts? Does one source illuminate another—perhaps commenting or clarifying or supplying additional data? Do two or more sources report studies that support a theory you've read about or an idea of your own?

Heed your own insights.

Apart from ideas prompted by your sources, you are sure to come up with independent thoughts: a conviction, a point of confusion that suddenly becomes clear, a question you haven't seen anyone else ask. These insights may occur at unexpected times, so it's good practice to keep a notebook or computer handy to record them.

Draw your own conclusions.

As your research proceeds, the responses, connections, and insights you form through synthesis will lead you to answer your starting research question with a statement of your thesis (see p. 117). They will also lead you to the main ideas supporting your thesis—conclusions you have drawn from your synthesis of sources, forming the main divisions of your paper.

Use sources to support your conclusions.

Effective synthesis requires careful handling of evidence from sources so that it meshes smoothly into your sentences and yet is clearly distinct from your own ideas. When drafting your paper, make sure that each paragraph focuses on an idea of your own, with the support for the idea coming from your sources. Generally, open each paragraph with your idea, provide evidence from a source or sources with appropriate citations, and close with an interpretation of the evidence. (For an example of such a paragraph, see page 7.)

38 Integrating Sources into Your Text

Integrating source material into your sentences is key to synthesizing others' ideas and information with your own. Evidence drawn from sources should *back up* your conclusions, not *be* your conclusions: you don't want to let your evidence overwhelm your own point of view. The point of research is to investigate and go beyond sources, to interpret them and use them to support your own independent ideas.

Integrating sources into your text may involve several conventions discussed elsewhere in this book:

- **Using commas to punctuate signal phrases** (p. 89).
- **Placing other punctuation marks with quotation marks** (pp. 96–97).
- **Using brackets and the ellipsis mark to indicate changes in quotations** (pp. 99–101).
- **Formatting long prose quotations and poetry quotations** (MLA, p. 197; APA, p. 217; and Chicago, p. 229).

38a Summary, paraphrase, and direct quotation

As you take notes from sources or work source material into your draft, you can summarize, paraphrase, quote, or combine methods. The choice should depend on why you are using a source.

Note Summaries, paraphrases, and quotations all require source citations. A summary or paraphrase without a source citation or a quotation without quotation marks is plagiarism. (See pp. 150–55 for more on plagiarism.)

Summary

When you **summarize,** you condense an extended idea or argument into a sentence or more in your own words. Summary is most useful when you want to record the gist of an author's idea without the background or supporting evidence. Here, for example, is a passage from a scholarly essay about consumption and its impact on the environment.

Original quotation

Such intuition is even making its way, albeit slowly, into scholarly circles, where recognition is mounting that ever-increasing pressures on ecosystems, life-supporting environmental services, and critical natural cycles are driven not only by the sheer number of resource users and the inefficiencies of their resource use, but also by the patterns of resource use themselves. In global environmental policymaking arenas, it is becoming more and more difficult to ignore the fact that the overdeveloped North must restrain its consumption if it expects the underdeveloped South to embrace a more sustainable trajectory.

—Thomas Princen, Michael Maniates, and Ken Conca, *Confronting Consumption,* p. 4

Summary

Overconsumption may be a more significant cause of environmental problems than increasing population is.

Paraphrase

When you **paraphrase,** you follow the author's original presentation much more closely, but you still restate it in your own words. Paraphrase is most useful when you want to reconstruct an author's line of reasoning but don't feel the original words merit direct quotation. Here is a paraphrase of the quotation from *Confronting Consumption.*

Paraphrase

Scholars are coming to believe that consumption is partly to blame for changes in ecosystems, reduction of essential natural resources, and changes in natural cycles. Policy makers increasingly see that wealthy nations have to start consuming less if they want developing nations to adopt practices that reduce pollution and waste. Rising population around the world does cause significant stress on the environment, but consumption is increasing even more rapidly than population.

Follow these guidelines when paraphrasing:

- **Read the material until you understand it.**
- **Restate the main ideas in your own words and sentence structures.** Use phrases if complete sentences seem cumbersome.
- **Be careful not to distort the author's meaning.**

For examples of poor and revised paraphrases, see page 154.

ESL If English is your second language, you may have difficulty paraphrasing the ideas in sources because synonyms don't occur to you or you don't see how to restructure sentences. Before attempting a paraphrase, read the original passage several times. Then, instead of "translating" line by line, try to state the gist of the passage without looking at it. Check your effort against the original to be sure you have captured the source author's meaning and emphasis without using his or her words and sentence structures. If you need a synonym for a word, look it up in a dictionary.

Direct quotation

Whether to quote a source instead of paraphrasing or summarizing it depends on the kind of source and on how important its exact words are. Quote extensively from primary sources that you are analyzing, such as historical documents or literary works. Quote selectively from secondary sources, such as other writers' views of primary sources. Summarize or paraphrase from secondary sources unless the material passes *both* of these tests:

- **The author's original satisfies one of these requirements:**

  The language is unusually vivid, bold, or inventive.
  The quotation cannot be paraphrased without distortion or loss of meaning.
  You take issue with the words themselves.
  The quotation represents and emphasizes the view of an important expert.
  The quotation is a graph, diagram, or table.

- **The quotation is as short as possible:**

  It includes only material relevant to your point.
  It is edited to eliminate examples and other unneeded material.

When taking a quotation from a source, copy the material *carefully.* Take down the author's exact wording, spelling, capitalization, and punctuation. Proofread every direct quotation *at least twice,* and be sure you have supplied big quotation marks so that later you won't confuse the direct quotation with a paraphrase or summary.

38b Introduction and interpretation of source material

Note Most examples in the following pages use the documentation style of the Modern Language Association (MLA) and also present-tense° verbs that are typical of much writing in the humanities. For specific variations in the academic disciplines, see pages 148–49.

°See Glossary of Terms, page 249.

Introduction

Work all quotations, paraphrases, and summaries smoothly into your own sentences, adding words as necessary to mesh structures.

Awkward One editor disagrees with this view and "a good reporter does not fail to separate opinions from facts" (Lyman 52).

Revised One editor disagrees with this view, maintaining that "a good reporter does not fail to separate opinions from facts" (Lyman 52).

To mesh your own and your source's words, you may sometimes need to make a substitution or addition to the quotation, signaling your change with brackets:

Words added

"The tabloids [of England] are a journalistic case study in bad reporting," claims Lyman (52).

Verb form changed

A bad reporter, Lyman implies, is one who "[fails] to separate opinions from facts" (52). [The bracketed verb replaces *fail* in the original.]

Capitalization changed

"[T]o separate opinions from facts" is a goal of good reporting (Lyman 52). [In the original, *to* is not capitalized.]

Noun supplied for pronoun

The reliability of a news organization "depends on [reporters'] trustworthiness," says Lyman (52). [The bracketed noun replaces *their* in the original.]

Interpretation

Even when it does not conflict with your own sentence structure, source material will be ineffective if you merely dump it in readers' laps without explaining how you intend it to be understood. In the following passage, we must figure out for ourselves that the writer's sentence and the quotation state opposite points of view.

Dumped Many news editors and reporters maintain that it is impossible to keep personal opinions from influencing the selection and presentation of facts. "True, news reporters, like everyone else, form impressions of what they see and hear. However, a good reporter does not fail to separate opinions from facts" (Lyman 52).

Revised Many news editors and reporters maintain that it is impossible to keep personal opinions from influencing the selection and presentation of facts.

> Yet not all authorities agree with this view. One editor grants that "news reporters, like everyone else, form impressions of what they see and hear." But, he insists, "a good reporter does not fail to separate opinions from facts" (Lyman 52).

Signal phrases

In the preceding revised passage, the words *One editor grants* and *he insists* are **signal phrases:** they tell readers who the source is and what to expect in the quotations. Signal phrases usually contain (1) the source author's name (or a substitute for it, such as *One editor* and *he*) and (2) a verb that indicates the source author's attitude or approach to what he or she says, as *grants* implies concession and *insists* implies argument.

Below are some verbs to use in signal phrases. For the appropriate tense° of such verbs (present,° as here, or past° or present perfect°) see pages 148–49.

Author is neutral	Author infers or suggests	Author argues	Author is uneasy or disparaging
comments	analyzes	claims	belittles
describes	asks	contends	bemoans
explains	assesses	defends	complains
illustrates	believes	disagrees	condemns
mentions	concludes	holds	deplores
notes	considers	insists	deprecates
observes	finds	maintains	derides
points out	predicts	**Author agrees**	laments
records	proposes	accepts	warns
relates	reveals	admits	
reports	shows	agrees	
says	speculates	concedes	
sees	suggests	concurs	
thinks	supposes	grants	
writes			

Note that some signal verbs, such as *describes* and *assesses,* cannot be followed by *that*.

Vary your signal phrases to suit your interpretation of source material and also to keep readers' interest. A signal phrase may precede, interrupt, or follow the borrowed material:

Signal phrase precedes

Lyman insists that "a good reporter does not fail to separate opinions from facts" (52).

Signal phrase interrupts

"However," Lyman insists, "a good reporter does not fail to separate opinions from facts" (52).

°See Glossary of Terms, page 249.

Signal phrase follows

"[A] good reporter does not fail to separate opinions from facts," Lyman insists (52).

Background information

You can add information to source material to integrate it into your text and inform readers why you are using it. Often, you may want to provide the author's name in the text:

Author named

Harold Lyman grants that "news reporters, like everyone else, form impressions of what they see and hear." But, Lyman insists, "a good reporter does not fail to separate opinions from facts" (52).

If the source title contributes information about the author or the context of the borrowed material, you can provide the title in the text:

Title given

Harold Lyman, in his book *The Conscience of the Journalist*, grants that "news reporters, like everyone else, form impressions of what they see and hear." But, Lyman insists, "a good reporter does not fail to separate opinions from facts" (52).

Finally, if the source author's background and experience reinforce or clarify the borrowed material, you can provide these credentials in the text:

Credentials given

Harold Lyman, a newspaper editor for more than forty years, grants that "news reporters, like everyone else, form impressions of what they see and hear." But, Lyman insists, "a good reporter does not fail to separate opinions from facts" (52).

You need not name the author, title, or credentials in your text when you are simply establishing facts or weaving together facts and opinions from varied sources to support a larger point. In the following passage, the information is more important than the source, so the author's name is confined to a parenthetical acknowledgment:

> To end the abuses of the British, many colonists were urging three actions: forming a united front, seceding from Britain, and taking control of their own international trade and diplomacy (Wills 325–36).

Discipline styles for interpreting sources

The preceding guidelines for interpreting source material apply generally across academic disciplines, but there are differences in verb tenses and documentation style.

English and some other humanities

Writers in English, foreign languages, and related disciplines use MLA style for documenting sources (see Chapter 40) and generally use the present tense° of verbs in signal phrases. (See the list of signal-phrase verbs on p. 146.) In discussing sources other than works of literature, the present perfect tense° is also sometimes appropriate:

Lyman insists . . . [present].
Lyman has insisted . . . [present perfect].

In discussing works of literature, use only the present tense to describe both the work of the author and the action in the work:

> Kate Chopin builds irony into every turn of "The Story of an Hour." For example, Mrs. Mallard, the central character, finds joy in the death of her husband, whom she loves, because she anticipates "the long procession of years that would belong to her absolutely" (23).

Avoid shifting tenses in writing about literature. You can, for instance, shorten quotations to avoid their past-tense° verbs:

Shift — Her freedom elevates her, so that "she carried herself unwittingly like a goddess of victory" (24).

No shift — Her freedom elevates her, so that she walks "unwittingly like a goddess of victory" (24).

History and other humanities

Writers in history, art history, philosophy, and related disciplines generally use the present tense or present perfect tense of verbs in signal phrases. (See the list of possible verbs on page 146.)

38b

> Lincoln persisted, as Haworth has noted, in "feeling that events controlled him."[3]

> What Miller calls Lincoln's "severe self-doubt"[6] undermined his effectiveness on at least two occasions.

The raised numbers after the quotations are part of the Chicago documentation style, used in history and other disciplines and discussed in Chapter 42.

Social and natural sciences

Writers in the sciences generally use a verb's present tense just for reporting the results of a study (*The data suggest* . . .). Otherwise, they use a verb's past tense or present perfect tense in a signal phrase, as when introducing an explanation, interpretation, or other commentary. (Thus, when you are writing for the sciences, generally convert the list of signal-phrase verbs on p. 146 from the present to the past or present perfect tense.)

°See Glossary of Terms, page 249.

> In an exhaustive survey of the literature published between 1990 and 2000, Walker (2001) found "no proof, merely a weak correlation, linking place of residence and rate of illness" (p. 121).
>
> Lin (1999) has suggested that preschooling may significantly affect children's academic performance through high school (p. 251).

These passages conform to the documentation style of the American Psychological Association (APA), discussed in Chapter 41. APA style or the similar CSE style (Chapter 43) is used in sociology, education, nursing, biology, and many other sciences.

38c Clear boundaries for source material

Position source citations in your text to accomplish two goals: (1) make it clear exactly where your borrowing of source material begins and ends; (2) keep the citations as unobtrusive as possible. You can accomplish both goals by placing an in-text citation at the end of the sentence element containing the borrowed material. This sentence element may be a phrase or a clause, and it may begin, interrupt, or conclude the sentence.

> The inflation rate might climb as high as 30 percent (Kim 164), an increase that could threaten the small nation's stability.
>
> The inflation rate, which might climb as high as 30 percent (Kim 164), could threaten the small nation's stability.
>
> The small nation's stability could be threatened by its inflation rate, which, one source predicts, might climb as high as 30 percent (Kim 164).

In the last example the addition of *one source predicts* clarifies that Kim is responsible only for the inflation-rate prediction, not for the statement about stability.

When your paraphrase or summary of a source runs longer than a sentence, clarify the boundaries by using the author's name in the first sentence and placing the parenthetical citation at the end of the last sentence.

> Juliette Kim studied the effects of acutely high inflation in several South American and African countries since World War II. She discovered that a major change in government accompanied or followed the inflationary period in 56 percent of cases (22-23).

39 Avoiding Plagiarism and Documenting Sources

The knowledge building that is the focus of academic writing rests on the honesty of all participants, including students, in using and crediting sources. This standard of honesty derives from the idea that the work of an author is his or her intellectual property: if you use that work, you must acknowledge the author's ownership. At the same time, source acknowledgments tell readers what your own writing is based on, creating the trust that knowledge building requires.

Plagiarism (from a Latin word for "kidnapper") is the presentation of someone else's work as your own. Whether deliberate or accidental, plagiarism is a serious offense. It breaks trust, and it undermines or even destroys your credibility as a researcher and writer. In most colleges, a code of academic honesty calls for severe consequences for plagiarism: a reduced or failing grade, suspension from school, or expulsion.

- ***Deliberate* plagiarism:**

  Copying or downloading a phrase, a sentence, or a longer passage from a source and passing it off as your own by omitting quotation marks and a source citation.

  Summarizing or paraphrasing someone else's ideas without acknowledging your debt in a source citation.

  Handing in as your own work a paper you have bought, copied off the Web, had a friend write, or accepted from another student.

- ***Accidental* plagiarism:**

  Reading a wide variety of print or Web sources on a subject without taking notes on them, and then not remembering the difference between what you recently learned and what you already knew.

  Forgetting to place quotation marks around another writer's words.

  Carelessly omitting a source citation for a paraphrase.

  Omitting a source citation for another's idea because you are unaware of the need to acknowledge the idea.

Visit *mycomplab.com* for more help with avoiding plagiarism and documenting sources.

Checklist for avoiding plagiarism

Type of source

- ☑ Are you using (1) your own independent material, (2) common knowledge, or (3) someone else's independent material? **You must acknowledge someone else's material.**

Quotations

- ☑ Do all quotations exactly match their sources? Check them.
- ☑ Have you inserted quotation marks around quotations that are run into your text?
- ☑ Have you shown omissions with ellipsis marks and additions with brackets?
- ☑ Does every quotation have a source citation?

Paraphrases and summaries

- ☑ Have you used your own words and sentence structures for every paraphrase and summary? If not, use quotation marks around the original author's words.
- ☑ Does every paraphrase and summary have a source citation?

The Web

- ☑ Have you obtained any necessary permission to use someone else's material on your Web site?

Source citations

- ☑ Have you acknowledged every use of someone else's material in each place where you use it?
- ☑ Does your list of works cited include all the sources you have used?

The way to avoid plagiarism is to acknowledge your sources by documenting them. This chapter discusses plagiarism and the Internet, shows how to distinguish what doesn't require acknowledgment from what does, and provides an overview of source documentation.

ESL The concept of intellectual property and thus the rules governing plagiarism are not universal. In some other cultures, for instance, students may be encouraged to copy the words of scholars without acknowledgment in order to demonstrate their mastery of or respect for the scholars' work. In the United States, however, it is plagiarism to copy an author's work without quotation marks and a source citation. If you're unsure about plagiarism after reading this chapter, ask your instructor for advice.

39a Plagiarism and the Internet

The Internet has made it easier to plagiarize than ever before, but it has also made plagiarism easier to catch.

Even honest students risk accidental plagiarism by downloading sources and importing portions into their drafts. Dishonest students may take advantage of downloading to steal others' work. They may also use the term-paper businesses on the Web, which offer both ready-made research and complete papers, usually for a fee. **Paying for research or a paper does not make it the buyer's work.** Anyone who submits someone else's work as his or her own is a plagiarist.

Students who plagiarize from the Internet both deprive themselves of an education in honest research and expose themselves to detection. Instructors can use search engines to locate specific phrases or sentences anywhere on the Web, including among scholarly publications, all kinds of Web sites, and term-paper collections. They can search the term-paper sites as easily as students can, looking for similarities with papers they have received. They can also use plagiarism-detection programs such as *Turnitin* that compare students' work with other work anywhere on the Internet, seeking matches as short as a few words.

Some instructors suggest that their students use plagiarism-detection programs to verify that their own work does not include accidental plagiarism, at least not from the Internet.

39b What *not* to acknowledge

Your independent material

You are not required to acknowledge your own observations, thoughts, compilations of facts, or experimental results, expressed in your own words and format.

Common knowledge

You need not acknowledge common knowledge: the standard information of a field of study as well as folk literature and commonsense observations.

If you do not know a subject well enough to determine whether a piece of information is common knowledge, make a record of the source. As you read more about the subject, the information may come up repeatedly without acknowledgment, in which case it is probably common knowledge. But if you are still in doubt when you finish your research, always acknowledge the source.

39c What *must* be acknowledged

You must always acknowledge other people's independent material—that is, any facts or ideas that are not common knowledge or your own. The source may be anything, including a book, an article, a movie, an interview, a microfilmed document, a Web page, a computer program, a newsgroup posting, or an opinion expressed on the radio. You must acknowledge summaries or paraphrases of ideas or facts as well as quotations of the language and format in which ideas or facts appear: wording, sentence structures, arrangement, and special graphics (such as a diagram). You must acknowledge another's material no matter how you use it, how much of it you use, or how often you use it.

Note See pages 144–46 on integrating quotations into your own text without plagiarism. And see pages 155–56 on acknowledging sources.

Copied language: Quotation marks and a source citation

The following example baldly plagiarizes the original quotation from Jessica Mitford's *Kind and Usual Punishment*, page 9. Without quotation marks or a source citation, the example matches Mitford's wording (underlined) and closely parallels her sentence structure:

Original quotation "The character and mentality of the keepers may be of more importance in understanding prisons than the character and mentality of the kept."

Plagiarism But the character of prison officials (the keepers) is of more importance in understanding prisons than the character of prisoners (the kept).

To avoid plagiarism, the writer has two options: (1) paraphrase and cite the source (see the examples on the next page) or (2) use Mitford's actual words *in quotation marks* and *with a source citation* (here, in MLA style):

Revision (quotation) According to one critic of the penal system, "The character and mentality of the keepers may be of more importance in understanding prisons than the character and mentality of the kept" (Mitford 9).

Even with a source citation and with a different sentence structure, the next example is still plagiarism because it uses some of Mitford's words (underlined) without quotation marks:

Plagiarism According to one critic of the penal system, the psychology of the kept may say less about prisons than the psychology of the keepers (Mitford 9).

Revision (quotation) According to one critic of the penal system, the psychology of "the kept" may say less about prisons than the psychology of "the keepers" (Mitford 9).

Paraphrase or summary: Your own words and a source citation

The example below changes Mitford's sentence structure, but it still uses her words (underlined) without quotation marks and without a source citation:

Plagiarism In understanding prisons, we should know more about the character and mentality of the keepers than of the kept.

To avoid plagiarism, the writer can use quotation marks and cite the source (previous page and above) or *use his or her own words* and still *cite the source* (because the idea is Mitford's, not the writer's):

Revision (paraphrase) Mitford holds that we may be able to learn more about prisons from the psychology of the prison officials than from that of the prisoners (9).

Revision (paraphrase) We may understand prisons better if we focus on the personalities and attitudes of the prison workers rather than those of the inmates (Mitford 9).

In the next example, the writer cites Mitford and does not use her words but still plagiarizes her sentence structure:

Plagiarism One critic of the penal system maintains that the psychology of prison officials may be more informative about prisons than the psychology of prisoners (Mitford 9).

39d

Revision (paraphrase) One critic of the penal system maintains that we may be able to learn less from the psychology of prisoners than from the psychology of prison officials (Mitford 9).

39d Online sources

You should acknowledge online sources when you would any other source: whenever you use someone else's independent material in any form. But online sources may present additional challenges as well:

- **Record complete publication information each time you consult an online source.** Online sources may change from one day to the next or even disappear entirely. See pages 120–21 for the information to record. If you do not have the proper information, you *may not* use the source.

- **Acknowledge linked sites.** If you use not only a Web site but also one or more of its linked sites, you must acknowledge the linked sites as well. One person's using a second person's work does not release you from the responsibility to cite the second work.
- **Seek the author's permission before using an e-mail message, discussion-group posting, or blog contribution.** Obtaining permission advises the author that his or her ideas are about to be distributed more widely and lets the author verify that you have not misrepresented the ideas.

If you want to use material in something you publish online, such as your own Web site, seek permission from the copyright holder in addition to citing the source. Generally, you can find information about copyright holders and permissions on the copyright page of a print publication (following the title page) and on a page labeled something like "Terms of Use" on a Web site. If you don't see an explicit release for student use, assume you must seek permission.

39e Documentation of sources

Every time you borrow the words, facts, or ideas of others, you must **document** the source—that is, supply a reference (or document) telling readers that you borrowed the material and where you borrowed it from.

Editors and instructors in most academic disciplines require special documentation formats (or styles) in their scholarly journals and in students' papers. All the styles share common features:

- **Citations in the text signal that material is borrowed and refer readers to detailed information about the sources.**
- **Detailed source information, either in footnotes or at the end of the paper, tells how to locate the sources.**

Aside from these essential similarities, the disciplines' documentation styles differ markedly in citation form, arrangement of source information, and other particulars. Each discipline's style reflects the needs of its practitioners for certain kinds of information presented in certain ways. For instance, the currency of a source is important in the social and natural sciences, where studies build on and correct each other; thus in-text citations in these disciplines usually include a source's date of publication. In the humanities, however, currency is less important, so in-text citations do not include date of publication.

The documentation formats of the disciplines are described in style guides, including those in the following list. This book presents the styles of the guides that are marked *.

Humanities

*The Chicago Manual of Style. 16th ed. 2010. (See pp. 219–31.)

*MLA Handbook for Writers of Research Papers. 7th ed. 2009. (See pp. 157–99.)

Social sciences

American Anthropological Association. *AAA Style Guide.* 2009. *aaanet.org/publications/guidelines.cfm.*

American Political Science Association. *Style Manual for Political Science.* 2006.

*American Psychological Association. *Publication Manual of the American Psychological Association.* 6th ed. 2010. (See pp. 200–19.)

American Sociological Association. *ASA Style Guide.* 3rd ed. 2007.

A Uniform System of Citation (law). 19th ed. 2010.

Sciences and mathematics

American Chemical Society. *ACS Style Guide: A Manual for Authors and Editors.* 3rd ed. 2006. *www.aip.org.*

American Institute of Physics. *Style Manual for Guidance in the Preparation of Papers.* 4th ed. 1997.

American Medical Association Manual of Style. 10th ed. 2007.

*Council of Science Editors. *Scientific Style and Format: The CSE Manual for Authors, Editors, and Publishers.* 7th ed. 2006. (See pp. 232–38.)

Ask your instructor which style you should use. If no style is required, use the guide from the preceding list that's most appropriate for the discipline in which you're writing. Do follow one system for citing sources—and one system only—so that you provide all the necessary information in a consistent format.

Note Bibliography software—*Zotero, Refworks, Endnote, Procite,* and others—can help you format your source citations in the style of your choice. Always ask your instructors if you may use such software for your papers. The programs prompt you for needed information (author's name, book title, and so on) and then format the information as required by the style. The programs remove some tedium from documenting sources, but they can't substitute for your own care and attention in giving your sources accurate and complete acknowledgment.

40 MLA Documentation and Format

English, foreign languages, and some other humanities use the documentation style of the Modern Language Association, recently updated in the *MLA Handbook for Writers of Research Papers*, 7th ed. (2009). The MLA's Web site, at *mla.org*, offers occasional updates and answers to frequently asked questions about MLA style.

In MLA style, brief parenthetical citations in the text (below) direct readers to a list of works cited at the end of the text (p. 162). This chapter also details the MLA format for papers (p. 196).

40a MLA parenthetical text citations

Citation formats

In-text citations of sources must include just enough information for the reader to locate both of the following:

- **The *source* in your list of works cited.**
- **The *place* in the source where the borrowed material appears.**

For any kind of source, you can usually meet both these requirements by providing the author's last name and (if the source uses them) the page numbers where the material appears. The reader can find the source in your list of works cited and find the borrowed material in the source itself.

1. Author not named in your text

When you have not already named the author in your sentence, provide the author's last name and the page number(s), with no punctuation between them, in parentheses.

One researcher concludes that "women impose a distinctive construction on moral problems, seeing moral dilemmas in terms of conflicting responsibilities" (Gilligan 105-06).

2. Author named in your text

When you have already given the author's name with the material you're citing, give just the page number(s) in parentheses.

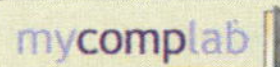

Visit *mycomplab.com* for more help with MLA documentation and format.

MLA parenthetical citations

Carol Gilligan concludes that "women impose a distinctive construction on moral problems, seeing moral dilemmas in terms of conflicting responsibilities" (105-06).

See models 6 and 10–11 for the forms to use when the source does not list an author or does not provide page numbers.

3. A work with two or three authors

If the source has two or three authors, give all their last names in the text or in the citation.

As Frieden and Sagalyn observe, "The poor and the minorities were the leading victims of highway and renewal programs" (29).

One textbook discusses the "ethical dilemmas in public relations practice" (Wilcox, Ault, and Agee 125).

4. A work with more than three authors

If the source has more than three authors, give all authors' last names or give only the first author's name followed by et al. (the abbreviation for the Latin *et alii,* meaning "and others"). Do the same in your list of works cited (see p. 165).

Increased competition means that employees of public relations firms may find their loyalty stretched in more than one direction (Cameron et al. 417).

Increased competition means that employees of public relations firms may find their loyalty stretched in more than one direction (Cameron, Wilcox, Reber, and Shin 417).

5. A work by an author of two or more cited works

If your list of works cited includes two or more works by the same author, then your citation should include the title of the particular work you are referring to. Use the full title in the text. In parentheses, give the full title only if it is brief; otherwise, shorten the title to the first one or two main words (excluding *A*, *An*, or *The*).

At about age seven, children begin to use appropriate gestures with their stories (Gardner, *Arts* 144-45).

6. An anonymous work

For a work with no named author or editor (whether an individual or an organization), use a full or shortened version of the title, as explained above.

One article notes that a death-row inmate may demand his own execution to achieve a fleeting notoriety ("Right" 16).

"The Right to Die" notes that a death-row inmate may demand execution to achieve a fleeting notoriety (16).

7. A work with a corporate author

Some works list as author a government body, committee, company, or other group. Cite such a work by the organization's name.

A 2008 report by the Hawaii Department of Education provides evidence of an increase in graduation rates (12).

8. A nonprint source

Cite a nonprint source such as a Web page or a DVD just as you would any other source, by the name of the author or other contributor (first example) or by the title (second example). See model 10 on the omission of page or other reference numbers for entire works or for works lacking such numbers.

Business forecasts for the fourth quarter are optimistic (White 4).

Many decades after its release, *Citizen Kane* is still remarkable for its rich black-and-white photography.

9. A multivolume work

If you consulted only one volume of a multivolume work, your list of works cited will say so (see model 28 on p. 176), and you can treat the volume as you would any book. If you consulted more than one volume of a multivolume work, give the appropriate volume before the page number (here, volume 5):

After issuing the Emancipation Proclamation, Lincoln said, "What I did, I did after very full deliberations, and under a very heavy and solemn sense of responsibility" (5: 438).

10. An entire work or a work with no page or other reference numbers

When you cite an entire work rather than a part of it, you may omit any page or other reference number. If the work you cite has an author, try to give the author's name in your text. You will not need a parenthetical citation then, but the source still must appear in your list of works cited.

Boyd deals with the need to acknowledge and come to terms with our fear of nuclear technology.

Use the same format when you cite a specific passage from a work with no page, paragraph, or other reference numbers, such as a Web source.

If the author's name does not appear in your text, put it in a parenthetical citation.

Almost 20 percent of commercial banks have been audited for the practice (Friis).

11. A work with numbered paragraphs or sections instead of pages

Give the paragraph or section number(s) and distinguish them from page numbers: after the author's name, put a comma, a space, and par. (one paragraph), pars. (more than one paragraph), sec., or secs.

Twins reared apart report similar feelings (Palfrey, pars. 6-7).

12. A source referred to by another source (indirect source)

When you want to use material that is quoted or paraphrased by your source, try to find the original source and work from it. If you can't find the original source, indicate that your use of it is indirect.

George Davino maintains that "even small children have vivid ideas about nuclear energy" (qtd. in Boyd 22).

The list of works cited then includes only Boyd (the work consulted), not Davino.

13. A literary work

Novels, plays, and poems are often available in many editions, so your instructor may ask you to provide information that will help readers find the passage you cite. For novels, follow the page number with the part, chapter, or other identifier.

Toward the end of James's novel, Maggie suddenly feels "the thick breath of the definite—which was the intimate, the immediate, the familiar, as she hadn't had them for so long" (535; pt. 6, ch. 41).

For poems that are not divided into parts, omit the page number and supply the line number(s) for the quotation, preceded by line or lines in the first citation.

In Shakespeare's Sonnet 73 the speaker identifies with the trees of late autumn, "Bare ruined choirs, where late the sweet birds sang" (line 4). "In me," Shakespeare writes, "thou seest the glowing of such fire / That on the ashes of his youth doth lie . . ." (9-10).

For verse plays and poems that are divided into parts, replace the page number(s) with the part and the line number(s)—in the following example, act 3, scene 4, line 147.

Later in Shakespeare's *King Lear* the disguised Edgar says, "The prince of darkness is a gentleman" (3.4.147).

For a prose play, provide the page number followed by the act and scene, if any.

14. The Bible

In a parenthetical citation of the Bible, abbreviate the title of any book longer than four letters, and then give chapter and verse(s).

According to the Bible, at Babel God "did . . . confound the language of all the earth" (Gen. 11.9).

15. Two or more works in the same citation

When you refer to more than one work in a single citation, separate the references with a semicolon.

Two recent articles point out that a computer badly used can be less efficient than no computer at all (Gough and Hall 201; Richards 162).

Footnotes or endnotes in special circumstances

Footnotes or endnotes may supplement parenthetical citations when you cite several sources at once, when you comment on a source, or when you provide information that does not fit easily in the text. Signal a footnote or endnote in your text with a numeral raised above the appropriate line. Then write a note with the same numeral.

Text At least five studies have confirmed these results.[1]

Note 1. Abbott and Winger 266-68; Casner 27; Hoyenga 78-79; Marino 36; Tripp, Tripp, and Walk 179-83.

Indent a note one-half inch, type the numeral on the text line, and follow the numeral with a period and a space. If the note appears as a footnote, place it at the bottom of the page on which the citation appears, set it off from the text with quadruple spacing, and double-space the note itself. If the note appears as an endnote, place it in numerical order with the other endnotes on a page between the text and the list of works cited. Double-space all the endnotes.

40b MLA list of works cited

On a new page at the end of your paper, a list titled Works Cited includes all the sources you quoted, paraphrased, or summarized in your paper. The format of the list is described below and illustrated on page 199.

Arrangement Arrange your sources in alphabetical order by the last name of the author (the first author if there is more than one). If an author is not given in the source, alphabetize the source by the first main word of the title (excluding *A*, *An*, or *The*).

Spacing and indention Double-space all entries. Type the first line of each entry at the left margin, and indent all subsequent lines one-half inch.

MLA 40b

Note MLA style requires that you give the medium for every source you cite, such as print, Web, DVD, or television.

Authors

The following models show how to handle authors' names in citing any kind of source.

1. One author

Ehrenreich, Barbara. *Dancing in the Streets: A History of Collective Joy.* New York: Metropolitan-Holt, 2006. Print.

Give the author's full name—last name first, a comma, first name, any middle name or initial, and a period. Omit any title, such as *Dr.* or *PhD.*

MLA works-cited models

(continued)

MLA works-cited models

(continued)

2. Two or three authors

Lifton, Robert Jay, and Greg Mitchell. *Who Owns Death: Capital Punishment, the American Conscience, and the End of Executions*. New York: Morrow, 2000. Print.

Wilcox, Dennis L., Phillip H. Ault, and Warren K. Agee. *Public Relations: Strategies and Tactics*. 8th ed. New York: Irwin, 2006. Print.

Give the authors' names in the order provided on the title page. Reverse the first and last names of the first author *only,* not of any other authors.

3. More than three authors

Cameron, Glen T., Dennis L. Wilcox, Bryan H. Reber, and Jae-Hwa Shin. *Public Relations Today: Managing Competition and Conflict*. New York: Pearson, 2007. Print.

Cameron, Glen T., et al. *Public Relations Today: Managing Competition and Conflict*. New York: Pearson, 2007. Print.

Give all authors' names, or give only the first author's name followed by et al. (Latin abbreviation for "and others"). Do the same in your in-text citations of the source.

4. The same author(s) for two or more works

Gardner, Howard. *The Arts and Human Development*. New York: Wiley, 1973. Print.

---. *Five Minds for the Future*. Boston: Harvard Business School P, 2007. Print.

Give the author's name only in the first entry. For the second and any subsequent works by the same author, substitute three hyphens for the author's name. Note that the three hyphens may substitute only for *exactly* the same name or names.

5. A corporate author

Vault Technologies. *Turnkey Parking Solutions*. Salt Lake City: Mills, 2008. Print.

Corporate authors include companies, government bodies, and other groups. List the name of the group as author when a source gives only that name and not an individual's name.

6. Author not named (anonymous)

The Dorling Kindersley World Reference Atlas. London: Dorling, 2007. Print.

"Let the Horse Race Begin." *Time* 31 Mar. 2008: 22. Print.

List a work that names no author—neither an individual nor a group—by its full title. Alphabetize the work by the title's first main word, excluding *A, An,* or *The* (Dorling in the first example and Let in the second).

Periodical print sources

Print periodicals include scholarly journals, newspapers, and magazines that are published at regular intervals (quarterly, monthly, weekly, or daily). For the distinction between journals and magazines, see pages 125–26.

Articles in scholarly journals

MLA 40b

7. An article in a journal with volume and issue numbers (print)

Bee, Robert. "The Importance of Preserving Paper-Based Artifacts in a Digital Age." *Library Quarterly* 78.2 (2008): 174-94. Print.

See pages 168–69 for the basic format for an article in a periodical (a journal) and the location of the required information in the journal.

8. An article in a journal with only issue numbers (print)

Rymhs, Deena. "David Collier's *Surviving Saskatoon* and New Comics." *Canadian Literature* 194 (2007): 75-92. Print.

If a scholarly journal numbers only issues, not volumes, give the issue number alone after the journal title.

9. An abstract of a journal article or a dissertation (print)

Lever, Janet. "Sex Differences in the Games Children Play." *Social Problems* 23.2 (1996): 478-87. *Psychological Abstracts* 63.5 (1996): item 1431. Print.

For an abstract of a journal article, give the publication information for the article as in model 7 and then the information for the abstract.

For an abstract appearing in *Dissertation Abstracts* (*DA*) or *Dissertation Abstracts International* (*DAI*), use the following format:

Steciw, Steven K. "Alterations to the Pessac Project of Le Corbusier." Diss. U of Cambridge, England, 1986. *DAI* 46.10 (1986): 565C. Print.

Articles in newspapers

10. An article in a national newspaper (print)

Rich, Motoko. "As E-Books Gain Popularity, You Can't Even Judge a Cover." *New York Times* 31 Mar. 2010, natl. ed.: A1+. Print.

If the newspaper is divided into sections and makes the section label part of the page number, do the same (A1+ above, with the plus sign indicating that the article continues on a later page). If the section label is not part of the page number, provide it before the colon—for instance, natl. ed., sec. 1: 3 or State and Local sec.: 4+.

11. An article in a local newspaper (print)

Perera, Dilshanie. "Shuttle Route to Extend Transit Coverage." *Town Topics* [Princeton] 10 Feb. 2010: 1+. Print.

If the city of publication does not appear in the title of a local newspaper, follow the title with the city name, not italicized, in brackets.

Articles in magazines

12. An article in a weekly or biweekly magazine (print)

Fortini, Amanda. "Pomegranate Princess." *New Yorker* 31 Mar. 2008: 92-99. Print.

Follow the magazine title with the day, the month, and the year of publication. (Abbreviate all months except May, June, and July.) Don't place the date in parentheses, and don't provide a volume or issue number.

(continued on p. 170)

Format for a print journal article

Journal cover

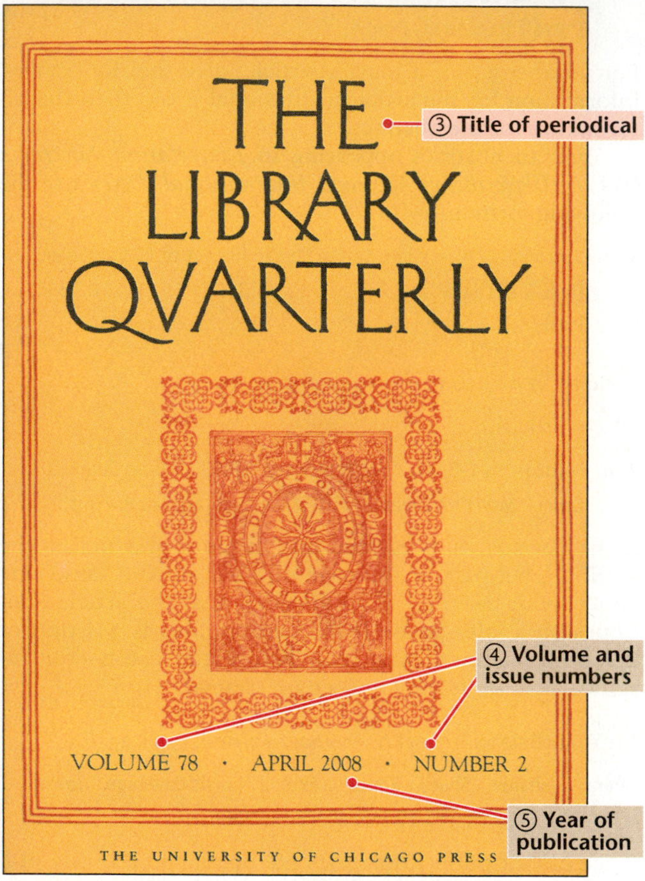

THE LIBRARY QVARTERLY
③ Title of periodical
④ Volume and issue numbers
VOLUME 78 · APRIL 2008 · NUMBER 2
⑤ Year of publication
THE UNIVERSITY OF CHICAGO PRESS

MLA 40b

First page of article

② Title of article

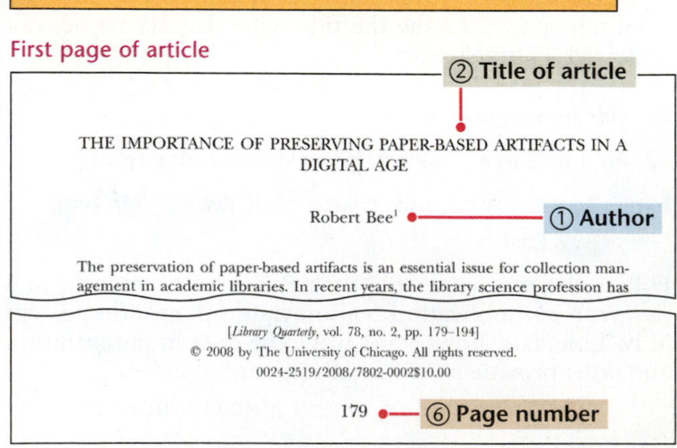

THE IMPORTANCE OF PRESERVING PAPER-BASED ARTIFACTS IN A DIGITAL AGE

Robert Bee[1] ① Author

The preservation of paper-based artifacts is an essential issue for collection management in academic libraries. In recent years, the library science profession has

[*Library Quarterly*, vol. 78, no. 2, pp. 179–194]

© 2008 by The University of Chicago. All rights reserved.

0024-2519/2008/7802-0002$10.00

179 ⑥ Page number

Bee, Robert. "The Importance of Preserving Paper-Based Artifacts in a Digital Age." *Library Quarterly* 78.2 (2008): 179-94. Print.

① Author. ② Title of article. ③ Title of periodical. ④ Volume and issue numbers. ⑤ Year of publication. ⑥ Inclusive page numbers. ⑦ Medium.

① **Author.** Give the full name—last name first, a comma, first name, and any middle name or initial. Omit *Dr., PhD,* or any other title. End the name with a period.

② **Title of article,** in quotation marks. Give the full title and any subtitle, separating them with a colon. End the title with a period inside the final quotation mark.

③ **Title of periodical,** in italics. Omit any *A, An,* or *The* from the beginning of the title. Do not end with a period.

④ **Volume and issue numbers,** in Arabic numerals, separated by a period. Do not add a period after the issue number.

⑤ **Year of publication,** in parentheses and followed by a colon.

⑥ **Inclusive page numbers of article,** without "pp." Provide only as many digits in the last number as needed for clarity, usually two.

⑦ **Medium.** Give the medium of the article, Print, followed by a period.

(continued from p. 167)

13. An article in a monthly or bimonthly magazine (print)

Douthat, Ross. "The Return of the Paranoid Style." *Atlantic Monthly* Apr. 2008: 52-59. Print.

Follow the magazine title with the month and the year of publication. (Abbreviate all months except May, June, and July.)

Reviews, editorials, letters to the editor, interviews

14. A review (print)

Glasswell, Kathryn, and George Kamberelis. "Drawing and Redrawing the Map of Writing Studies." Rev. of *Handbook of Writing Research*, by Charles A. MacArthur, Steve Graham, and Jill Fitzgerald. *Reading Research Quarterly* 42.2 (2007): 304-23. Print.

Rev. is an abbreviation for "Review." The names of the authors of the work being reviewed follow the title of the work, a comma, and by. If the review has no title of its own, then Rev. of and the title of the reviewed work immediately follow the name of the reviewer.

15. An editorial (print)

"A Global AIDS Campaign Stalled." Editorial. *New York Times* 21 June 2008, natl. ed.: A18. Print.

For an editorial with no named author, begin with the title and add the word Editorial after the title, as in the example. For an editorial with a named author, give his or her name at the start.

MLA 40b

16. A letter to the editor (print)

McBride, Thad. "Swapping the Suit and Tie." Letter. *Economist* 29 Mar. 2008: 30. Print.

Add the word Letter after the title, if there is one, or after the author's name.

17. An interview (print)

Aloni, Shulamit. Interview. *Palestine-Israel Journal of Politics, Economics, and Culture* 14.4 (2007): 63-68. Print.

Begin with the name of the person interviewed. If the interview does not have a title (as in the example), add Interview after the name. (Replace this description with the title if there is one.) You may also add the name of the interviewer if you know it—for example, Interview by Benson

Wright. See model 73 (p. 194) to cite a broadcast interview or an interview you conduct yourself.

Nonperiodical print sources

Nonperiodical print sources are works that are not published at regular intervals, such as books, government publications, and pamphlets.

Books

18. Basic format for a book (print)

Lahiri, Jhumpa. *Unaccustomed Earth*. New York: Knopf, 2008. Print.

The next two pages show the basic format for a book and the location of the required information in the book.

19. A second or subsequent edition (print)

Bolinger, Dwight L. *Aspects of Language*. 3rd ed. New York: Harcourt, 1981. Print.

Place the edition number or other designation (such as Rev. ed.) after the title. (If an editor's name follows the title, place the edition number after the name. See model 24.)

20. A book with an editor (print)

Holland, Merlin, and Rupert Hart-Davis, eds. *The Complete Letters of Oscar Wilde*. New York: Holt, 2000. Print.

Handle editors' names like authors' names (models 1–4), but add a comma and the abbreviation ed. or eds. after the last editor's name.

21. A book with an author and an editor (print)

Mumford, Lewis. *The City in History*. Ed. Donald L. Miller. New York: Pantheon, 1986. Print.

When citing the work of the author, give his or her name first, and give the editor's name after the title, preceded by Ed. (singular only, meaning "Edited by"). When citing the work of the editor, use model 20 for a book with an editor, adding By and the author's name after the title:

Miller, Donald L., ed. *The City in History*. By Lewis Mumford. New York: Pantheon, 1986. Print.

22. A book with a translator (print)

Alighieri, Dante. *The Inferno*. Trans. John Ciardi. New York: NAL, 1971. Print.

(continued on p. 174)

Format for a print book

Title page

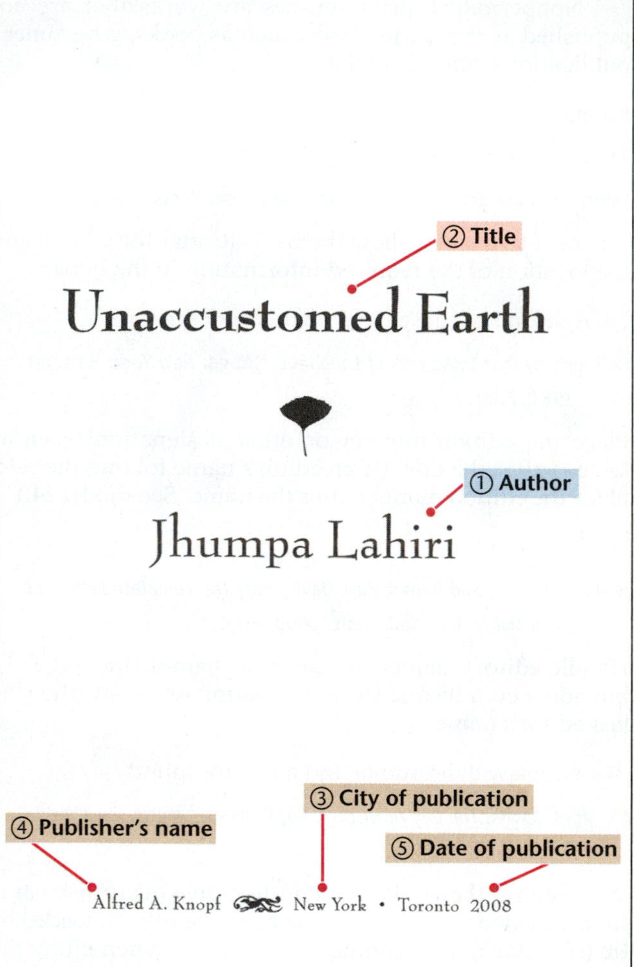

MLA 40b

① ② ③ ④
Lahiri, Jhumpa. *Unaccustomed Earth.* New York: Knopf,
⑤ ⑥
2008. Print.

① **Author.** Give the full name—last name first, a comma, first name, and any middle name or initial. Omit *Dr., PhD,* or any other title. End the name with a period.

② **Title,** in italics. Give the full title and any subtitle, separating them with a colon. End the title with a period.

③ **City of publication.** Precede the publisher's name with its city, followed by a colon. Use only the first city if the title page lists more than one.

④ **Publisher's name.** Shorten most publishers' names ("UP" for University Press, "Little" for Little, Brown). Give both imprint and publisher's names when they appear on the title page: e.g., "Vintage-Random" for Vintage Books and Random House.

⑤ **Date of publication.** If the date doesn't appear on the title page, look for it on the next page. End the date with a period.

⑥ **Medium.** Give the medium of the book, Print, followed by a period.

(continued from p. 171)

When citing the work of the author, give his or her name first, and give the translator's name after the title, preceded by Trans. ("Translated by"). When citing the work of the translator, give his or her name first, followed by a comma and trans. Follow the title with By and the author's name:

Ciardi, John, trans. *The Inferno*. By Dante Alighieri. New York: NAL, 1971. Print.

23. An anthology (print)

Kennedy, X. J., and Dana Gioia, eds. *Literature: An Introduction to Fiction, Poetry, and Drama*. 11th ed. New York: Longman, 2010. Print.

Cite an entire anthology only when citing the work of the editor or editors or when your instructor permits cross-referencing like that shown in model 25.

24. A selection from an anthology (print)

Mason, Bobbie Ann. "Shiloh." *Literature: An Introduction to Fiction, Poetry, and Drama*. Ed. X. J. Kennedy and Dana Gioia. 11th ed. New York: Longman, 2010. 569-79. Print.

This listing adds the following to the anthology entry in model 23: author of selection, title of selection (in quotation marks), and inclusive page numbers for the selection (without the abbreviation "pp."). If you wish, you may also supply the original date of publication for the work you are citing, after its title. See model 30.

If the work you cite comes from a collection of works by one author that has no editor, use the following form:

Auden, W. H. "Family Ghosts." *The Collected Poetry of W. H. Auden*. New York: Random, 1945. 132-33. Print.

If the work you cite is a scholarly article that was previously printed elsewhere, provide the complete information for the earlier publication of the piece, followed by Rpt. in ("Reprinted in") and the information for the source in which you found the piece:

Molloy, Francis C. "The Suburban Vision in John O'Hara's Short Stories." *Critique: Studies in Modern Fiction* 25.2 (1984): 101-13. Rpt. in *Short Story Criticism: Excerpts from Criticism of the Works of Short Fiction Writers*. Ed. David Segal. Vol. 15. Detroit: Gale, 1989. 287-92. Print.

25. Two or more selections from the same anthology (print)

Cisneros, Sandra. "The House on Mango Street." Kennedy and Gioia 518-19.

Kennedy, X. J., and Dana Gioia, eds. *Literature: An Introduction to Fiction, Poetry, and Drama*. 11th ed. New York: Longman, 2010. Print.

Merwin, W. S. "For the Anniversary of My Death." Kennedy and Gioia 834.

Stevens, Wallace. "Thirteen Ways of Looking at a Blackbird." Kennedy and Gioia 838-40.

When you are citing more than one selection from the same anthology, your instructor may allow you to avoid repetition by giving the anthology information in full (as in the Kennedy and Gioia entry) and then simply cross-referencing it in entries for the works you used (Kennedy and Gioia plus page numbers). Because the selection entries cross-reference the Kennedy anthology, they do not require the medium.

26. An article in a reference work (print)

"Reckon." *Merriam-Webster's Collegiate Dictionary*. 11th ed. 2008. Print.

Wenner, Manfred W. "Arabia." *The New Encyclopaedia Britannica: Macropaedia*. 15th ed. 2007. Print.

List an article in a reference work by its title (first example) unless the article is signed (second example). For works with entries arranged alphabetically, you need not include volume or page numbers. For works that are widely used and often revised, like those above, you may omit the editors' names, place of publication, and publisher's name. For works that are specialized—with narrow subjects and audiences—give full publication information:

"Hungarians in America." *The Ethnic Almanac*. Ed. Stephanie Bernardo Johns. 6th ed. New York: Doubleday, 2002. 121-23. Print.

See also models 46 (p. 184) and 66 (p. 192), respectively, to cite reference works appearing on the Web or on a CD-ROM or DVD-ROM.

27. An illustrated book or graphic narrative (print)

Wilson, G. Willow. *Cairo*. Illus. M. K. Perker. New York: Vertigo-DC Comics, 2005. Print.

When citing the work of the writer of a graphic narrative or illustrated book, give the author's name, title, Illus. ("Illustrated by"), and the illustrator's name. When citing the work of an illustrator, list his or her name first, followed by a comma and illus. ("illustrator"). After the title and By, list the author's name.

Williams, Garth, illus. *Charlotte's Web.* By E. B. White. 1952. New York: Harper, 1999. Print.

28. A multivolume work (print)

Lincoln, Abraham. *The Collected Works of Abraham Lincoln*. Ed. Roy P. Basler. Vol. 5. New Brunswick: Rutgers UP, 1953. Print. 8 vols.

If you use only one volume of a multivolume work, give that volume number before the publication information (Vol. 5 in the preceding example). You may add the total number of volumes at the end of the entry (8 vols. in the example).

If you use two or more volumes of a multivolume work, give the work's total number of volumes before the publication information (8 vols. in the following example). Your text citation will indicate which volume you are citing (see pp. 159–60).

Lincoln, Abraham. *The Collected Works of Abraham Lincoln*. Ed. Roy P. Basler. 8 vols. New Brunswick: Rutgers UP, 1953. Print.

29. A series (print)

Bergman, Ingmar. *The Seventh Seal*. New York: Simon, 1995. Print. Mod. Film Scripts Ser. 12.

Place the name of the series (not quoted or italicized) at the end of the entry. Abbreviate common words such as *modern* and *series.*

30. A republished book (print)

James, Henry. *The Bostonians*. 1886. New York: Penguin, 2001. Print.

Insert the original publication date between the title and the full publication information for the source you are using.

31. The Bible (print)

The Bible. Print. King James Vers.

The Holy Bible. Trans. Ronald Youngblood et al. Grand Rapids: Zondervan, 1984. Print. New Intl. Vers.

When citing a standard version of the Bible (first example), do not italicize the title or the name of the version at the end. You need not provide publication information. For an edition of the Bible (second example), italicize the title, provide editors' and/or translators' names, give full publication information, and add the version name at the end.

32. A book with a title in its title (print)

Eco, Umberto. *Postscript to* The Name of the Rose. Trans. William Weaver. New York: Harcourt, 1983. Print.

When a book's title contains another book title, do not italicize the second title. When a book's title contains a quotation or the title of a work normally placed in quotation marks, keep the quotation marks and italicize both titles: *Critical Response to Henry James's "The Beast in the Jungle."*

33. Published proceedings of a conference (print)

Stimpson, Bill, ed. *AWEA Annual Conference and Exhibition.* Proc. of Amer. Wind Energy Assn. Conf., 3-6 June 2007, New York. Red Hook: Curran, 2008. Print.

Treat the published proceedings of a conference like a book. Between the title and the publication data, add information about the conference, such as its name, date, and location.

34. An introduction, preface, foreword, or afterword (print)

Donaldson, Norman. Introduction. *The Claverings*. By Anthony Trollope. New York: Dover, 1977. vii-xv. Print.

Give the author of the introduction, foreword, or afterword followed by the name of the piece. Follow the title of the book with By and the book author's name. Give the inclusive page numbers of the part you cite.

When the author of a preface or introduction is the same as the author of the book, give only the last name after the title:

Gould, Stephen Jay. Prologue. *The Flamingo's Smile: Reflections in Natural History*. By Gould. New York: Norton, 1985. 13-20. Print.

35. A book lacking publication information or pagination (print)

Carle, Eric. *The Very Busy Spider.* New York: Philomel, 1984. N. pag. Print.

Provide as much information as you can and indicate the missing information with an abbreviation: N.p. if no city of publication, n.p. if no publisher, n.d. if no publication date, and N. pag. if no page numbers.

Other nonperiodical print sources

36. A government publication (print)

United Nations. Dept. of Economic and Social Affairs. *World Youth Report 2007: Young People's Transition to Adulthood—Progress and Challenges*. New York: United Nations, 2008. Print.

United States. Cong. House. Committee on Agriculture, Nutrition, and Forestry. *Food and Energy Act of 2007*. 110th Cong., 1st sess. Washington: GPO, 2007. Print.

Wisconsin. Dept. of Public Instruction. *Bullying Prevention Program: Grades 6-8*. Madison: Wisconsin Dept. of Public Instruction, 2007. Print.

If a government publication does not list a person as author or editor, give as author the name of the government and the name of the agency (which may be abbreviated). For a congressional publication (second example), give the house and committee involved before the title, and give the number and session of Congress after the title.

If a government publication lists a person as author or editor, treat the source as an authored or edited book:

Putko, Michelle. *Women in Combat Compendium*. Carlisle: US Army War Coll., Strategic Studies Inst., 2008. Print.

See model 45 (p. 184) to cite a government publication you find on the Web.

37. A pamphlet or brochure (print)

Understanding Childhood Obesity. Tampa: Obesity Action Coalition, 2010. Print.

Most pamphlets and brochures can be treated as books.

38. A dissertation (print)

McFaddin, Marie Oliver. *Adaptive Reuse: An Architectural Solution for Poverty and Homelessness*. Diss. U of Maryland, 2007. Ann Arbor: UMI, 2007. Print.

Treat a published dissertation like a book, but after the title insert Diss. ("Dissertation"), the institution granting the degree, and the year.

For an unpublished dissertation, use quotation marks rather than italics for the title and omit publication information:

Wilson, Stuart M. "John Stuart Mill as a Literary Critic." Diss. U of Michigan, 1990. Print.

39. A letter (print)

Buttolph, Mrs. Laura E. Letter to Rev. and Mrs. C. C. Jones. 20 June 1857. *The Children of Pride: A True Story of Georgia and the Civil War*. Ed. Robert Manson Myers. New Haven: Yale UP, 1972. 334-35. Print.

List a published letter under the writer's name. Specify that the source is a letter and to whom it was addressed, and give the date on which it was written.

For an unpublished letter in the collection of a library or archive, specify the writer, recipient, and date, as for a published letter. Then provide the medium, either MS ("manuscript") or TS ("typescript"). End with the name and location of the archive.

James, Jonathan E. Letter to his sister. 16 Apr. 1970. MS. Jonathan E. James Papers. South Dakota State Archive, Pierre.

For a letter you received, specify yourself as recipient and give the date and the medium, MS or TS.

Wynne, Ava. Letter to the author. 6 Apr. 2008. MS.

To cite an e-mail message or a discussion-group posting, see models 68–69 (p. 192).

Nonperiodical Web sources

This section shows how to cite nonperiodical sources that you find on the Web. These sources may be published only once or occasionally, or they may be updated frequently but not regularly. (Most online magazines and newspapers fall into the latter category. See pp. 181 and 184.) Some nonperiodical Web sources are available only on the Web (next page); others are available in other media as well (p. 187). See also models 60–65 (pp. 188–91) to cite a scholarly journal that you find on the Web and any periodical that you find in an online database.

The MLA does not require a URL (electronic address) in Web source citations unless a source is hard to find without it or could be confused with another source. See model 59 (p. 188) for the form to use when citing a URL.

Note The *MLA Handbook* does not label its examples of nonperiodical Web sources as particular types. For ease of reference, the following models identify and illustrate the kinds of Web sources you are likely to encounter. If you don't see just what you need, consult the index of models on pages 163–65 for a similar source type whose format you can adapt. If your source does not include all of the information needed for a complete citation, find and list what you can.

Nonperiodical sources available only on the Web

Many nonperiodical Web sources are available only online. The following list, adapted from the *MLA Handbook,* itemizes the possible elements in a nonperiodical Web publication, in order of their appearance in a works-cited entry:

1. **Name of the author or other person responsible for the source,** such as an editor, translator, or performer.
2. **Title of the cited work.** Use quotation marks for titles of articles, blog entries, and other sources that are parts of larger works. Use italics for books, plays, and other sources that are published independently.
3. **Title of the Web site,** in italics.
4. **Version or edition cited,** if any, following model 19 (p. 171)—for example, *Index of History Periodicals.* 2nd ed.
5. **Publisher or sponsor of the site,** followed by a comma. If you cannot find a publisher or sponsor, use N.p. ("No publisher") instead.
6. **Date of electronic publication, latest revision, or posting.** If no date is available, use n.d. ("no date") instead.
7. **Medium of publication:** Web.
8. **Date of your access:** day, month, year.

For some Web sources, you may want to include information that is not on this list, such as the names of both the writer and the performers on a television show.

40. A short work with a title (Web)

Molella, Arthur. "Cultures of Innovation." *The Lemelson Center for the Study of Invention and Innovation.* Smithsonian Inst., Natl. Museum of Amer. Hist., Spring 2005. Web. 3 Aug. 2010.

MLA 40b

See pages 182–83 for an analysis of this entry and the location of the required information on the Web site. If the short work you are citing lacks an author, start the entry with the title of the work:

"Clean Energy." *Union of Concerned Scientists: Citizens and Scientists for Environmental Solutions.* Union of Concerned Scientists, 5 Feb. 2010. Web. 11 Mar. 2010.

To cite a short Web source that also appears in another medium (such as print), see models 54–58 (pp. 186–87). To cite an article from a Web journal or from an online database, see models 60–65 (pp. 188–91).

41. A short work without a title (Web)

Crane, Gregory, ed. Home page. *The Perseus Digital Library.* Dept. of Classics, Tufts U, n.d. Web. 21 July 2010.

If you are citing an untitled short work from a Web site, such as the home page of a site or a posting to a blog, insert Home page, Online posting, or another descriptive label in place of the title. Note that this source lacks a publication date, indicated by n.d. after the sponsor's name.

42. An entire site (Web)

Cheit, Ross E., ed. *The Recovered Memory Project.* Taubman Center for Public and Amer. Insts., Brown U, July 2007. Web. 8 Oct. 2010.

When citing an entire Web site, include the name of the editor, author, or compiler (if available); the title of the site; the sponsor; the date of publication or most recent update; the medium (Web); and your date of access.

If your source lacks a named author or editor, begin with the site title:

Union of Concerned Scientists: Citizens and Scientists for Environmental Solutions. Union of Concerned Scientists, 5 Feb. 2010. Web. 11 Mar. 2010.

If your source lacks a sponsor, use the abbreviation N.p. ("No publisher"). If it lacks a publication date, use the abbreviation n.d. The source below lacks both a sponsor and a publication date:

Corbett, John. *STARN: Scots Teaching and Resource Network.* N.p., n.d. Web. 26 Nov. 2009.

43. An article in a newspaper (Web)

Ratliff, Ben. "Musicians without Borders." *New York Times.* New York Times, 29 Mar. 2010. Web. 8 Apr. 2010.

Even when an online periodical relates to a printed version, treat it as a nonperiodical because the online content may change often and unpredictably. For an online newspaper article, list the author, article title, and newspaper title, as in model 10 or 11 (p. 167). Then give the publisher's name, the date, the medium (Web), and the date of your access.

Use the preceding format to adapt the models for print periodicals if you need to cite a Web newspaper review, editorial, letter to the editor, or interview (models 14–17, p. 170). See model 64 to cite a newspaper article in an online database.

44. An article in a magazine (Web)

Baird, Julie. "The Moral Weight of War." *Newsweek.* Newsweek, 5 Apr. 2010. Web. 15 May 2010.

(continued on p. 184)

Format for a short work on the Web

Top of page

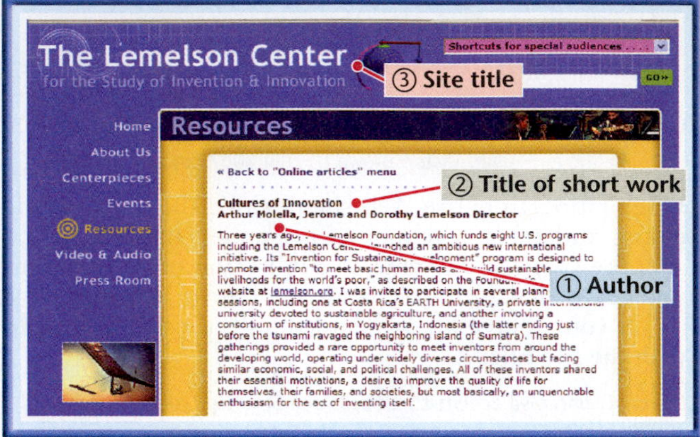

Bottom of page

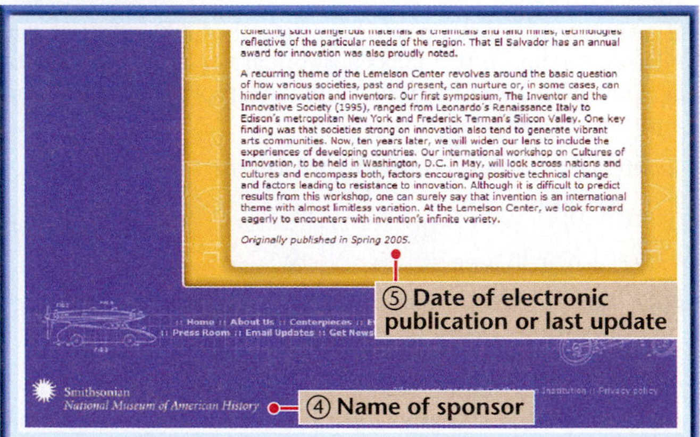

MLA
40b

① Molella, Arthur. ② "Cultures of Innovation." ③ *The Lemelson Center for the Study of Invention and Innovation.* ④ Smithsonian Inst., Natl. Museum of Amer. Hist., ⑤ Spring 2005. ⑥ Web. ⑦ 3 Aug. 2010.

① **Author.** Give the full name—last name first, a comma, first name, and any middle name or initial. Omit *Dr., PhD,* or any other title. End the name with a period. If you don't see the author's name at the top of the page, look at the bottom. If no author is listed, begin with the title of the short work.

② **Title of the short work,** in quotation marks. End the title with a period inside the final quotation mark.

③ **Site title,** italicized and ending with a period.

④ **Name of the sponsor,** ending with a comma.

⑤ **Date of electronic publication or last update.** For dates that include day and month, give the day first, then month, then year. Abbreviate all months except May, June, and July. End the date with a period.

⑥ **Medium.** Give the medium of the article, Web, followed by a period.

⑦ **Date of your access.** Give the day first, then month, then year. Abbreviate all months except May, June, and July. End the date with a period.

(continued from p. 181)

See the explanation with model 43 (p. 181) for why an online magazine is treated as a nonperiodical. List the author, article title, and magazine title, as in model 12 or 13 (pp. 167 and 170). Then give the publisher's name, the date, the medium (Web), and the date of your access.

Use the preceding format to adapt the models for print periodicals if you need to cite a Web magazine review, editorial, letter to the editor, or interview (models 14–17, p. 170). See model 65 to cite a magazine article in an online database.

45. A government publication (Web)

United States. Dept. of Agriculture. "Inside the Pyramid." *MyPyramid.gov.* US Dept. of Agriculture, n.d. Web. 1 Mar. 2010.

See model 36 for examples of government publications in print. Provide the same information for online publications, substituting Web for print publication information and adding your date of access.

46. An article in a reference work (Web)

"Yi Dynasty." *Encyclopaedia Britannica Online*. Encyclopaedia Britannica, 2010. Web. 7 Apr. 2010.

This source does not list an author, so the entry begins with the title of the article and then proceeds as for other Web sources. If a reference article has an author, place the name before the article title.

For reference works that you find in print or on CD-ROM or DVD-ROM, see models 26 (p. 175) and 66 (p. 192), respectively.

47. An image (Web)

The following examples show formats for a range of images that are available only on the Web.

A work of visual art:

Simpson, Rick. *Overload. Museum of Computer Art.* Museum of Computer Art, 2008. Web. 1 Apr. 2010.

A photograph:

Touboul, Jean. *Desert 1*. 2002. Photograph. *Artmuse.net.* Jean Touboul, 2008. Web. 14 Nov. 2010.

An advertisement:

FreeCreditReport.com. Advertisement. *Facebook*. Facebook, 2010. Web. 6 May 2010.

A map, chart, graph, or diagram:

"Greenhouse Effect." Diagram. *Earthguide.* Scripps Inst. of Oceanography, 2010. Web. 17 July 2010.

See also model 58 (p. 187) to cite an image that appears both on the Web and in another medium; model 71 (p. 193) to cite an image in a digital file; and models 76–80 (pp. 194–96) to cite an image that isn't on a computer.

48. A television or radio program (Web)

Seabrook, Andrea, host. *All Things Considered.* Natl. Public Radio, 6 Apr. 2010. Web. 21 Apr. 2010.

Cite television or radio content on the Web by its title or by the name of the person whose work you are citing. Identify the role of anyone but an author (host in the example). You may also cite other contributors (and their roles) after the title, as in model 50. See also model 72 (p. 193) to cite a television or radio program that isn't on the Web.

49. A video recording (Web)

Green Children Foundation, prod. *The Green Children Visit China. YouTube.* YouTube, 7 Jan. 2008. Web. 28 June 2010.

Cite a video on the Web either by its title or by the name of the person whose work you are citing. Identify the role of anyone but an author (prod. in the example). You may also cite other contributors (and their roles) after the title, as in model 50.

See also model 51 to cite a podcast of a video recording; model 57 (p. 187) to cite a video recording or film that appears both on the Web and in another medium (such as DVD); and model 75 (p. 194) to cite a film, DVD, or video recording that isn't on the Web.

50. A sound recording (Web)

Beglarian, Eve. *Five Things.* Perf. Beglarian et al. *Kalvos and Damian.* N.p., 23 Oct. 2001. Web. 8 Mar. 2010.

Cite a musical sound recording by its title or by the name of the person whose work you are citing—in this example, the composer. This example also gives the performers of the work after the title. Use the same format for a spoken-word recording that you find on the Web:

Wasserstein, Wendy, narr. "Afternoon of a Faun." By Wasserstein. *The Borzoi Reader Online.* Knopf, 2001. Web. 14 Feb. 2008.

See also the next model to cite a sound podcast; model 56 to cite a sound recording that appears both on the Web and in another medium (such as CD); and model 74 (p. 194) to cite a sound recording that isn't on the Web.

51. A podcast (Web)

Cobiella, Kelly. "Exonerated." *60 Minutes. CBS News.* CBS News, 19 Apr. 2009. Web. 6 June 2010.

This podcast from a news program lists the author of a story on the show, the title of the story (in quotation marks), and the program (italicized).

52. A blog entry (Web)

Marshall, Joshua Micah. "When Did the Dust Settle?" *Talking Points Memo.* TPM Media, 23 Feb. 2010. Web. 29 Mar. 2010.

This blog entry gives the title of the entry (in quotation marks) and the title of the blog or site (in italics). See model 41 (p. 180) to cite a blog entry without a title.

53. A wiki (Web)

"Podcast." *Wikipedia.* Wikimedia, n.d. Web. 20 June 2010.

To cite an entry from a wiki, give the entry title, site title, sponsor, and publication date (here n.d. because the wiki entry is undated). Begin with the site title if you are citing the entire wiki.

Nonperiodical Web sources also available in print

Some sources you find on the Web may be books, poems, short stories, and other works that have been scanned from print versions. To cite such a source, generally provide the information for original print publication as well as that for Web publication. Begin your entry as if you were citing the print work, consulting models 18–39 for an appropriate format. Then, instead of giving "Print" as the medium, provide the title of the Web site you used, any version or edition number, the medium you used (Web), and the date of your access.

54. A short work with print publication information (Web)

Wheatley, Phillis. "On Virtue." *Poems on Various Subjects, Religious and Moral.* London, 1773. N. pag. *American Verse Project.* Web. 21 July 2010.

The print information for this poem follows model 24 (p. 174) for a selection from an anthology, but it omits the publisher's name because the anthology was published before 1900. The print information ends with N. pag. because the original source has no page numbers.

55. A book with print publication information (Web)

James, Henry. *The Ambassadors*. 1903. New York: Scribner's, 1909. *Oxford Text Archive*. Web. 5 May 2010.

The print information for this novel follows model 30 (p. 176) for a republished book, so it includes both the original date of publication (1903) and the publication information for the scanned book.

Nonperiodical Web sources also available in other media

Some images, films, and sound recordings that you find on the Web may have been published before in other media and then scanned or digitized for the Web. To cite such a source, generally provide the information for original publication as well as that for Web publication. Begin your entry as if you were citing the original, consulting models 72–82 (pp. 193–96) for an appropriate format. Then, instead of giving the original medium of publication, provide the title of the Web site you used, the medium you used (Web), and your date of access.

56. A sound recording with other publication information (Web)

"Rioting in Pittsburgh." CBS Radio, 1968. *Vincent Voice Library*. Web. 7 Dec. 2009.

For Web sound recordings with original publication information, base citations on model 74 (p. 194), adding the information for Web publication.

57. A film or video recording with other publication information (Web)

Coca-Cola. Advertisement. Dir. Haskell Wexler. 1971. *American Memory*. Lib. of Cong. Web. 8 Apr. 2010.

For Web films or videos with original publication information, base citations on model 75 (p. 194), adding the information for Web publication.

58. An image with other publication information (Web)

Pollock, Jackson. *Lavender Mist: Number 1*. 1950. Natl. Gallery of Art, Washington. *WebMuseum*. Web. 7 Apr. 2010.

Keefe, Mike. "FAA Inspector in a Quandary." Cartoon. *Denver Post* 5 Apr. 2008. *PoliticalCartoons.com*. Web. 7 Apr. 2010.

For Web images with original publication information, base citations on models 76–80 (pp. 194–96), adding the information for Web publication.

Citation of a URL

59. A source requiring citation of the URL (Web)

Joss, Rich. "Dispatches from the Ice: The Second Season Begins." *Antarctic Expeditions*. Smithsonian Natl. Zoo and Friends of the Natl. Zoo, 26 Oct. 2007. Web. 26 Sept. 2010. <http://nationalzoo.si.edu/ConservationAndScience/AquaticEcosystems/Antarctica/Expedition/FieldNew/2-FieldNews.cfm>.

Give the URL of a source when readers may not be able to locate the source without one. For example, using a search engine to find "Dispatches from the Ice" (the title in the example) yields more than ten hits, one of which links to the correct site but the wrong document.

Journals on the Web and periodicals in online databases

This section covers scholarly journals that you reach directly on the Web and journals, newspapers, and magazines that you reach through online databases. Treat newspapers and magazines that you reach directly on the Web as periodicals: see models 43 and 44 (pp. 181 and 184).

Web journals consulted directly

60. An article in a scholarly journal (Web)

Polletta, Francesca. "Just Talk: Public Deliberation after 9/11." *Journal of Public Deliberation* 4.1 (2008): n. pag. Web. 7 Apr. 2010.

For a journal article you find directly on the Web, use the format for a print journal (pp. 168–69), but replace the medium "Print" with Web and add your access date. Because many Web journals do not number pages, you may have to substitute n. pag. for page numbers, as in the preceding example.

Use the same format to adapt the models for print periodicals if you need to cite a Web journal review, editorial, letter to the editor, or interview (models 14–17, pp. 170–71). For a journal article reached in an online database, see model 62.

61. An abstract of a journal article (Web)

Polletta, Francesca. "Just Talk: Public Deliberation after 9/11." *Journal of Public Deliberation* 4.1 (2008): n. pag. Abstract. Web. 7 Apr. 2010.

Treat a Web abstract like a Web journal article, but add Abstract between the publication information and the medium. (You may omit this label if the journal title clearly indicates that the cited work is an abstract.) See model 63 to cite an abstract in an online database.

Web periodicals consulted in online databases

To cite articles in journals, newspapers, and magazines that you find in online databases, follow models 7–17 (pp. 166–71) for print periodicals, but replace "Print" with the title of the database you consulted, the medium (Web), and the date of your access.

62. An article in a scholarly journal (online database)

Gorski, Paul C. "Privilege and Repression in the Digital Era: Rethinking the Sociopolitics of the Digital Divide." *Race, Gender and Class* 10.4 (2003): 145-76. *Ethnic NewsWatch*. Web. 23 Apr. 2010.

See the next two pages for an analysis of the preceding entry and the location of the required information in the database.

63. An abstract of a journal article (online database)

Gorski, Paul C. "Privilege and Repression in the Digital Era: Rethinking the Sociopolitics of the Digital Divide." *Race, Gender and Class* 10.4 (2003): 145-76. Abstract. *Ethnic NewsWatch*. Web. 23 Apr. 2010.

Treat an abstract in an online database like a journal article in a database, but add Abstract between the publication information and the database title. (You may omit this label if the journal title clearly indicates that the cited work is an abstract.)

64. An article in a newspaper (online database)

Buckman, Rebecca. "Driver Cell Phone Bans Questioned." *Wall Street Journal* 13 May 2008, eastern ed.: D2+. *ProQuest*. Web. 12 Oct. 2010.

Follow model 10 or 11 (p. 167) for citing a newspaper article, and add the title of the database, the medium (Web), and the date of your access.

65. An article in a magazine (online database)

Brown, Kathryn. "The Skinny on the Environment." *Scientific American* Jan. 2008: 30-37. *Academic Search Complete*. Web. 3 July 2010.

Follow model 12 or 13 (pp. 167 and 170) for citing a magazine article, and add the title of the database, the medium (Web), and the date of your access.

(continued on p. 192)

MLA 40b

Format for a journal article in an online database

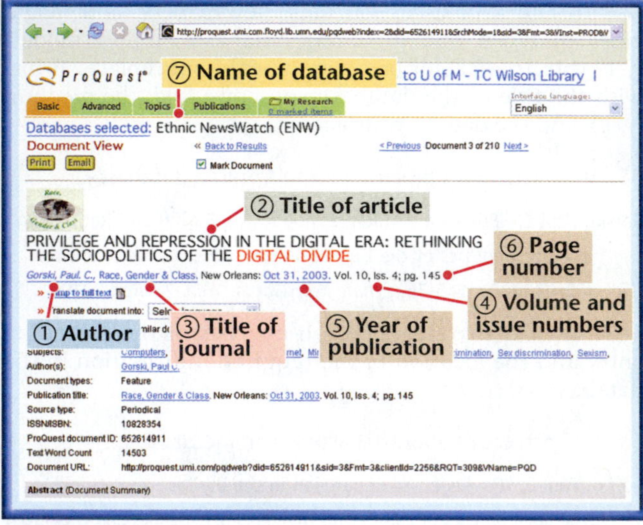

MLA 40b

① ②

Gorski, Paul C. "Privilege and Repression in the Digital Era: Rethinking the Sociopolitics of the Digital Divide."

③ ④ ⑤ ⑥

Race, Gender and Class 10.4 (2003): 145-76. *Ethnic*

⑦ ⑧ ⑨

NewsWatch. Web. 23 Apr. 2010.

① **Author.** Give the full name—last name first, a comma, first name, and any middle name or initial. Omit *Dr., PhD,* or any other title. End the name with a period.

② **Title of the article,** in quotation marks. End the title with a period inside the final quotation mark.

③ **Title of the journal,** in italics. Omit any *A, An,* or *The* from the beginning of the title. Do not end with a period.

④ **Volume and issue numbers,** in Arabic numerals, separated by a period. Do not add a period after the issue number.

⑤ **Year of publication,** in parentheses and followed by a colon.

⑥ **Inclusive page numbers** of article, without "pp." Provide only as many digits in the last number as needed for clarity, usually two. If no page numbers are given, insert n. pag. in their place.

⑦ **Name of the database,** in italics, ending with a period.

⑧ **Medium.** Give the medium of the article, Web, followed by a period.

⑨ **Date of your access.** Give the day first, then month, then year. Abbreviate all months except May, June, and July. End the date with a period.

(continued from p. 189)

Other electronic sources

Publications on CD-ROM or DVD-ROM

66. A nonperiodical CD-ROM or DVD-ROM

Nunberg, Geoffrey. "Usage in the Dictionary." *The American Heritage Dictionary of the English Language.* 4th ed. Boston: Houghton, 2008. CD-ROM.

Single-issue CD-ROMs may be encyclopedias, dictionaries, books, and other resources that are published just once, like print books. Follow models 18–35 for print books (pp. 171–77), but replace "Print" with CD-ROM or DVD-ROM. If the disc has a vendor that differs from the publisher of the work, add the vendor's place of publication, name, and publication date after the medium.

See also models 26 (p. 175) and 46 (p. 184) to cite reference works in print and on the Web.

67. A periodical CD-ROM or DVD-ROM

Kolata, Gina. "Gauging Body Mass Index in a Changing Body." *New York Times* 28 June 2005, natl. ed.: D1+. CD-ROM. *New York Times Ondisc.* UMI-ProQuest. Sept. 2005.

Cite an article or a periodical CD-ROM or DVD-ROM as you would a print article (pp. 166–70), but replace "Print" with CD-ROM or DVD-ROM and add the database title, the vendor's name, and the database publication date.

E-mail and discussion-group postings

68. An e-mail message

MLA 40b

Bailey, Elizabeth. "Re: London." Message to the author. 27 Mar. 2010. E-mail.

For the title of an e-mail, use the subject heading in quotation marks. Name the recipient, whether yourself (the author) or someone else.

69. A posting to a discussion group

Williams, Frederick. "Circles as Primitive." *The Math Forum @ Drexel.* Drexel U, 28 Feb. 2008. E-mail.

If a discussion-group posting does not have a title, say Online posting instead. Give the title of the discussion list as well as the name of the sponsor.

Digital files

You may want to cite a digital file that is not on the Web or on a disc, such as a PDF document, a JPEG image, or an MP3 sound recording that you downloaded onto your computer. Use the appropriate model for your kind of source (for instance, model 77 for a personal photograph), but replace the medium with the file format you're using. If you don't know the file format, use Digital file.

70. A text file (digital)

Berg, John K. "Estimates of Persons Driving While Intoxicated." *Law Enforcement Today* 17 Apr. 2008. PDF file.

Fernandez, Carlos. "Summers in Spain." 2010. *Microsoft Word* file.

71. A media file (digital)

Springsteen, Bruce. "This Life." *Working on a Dream*. Columbia, 2009. MP3 file.

Boys playing basketball. Personal photograph by Granger Goetz. 2010. JPEG file.

Other sources

The source types covered in this section are not on a computer or, generally, in printed sources. Most of them have parallel citation formats elsewhere in this chapter when you reach them through electronic and print media. See model 17 (p. 170) to cite an interview in print. See models 47–50 (pp. 184–85) to cite images, television and radio programs, video recordings, and sound recordings that are available only on the Web. See models 56–58 (p. 187) to cite such sources when they are available on the Web and in other media. And see model 71 to cite such sources in digital files.

72. A television or radio program

"The Time Warp." By Zoanne Clark. Dir. Rob Corn. *Grey's Anatomy*. ABC. KGO, San Francisco, 18 Feb. 2010. Television.

Start with the title unless you are citing the work of a person or persons. The example here cites an episode title (in quotation marks) and the names of the episode's writer and director. It also gives the name of the network and the call letters and city of the local station. If you list individuals who worked on the entire program rather than an episode, put their names after the program title.

73. A personal or broadcast interview

Paul, William. Personal interview. 6 June 2008.

Filkins, Dexter. Interview by Terry Gross. *Fresh Air*. Natl. Public Radio. WGBH, Boston, 20 Apr. 2010. Radio.

Begin with the name of the person interviewed. For an interview you conducted, specify Personal interview or the medium (such as Telephone interview or E-mail interview), and then give the date. For an interview you heard or saw, provide the title if any or Interview if there is no title. Add the name of the interviewer if he or she is identified.

74. A sound recording

Rubenstein, Artur, perf. Piano Concerto no. 2 in B-flat. By Johannes Brahms. Cond. Eugene Ormandy. Philadelphia Orch. RCA, 1972. LP.

Springsteen, Bruce. "This Life." *Working on a Dream*. Columbia, 2009. CD.

Begin with the name of the individual whose work you are citing. Unless this person is the composer, identify his or her role, as with perf. ("performer") in the first example. If you're citing a work identified by form, number, and key (first example), do not use quotation marks or italics for the title. If you're citing a song or song lyrics (second example), give the title in quotation marks; then provide the title of the recording in italics. Following the title, name and identify other contributors you want to mention. Then provide the manufacturer of the recording, the date of release, and the medium.

75. A film, DVD, or video recording

The Joneses. Dir. Chris Tyrrell. Bjort, 2010. Film.

MLA 40b

Start with the title of the work unless you are citing the work of a person (see the next example). Generally, identify and name the director. You may list other participants (writer, lead performers, and so on) as you judge appropriate. For a film, end with the distributor, date, and medium (Film).

For a DVD or videocassette, include the original release date (if any), the distributor's name and release date, and the medium.

Balanchine, George, chor. *Serenade*. Perf. San Francisco Ballet. Dir. Hilary Bean. 1991. PBS Video, 2006. DVD.

76. A painting, photograph, or other work of visual art

Arnold, Leslie. *Seated Woman*. N.d. Oil on canvas. DeYoung Museum, San Francisco.

Sugimoto, Hiroshi. *Pacific Ocean, Mount Tamalpais.* 1994. Photograph. Private collection.

To cite an actual work of art, name the artist and give the title (in italics) and the date of creation (or N.d. if the date is unknown). Then provide the medium of the work and the name and location of the owner, if known. (Use Private collection if not.)

For a work you see only in a reproduction, provide the complete publication information for the source you used. Omit the medium of the work itself, and replace it with the medium of the reproduction (Print in the following example). Omit such information only if you examined the actual work.

Hockney, David. *Place Furstenberg, Paris.* 1985. Coll. Art Gallery, New Paltz. *David Hockney: A Retrospective.* Ed. Maurice Tuchman and Stephanie Barron. Los Angeles: Los Angeles County Museum of Art, 1988. 247. Print.

77. A personal photograph

Common milkweed on Lake Michigan shoreline. Personal photograph by the author. 22 Aug. 2008.

For a personal photograph by you or by someone else, describe the subject, name the photographer, and add the date. The current edition of the *MLA Handbook* does not cover personal photographs. This format comes from the previous edition.

78. A map, chart, graph, or diagram

"The Sonoran Desert." Map. *Sonoran Desert: An American Deserts Handbook.* By Rose Houk. Tucson: Western Natl. Parks Assn., 2000. 12. Print.

Unless the creator of an illustration is given on the source, list the illustration by its title. Put the title in quotation marks if it comes from another publication or in italics if it is published independently. Then add a description (Map, Chart, and so on).

79. A cartoon or comic strip

Trudeau, Garry. "Doonesbury." Comic strip. *San Francisco Chronicle* 28 Aug. 2010: E6. Print.

Cite a cartoon or comic strip with the artist's name, the title (in quotation marks), and the description Cartoon or Comic strip.

80. An advertisement

iPad. Advertisement. *New Yorker* 21 Apr. 2010: 3. Print.

Cite an advertisement with the name of the product or company advertised and the description Advertisement.

81. A performance

Levine, James, cond. Boston Symphony Orch. Symphony Hall, Boston. 2 May 2010. Performance.

The New Century. By Paul Rudnick. Dir. Nicholas Martin. Mitzi E. Newhouse Theater, New York. 6 May 2010. Performance.

For a live performance, generally base your citation on film citations (model 75). Place the title first (second example) unless you are citing the work of an individual (first example). After the title, provide relevant information about participants as well as the theater, city, and performance date.

82. A lecture, speech, address, or reading

Fontaine, Claire. "Economics." Museum of Contemporary Art. North Miami. 5 June 2010. Address.

Give the speaker's name and title (if any), the title of the meeting (if any), the name of the sponsoring organization, the location of the presentation, the date, and the type of presentation (Lecture, Speech, Address, Reading).

Although the MLA does not provide a specific style for citing classroom lectures in your courses, you can adapt the preceding format for this purpose.

Cavanaugh, Carol. Class lecture on teaching mentors. Lesley U. 4 Apr. 2008. Lecture.

40c MLA paper format

The document format recommended by the *MLA Handbook* is fairly simple, with just a few elements. See pages 198–99 for illustrations of the elements. See also pages 22–25 for guidelines on type fonts, headings, lists, illustrations, and other features that are not specified in MLA style.

Margins Use minimum one-inch margins on all sides of every page.

Spacing and indentions Double-space throughout. Indent the first lines of paragraphs one-half inch. (See opposite for indention of poetry and long prose quotations.)

Paging Begin numbering on the first page, and number consecutively through the end (including the list of works cited). Type Arabic numerals (1, 2, 3) in the upper right about one-half inch from the top. Place your last name before the page number in case the pages later become separated.

Identification and title In the upper left of the first page, give your name, your instructor's name, the course title, and the date—all double-spaced. Center the title. Do not type it in all-capitals or italics or place it between quotation marks.

Poetry and long prose quotations Treat a single line of poetry like any other quotation, running it into your text and enclosing it in quotation marks. You may run in two or three lines of poetry as well, separating the lines with a slash:

> An example of Robert Frost's incisiveness is in two lines from "Death of the Hired Man": "Home is the place where, when you have to go there / They have to take you in" (119-20).

Always separate quotations of more than three lines of poetry from your text. Use double spacing and a one-inch indention. *Do not add quotation marks.*

> Emily Dickinson stripped ideas to their essence, as in this description of "A narrow Fellow in the Grass," a snake:
>
> > I more than once at Noon
> > Have passed, I thought, a Whip lash
> > Unbraiding in the Sun
> > When stopping to secure it
> > It wrinkled, and was gone – (12-16)

Also separate prose quotations of five or more typed lines. *Do not add quotation marks.*

> In his 1967 study of the lives of unemployed black men, Elliot Liebow observes that "unskilled" construction work requires more experience and skill than is generally assumed:
>
> > A healthy, sturdy, active man of good intelligence requires from two to four weeks to break in on a construction job. . . . It frequently happens that his foreman or the craftsman he services is not willing to wait that long for him to get into condition or to learn at a glance the difference in size between a rough 2 x 8 and a finished 2 x 10. (62)

40d Sample pages in MLA style

The samples on these two pages show the main elements of MLA document format along with their spacing and indentions.

First page

1/2″

Haley 1

All double-spaced

Vanessa Haley

Professor Moisan

English 101

24 March 2007

Annie Dillard's Healing Vision ← Center

1/2″

It is almost a commonplace these days that human arrogance is destroying the environment. Environmentalists, naturalists, and now the man or woman on the street seem to agree: the long-held belief that human beings are separate from nature, destined to rise above its laws and conquer it, has been ruinous.

1″ 1″

Unfortunately, much writing about nature goes to the opposite extreme, viewing nature as pure and harmonious, humanity as corrupt and dangerous. One nature writer who seems to recognize the naturalness of humanity is Annie Dillard. In her best-known work, the Pulitzer Prize-winning *Pilgrim at Tinker Creek*, she is a solitary person encountering the natural world, and some critics fault her for turning her back on society. But in those encounters with nature, Dillard probes a spiritual as well as a physical identity between human beings and nature that could help to heal the rift between them.

Dillard is not renowned for her sense of involvement with human society. Like Henry David Thoreau, with whom she is often compared, she retreats from rather than confronts human society. The critic Gary McIlroy points out that although Thoreau discusses society a great deal in *Walden*, he makes no attempt "to find a middle ground between it and his experiment in the woods" (113). Dillard has been similarly criticized. For instance, the writer Eudora Welty comments that

1″

> Annie Dillard is the only person in her book, substantially the only one in her world; I recall no outside human speech coming to break the long soliloquy

1″

MLA 40d

Second page

Haley 2

> of the author. Speaking of the universe very often, she is yet self-surrounded and, beyond that, book-surrounded. Her own book might have taken in more of human life without losing a bit of the wonder she was after. (37)

It is true, as Welty says, that in *Pilgrim* Dillard seems detached from human society. However, she actually was always close to it at Tinker Creek. In a later book, *Teaching a Stone to Talk*, she says of the neighborhood, "This is, mind you, suburbia. It is a five-minute walk in three directions to rows of houses. . . . There's a 55 mph highway at one end of the pond, and a nesting pair of wood ducks at the other" (qtd. in Suh).

Rather than hiding from humanity, Dillard seems to be trying to understand it through nature. In *Pilgrim* she reports buying a goldfish, which she names Ellery Channing. She recalls once seeing through a microscope "red blood cells whip, one by one, through the capillaries" of yet another goldfish (124). Now watching Ellery Channing, she sees the blood in his body as a bond between fish and human being: "Those red blood cells are

Works cited

1/2″

Haley 6

All double-spaced

Works Cited ← Center

Becker, John E. "Science and the Sacred: From Walden to Tinker Creek." *Thought: A Review of Culture and Ideas* 62 (1987): 400-13. Print.

1/2″

Dillard, Annie. *Pilgrim at Tinker Creek*. New York: Harper, 1974. Print.

1″ McIlroy, Gary. "*Pilgrim at Tinker Creek* and the Social Legacy of Walden." *South Atlantic Quarterly* 85.2 (1986): 111-16. Print. 1″

Suh, Grace. "Ideas Are Tough, Irony Is Easy." *Yale Herald*. Yale U, 4 Oct. 2005. Web. 22 Jan. 2007.

Welty, Eudora. Rev. of *Pilgrim at Tinker Creek*, by Annie Dillard. *New York Times Book Review* 24 Mar. 1974: 36-37. *ProQuest Historical Newspapers*. Web. 20 Jan. 2007.

MLA 40d

41 APA Documentation and Format

The documentation style of the American Psychological Association is used in psychology and some other social sciences and is very similar to the styles in sociology, economics, and other disciplines. The following adapts the APA style from the *Publication Manual of the American Psychological Association*, 6th ed. (2010).

Note The APA provides answers to frequently asked questions at *www.apastyle.org/learn/faqs/index.aspx*.

41a APA parenthetical text citations

Citation formats

In APA style, parenthetical citations in the text refer to a list of sources at the end of the text. The basic parenthetical citation contains the author's last name and the date of publication. If you name the author in your text, then the citation includes just the date. Unless none is available, the APA also requires a page or other identifying number for a direct quotation and recommends an identifying number for a paraphrase.

1. Author not named in your text

One critic of Milgram's experiments insisted that the subjects "should have been fully informed of the possible effects on them" (Baumrind, 1988, p. 34).

APA 41a

APA parenthetical text citations

mycomplab

Visit *mycomplab.com* for more help with APA documentation and format.

2. Author named in your text

Baumrind (1988) insisted that the subjects in Milgram's study "should have been fully informed of the possible effects on them" (p. 34).

3. A work with two authors

Pepinsky and DeStefano (1997) demonstrated that a teacher's language often reveals hidden biases.

One study (Pepinsky & DeStefano, 1997) demonstrated the hidden biases often revealed in a teacher's language.

4. A work with three to five authors

First reference:

Pepinsky, Dunn, Rentl, and Corson (1999) further demonstrated the biases evident in gestures.

Later references:

In the work of Pepinsky et al. (1999), the loaded gestures included head shakes and eye contact.

5. A work with six or more authors

One study (Rutter et al., 2003) attempted to explain these geographical differences in adolescent experience.

6. A work with a group author

The students' later work improved significantly (Lenschow Research, 2009).

Use this model for works that list an agency, institution, corporation, or other group as the author.

7. A work with no author or an anonymous work

One article ("Right to Die," 1996) noted that a death-row inmate may crave notoriety.

For a work that lists "Anonymous" as the author, use that word in the citation: (Anonymous, 2010).

8. One of two or more works by the same author(s)

At about age seven, most children begin to use appropriate gestures to reinforce their stories (Gardner, 1973a).

(See the reference for this source on p. 205.)

9. Two or more works by different authors

Two studies (Marconi & Hamblen, 1999; Torrence, 2007) found that monthly safety meetings can dramatically reduce workplace injuries.

10. An indirect source

Supporting data appeared in a study by Chang (as cited in Torrence, 2007).

11. An electronic source

Ferguson and Hawkins (2006) did not anticipate the "evident hostility" of participants (para. 6).

Electronic sources can be cited like printed sources, usually with the author's last name and the publication date. When quoting or paraphrasing electronic sources that number paragraphs instead of pages, provide the paragraph number preceded by para.

41b APA reference list

In APA style, the in-text parenthetical citations refer to the list of sources at the end of the text. Title this list References, and include in it the full publication information for every source you cited in your paper. Place the list at the end of the paper, and number its page(s) in sequence with the preceding pages. For an illustration of the following elements and their spacing, see page 219.

Arrangement Arrange sources alphabetically by the author's last name. If there is no author, alphabetize by the first main word of the title.

Spacing Double-space everything in the references unless your instructor requests single spacing. (If you do single-space the entries themselves, always double-space *between* them.)

Indention Begin each entry at the left margin, and indent the second and subsequent lines five to seven spaces or one-half inch.

Punctuation Separate the parts of the reference (author, date, title, and publication information) with a period and one space. Do not use a final period in references that conclude with a DOI or URL (see p. 209).

Authors For works with up to seven authors, list all authors with last name first, separating names and parts of names with commas. Use initials for first and middle names even when names are listed fully on the source itself. Use an ampersand (&) before the last author's name. See model 3, opposite, for the treatment of eight or more authors.

Publication date Place the publication date in parentheses after the author's or authors' names, followed by a period. Generally, this date is the year only, though for some sources (such as magazine and newspaper articles) it includes the month and sometimes the day as well.

Titles In titles of books and articles, capitalize only the first word of the title, the first word of the subtitle, and proper nouns; all other words begin with small letters. In titles of journals, capitalize all significant words (see pp. 108–09 for guidelines). Italicize the titles of books and journals. Do not italicize or use quotation marks around the titles of articles.

City and state of publication For sources that are not periodicals (such as books or government publications), give the city of publication, a comma, the two-letter postal abbreviation of the state, and a colon. Omit the state if the publisher is a university whose name includes the state name, such as University of Arizona.

Publisher's name Also for nonperiodical sources, give the publisher's name after the place of publication and a colon. Shorten names of many publishers (such as Morrow for William Morrow), and omit *Co., Inc.,* and *Publishers*. However, give full names for associations, corporations, and university presses (such as Harvard University Press), and do not omit *Books* or *Press* from a publisher's name.

Page numbers Use the abbreviation p. or pp. before page numbers in books and in newspapers. Do *not* use the abbreviation for journals and magazines. For inclusive page numbers, include all figures: 667-668.

Authors

1. One author

Rodriguez, R. (1982). *A hunger of memory: The education of Richard Rodriguez.* Boston, MA: Godine.

2. Two to seven authors

Nesselroade, J. R., & Baltes, P. B. (1999). *Longitudinal research in behavioral studies.* New York, NY: Academic Press.

Separate authors' names with commas and use an ampersand (&) before the last author's name.

3. Eight or more authors

Wimple, P. B., Van Eijk, M., Potts, C. A., Hayes, J., Obergau, W. R., Smith, H., . . . Zimmer, S. (2001). *Case studies in moral decision making among adolescents.* San Francisco, CA: Jossey-Bass.

List the first six authors' names, insert an ellipsis mark (three spaced periods), and then give the last author's name.

APA reference-list models

4. A group author

Lenschow Research. (2008). *Trends in secondary curriculum.* Baltimore, MD: Arrow Books.

5. Author not named (anonymous)

Merriam-Webster's collegiate dictionary (11th ed.). (2008). Springfield, MA: Merriam-Webster.

Heroes of the environment. (2009, October 5). *Time, 174*(13), 45-54.

For a work whose author is actually given as "Anonymous," use and alphabetize that word as if it were a name:

Anonymous. (2006). *Teaching research.* New York, NY: Alpine Press.

6. Two or more works by the same author(s) published in the same year

Gardner, H. (1973a). *The arts and human development.* New York, NY: Wiley.

Gardner, H. (1973b). *The quest for mind: Piaget, Lévi-Strauss, and the structuralist movement*. New York, NY: Knopf.

Print periodicals: Journals, newspapers, magazines

7. An article in a journal (print)

Selwyn, N. (2005). The social processes of learning to use computers. *Social Science Computer Review, 23*, 122-135.

See the next two pages for the basic format for a print journal article and the location of the required information in the journal. If the print article has a Digital Object Identifier, add it at the end of the entry. See model 18.

Note For journals that number the pages of issues consecutively through an annual volume, give the volume number (in italics) after the title, as in the example above. For magazines and for journals that start each issue with page 1, give the issue number after the volume number, in parentheses and not italicized. See model 10.

(continued on p. 208)

Format for a print journal article

Journal cover

APA 41b

① ② ③
Selwyn, N. (2005). The social processes of learning to use computers. ④ *Social Science Computer Review,* ⑤ *23,* ⑥ 122-135.

① **Author.** Give the last name first, a comma, the initial of the first name, and any middle initial, following each initial with a period. Omit *Dr., PhD,* or any other title.

② **Year of publication,** in parentheses and followed by a period.

③ **Title of the article.** Give the full article title and any subtitle, separating them with a colon. Capitalize only the first words of the title and subtitle, and do not place the title in quotation marks.

④ **Title of the periodical,** in italics. Capitalize all significant words and end with a comma.

⑤ **Volume number,** italicized and followed by a comma. See page 205 for when to include the issue number.

⑥ **Inclusive page numbers of article,** without "pp." Do not omit any numerals.

(continued from p. 205)

8. An abstract of a journal article (print)

Emery, R. E. (2006). Marital turmoil: Interpersonal conflict and the children of discord and divorce. *Psychological Bulletin, 92*, 310-330. Abstract obtained from *Psychological Abstracts*, 2007, *69*, Item 1320.

9. An article in a newspaper (print)

Stout, D. (2008, May 28). Blind win court ruling on U.S. currency. *The New York Times*, p. A23.

10. An article in a magazine (print)

Newton-Small, J. (2009, October 5). Divided loyalties. *Time, 174*(13), 38.

11. A review (print)

Dinnage, R. (1987, November 29). Against the master and his men [Review of the book *A mind of her own: The life of Karen Horney*, by S. Quinn]. *The New York Times Book Review*, 10-11.

Print books

12. Basic format for a book (print)

Ehrenreich, B. (2007). *Dancing in the streets: A history of collective joy.* New York, NY: Holt.

13. A book with an editor (print)

Dohrenwend, B. S., & Dohrenwend, B. P. (Eds.). (1999). *Stressful life events: Their nature and effects*. New York, NY: Wiley.

APA 41b

14. A book with a translator (print)

Trajan, P. D. (1927). *Psychology of animals* (H. Simone, Trans.). Washington, DC: Halperin.

15. A later edition (print)

Bolinger, D. L. (1981). *Aspects of language* (3rd ed.). New York, NY: Harcourt Brace Jovanovich.

16. A work in more than one volume (print)

Reference to a single volume:

Lincoln, A. (1953). *The collected works of Abraham Lincoln* (R. P. Basler, Ed.). (Vol. 5). New Brunswick, NJ: Rutgers University Press.

Reference to all volumes:

Lincoln, A. (1953). *The collected works of Abraham Lincoln* (R. P. Basler, Ed.). (Vols. 1-8). New Brunswick, NJ: Rutgers University Press.

17. An article or a chapter in an edited book (print)

Paykel, E. S. (1999). Life stress and psychiatric disorder: Applications of the clinical approach. In B. S. Dohrenwend & B. P. Dohrenwend (Eds.), *Stressful life events: Their nature and effects* (pp. 239-264). New York, NY: Wiley.

Web and other electronic sources

In APA style, most electronic references begin the same way as print references do: author, date, and title. Then you add information on how to retrieve the source, generally giving a Digital Object Identifier (DOI) or a URL. A DOI is a unique identifier that many publishers assign to journal articles and other documents.

- **Give the DOI, not the URL, when one is available.** (See models 18 and 25.)
- **Give the URL when a DOI is not available.** Provide the URL in a statement beginning Retrieved from. For most sources, use the home page URL of the Web site where your source can be found. (See models 19 and 23.) Use the complete URL only if the source is hard to find from the home page. (See model 32.)
- **Do not add a period after a DOI or a URL.**
- **Break a DOI or URL from one line to the next only before punctuation,** such as a period or a slash. (But break after the two slashes in http://.) Do not hyphenate a URL or a DOI.

Provide the date of your access to an electronic source only if the source lacks a publication date or edition or version number or if the source is likely to change. (See models 26 and 29.)

18. A journal article with a Digital Object Identifier (DOI) (Web)

Cunningham, J. A., & Selby, P. (2007). Relighting cigarettes: How common is it? *Nicotine and Tobacco Research, 9*, 621-623. doi:10.1080/14622200701239688

See the next two pages for the basic format for a periodical article that you access either directly online or through an online database as well as the location of the required information on the source.

(continued on p. 212)

Format for a journal article on the Web

Top of page

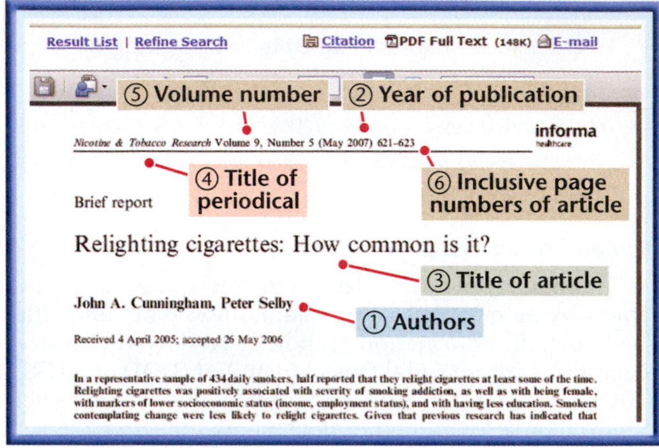
Result List | Refine Search

Citation PDF Full Text (148K) E-mail

informa healthcare

Nicotine & Tobacco Research Volume 9, Number 5 (May 2007) 621–623

Brief report

Relighting cigarettes: How common is it?

John A. Cunningham, Peter Selby

Received 4 April 2005; accepted 26 May 2006

In a representative sample of 434 daily smokers, half reported that they relight cigarettes at least some of the time. Relighting cigarettes was positively associated with severity of smoking addiction, as well as with being female, with markers of lower socioeconomic status (income, employment status), and with having less education. Smokers contemplating change were less likely to relight cigarettes. Given that previous research has indicated that

Bottom of page

more or less harmful (but never safe; Cunningham, Faulkner, Selby, & Cordingley, 2006; Kozlowski et al., 1999).

What other behaviors make a cigarette more harmful? Some evidence indicates that relighting a cigarette might make it more harmful. Two studies have found that smokers who reported relighting cigarettes were more likely to develop some types of

John A. Cunningham, Ph.D., Peter Selby, MBBS, Centre for Addiction and Mental Health and University of Toronto, Ontario, Canada.

Correspondence: John Cunningham, Centre for Addiction and Mental Health, 33 Russell Street, Toronto, Ontario, M5S 2S1, Canada. Tel: +1 (416) 535-8501; Fax: +1 (416) 595-6899; E-mail: john_cunningham@camh.net

ettes are smoked per day and how soon after waking the first cigarette is usually smoked (Heatherton, Kozlowski, Frecker, & Robinson, 1989), and the stage of change algorithm (Prochaska & DiClemente, 1983) also were used. Demographic characteristics were recorded. Results are reported as weighted values to adjust for the number of adults in surveyed households. Sample sizes are presented as unweighted values.

Results

Of daily smokers, 17% reported frequently relighting cigarettes and 36% reported sometimes relighting (5

ISSN 1462-2203 print/ISSN 1469-994X online © 2007 Society for Research on Nicotine and Tobacco

DOI: 10.1080/14622200701239688

⑦ **Retrieval information**

APA 41b

① ② ③
Cunningham, J. A., & Selby, P. (2007). Relighting cigarettes:

④ ⑤
How common is it? *Nicotine and Tobacco Research, 9,*

⑥ ⑦
621-623. doi:10.1080/14622200701239688

① **Authors.** Give each author's last name, first initial, and any middle initial. Separate names from initials with commas, and use & before the last author's name. Omit *Dr., PhD,* or any other title. See models 1–4 (pp. 203–04) to cite single and multiple authors.

② **Year of publication,** in parentheses and followed by a period.

③ **Title of the article.** Give the full article title and any subtitle, separating them with a colon. Capitalize only the first words of the title and subtitle, and do not place the title in quotation marks.

④ **Title of the periodical,** in italics. Capitalize all significant words and end with a comma.

⑤ **Volume number,** italicized and followed by a comma. See page 205 for when to include the issue number.

⑥ **Inclusive page numbers of article,** without "pp." Do not omit any numerals.

⑦ **Retrieval information,** either a DOI (shown here) or a URL (model 19). See model 20 for how to cite an article without a DOI that you retrieve from a database.

(continued from p. 209)

19. A journal article without a DOI (Web)

Polletta, F. (2008). Just talk: Public deliberation after 9/11. *Journal of Public Deliberation, 4*(1). Retrieved from http://services.bepress .com/jpd

20. A periodical article in an online database (Web)

Rosen, I. M., Maurer, D. M., & Darnall, C. R. (2008). Reducing tobacco use in adolescents. *American Family Physician, 77*, 483-490. Retrieved from http://www.aafp.org/online/en/home /publications/journals/afp.html

The preceding example gives the URL of the journal's home page. If you don't find the home page of the periodical, give the database name in your retrieval statement:

Smith, E. M. (1926, March). Equal rights—internationally! *Life and Labor Bulletin, 4,* 1-2. Retrieved from Women and Social Movements in the United States, 1600-2000, database.

21. An abstract of a journal article (Web)

Polletta, F. (2008). Just talk: Public deliberation after 9/11. *Journal of Public Deliberation, 4*(1). Abstract retrieved from http://services .bepress.com/jpd

22. An article in a newspaper (Web)

Gootman, E. (2008, June 19). Gifted programs in the city are less diverse. *The New York Times*. Retrieved from http://www.nytimes.com

23. An article in a magazine (Web)

Young, E. (2009, February 21). Sleep well, keep sane. *New Scientist, 201*(26), 34-37. Retrieved from http://www.newscientist.com

24. Supplemental periodical content that appears only online (Web)

Gawande, A. (2009, June 1). More is less [Supplemental material]. *The New Yorker*. Retrieved from http://www.newyorker.com

25. A review (Web)

Bond, M. (2008, December 18). Does genius breed success? [Review of the book *Outliers: The story of success,* by M. Gladwell]. *Nature, 456,* 785. doi:10.1038/456874a

26. A report or other material from the Web site of an organization or government (Web)

Ellerman, D., & Joskow, P. L. (2008, May). *The European Union's emissions trading system in perspective.* Retrieved from the Pew Center on Global Climate Change website: http://www.pewclimate.org

If the document you cite is difficult to locate from the organization's home page, give the complete URL in the retrieval statement:

Union of Concerned Scientists. *Clean vehicles.* (2009, April 24). Retrieved from http://www.ucsusa.org/clean_vehicles

If the document you cite is undated, use the abbreviation n.d. in place of the publication date and give the date of your access in the retrieval statement:

U.S. Department of Agriculture. (n.d.). *Inside the pyramid.* Retrieved April 23, 2010, from http://www.mypyramid.gov

27. A book (Web)

Hernandez, L. M., & Munthali, A. W. (Eds.). (2007). *Training physicians for public health careers.* Retrieved from http://books.nap.edu /catalog.php?record_id=11915

28. An article in a reference work (Web)

Perception. (2008). In *Encyclopaedia Britannica Online.* Retrieved from http://www.britannica.com/EBchecked/topic/451015/perception

29. An article in a wiki (Web)

Clinical neuropsychology. (2008, January 27). Retrieved August 3, 2009, from Wikipedia: http://en.wikipedia.org/wiki /Clinical_neuropsychology

30. A dissertation (Web)

A dissertation in a commercial database:

McFaddin, M. O. (2007). *Adaptive reuse: An architectural solution for poverty and homelessness* (Doctoral dissertation). Available from ProQuest Dissertations and Theses database. (ATT 1378764)

A dissertation in an institutional database:

Chang, J. K. (2003). *Therapeutic intervention in treatment of injuries to the hand and wrist* (Doctoral dissertation). Retrieved from http://medsci.archive.liasu.edu/61724

31. A podcast (Web)

Ferracca, J. (Producer). (2008, June 11). Who owns antiquities? [Audio podcast]. *Here on earth: Radio without borders.* Retrieved from http://www.wpr.org/hereonearth

32. A film or video recording (Web)

Green Children Foundation (Producer). (2008, January 7). *The green children visit China* [Video file]. Retrieved from http://youtube.com/watch?v=uD4xfLTxCsY

33. An image (Web)

United Nations Population Fund (Cartographer). (2005). *Percent of population living on less than $1/day* [Demographic map]. Retrieved from http://www.unfpa.org

34. A message posted to a blog or discussion group (Web)

Munger, D. (2010, May 9). Does recess really improve classroom behavior? [Web log post]. Retrieved from http://scienceblogs.com/cognitivedaily

35. A personal communication (text citation)

At least one member of the research team has expressed reservations about the design of the study (L. Kogod, personal communication, February 6, 2010).

Personal e-mail and other online postings that are not retrievable by others should be cited only in the text, as here, not in the list of references.

Other sources

36. A report (print)

Gerald, K. (2003). *Medico-moral problems in obstetric care* (Report No. NP-71). St. Louis, MO: Catholic Hospital Association.

Jolson, M. K. (2001). *Music education for preschoolers* (Report No. TC-622). New York, NY: Teachers College, Columbia University. (ERIC Document Reproduction Service No. ED264488)

37. A government publication (print)

Hawaii. Department of Education. (2010). *Kauai district schools, profile 2009-10*. Honolulu, HI: Author.

Medicare payment for outpatient physical and occupational therapy services: Hearing before the Committee on Ways and Means, House of Representatives, 110th Cong. 3 (2007).

Stiller, A. (2008). *Historic preservation and tax incentives*. Washington, DC: U.S. Department of the Interior.

38. A dissertation (print)

A dissertation abstracted in DAI:

Steciw, S. K. (1986). Alterations to the Pessac project of Le Corbusier. *Dissertation Abstracts International, 46*(6), 565C.

An unpublished dissertation:

Holcomb, C. M. (2008). *Dance as therapy for reducing anxiety in elementary-age children: Case studies in grades 1 through 6* (Unpublished doctoral dissertation). University of Washington.

39. An interview (print)

Schenker, H. (2007). No peace without third-party intervention [Interview with Shulamit Aloni]. *Palestine-Israel Journal of Politics, Economics, and Culture, 14*(4), 63-68.

For an interview you conduct yourself, use an in-text parenthetical citation, as shown in model 35 for a personal communication.

40. A motion picture

American Psychological Association (Producer). (2001). *Ethnocultural psychotherapy* [DVD]. Available from http://www.apa.org/videos

Tyrrell, C. (Director). (2010). *The Joneses* [Motion picture]. United States: Bjort Productions.

41. A musical recording

Springsteen, B. (2002). Empty sky. On *The rising* [CD]. New York, NY: Columbia.

42. A television series or episode

Rhimes, S. (Executive Producer). (2010). *Grey's anatomy* [Television series]. New York, NY: CBS.

Clark, Z. (Writer), & Corn, R. (Director). (2010). The time warp [Television series episode]. In S. Rhimes (Executive Producer), *Grey's anatomy*. New York, NY: CBS.

APA 41c

41c APA paper format

The following guidelines for document format reflect the second printing of the APA *Publication Manual*, 6th edition, which corrected some errors in the first printing. Your instructor may modify this format.

For illustrations of the following elements, see the next two pages. And see pages 22–25 for guidelines on type fonts, lists, tables and figures, and other elements of document design.

Margins Use one-inch margins on the top, bottom, and both sides.

Spacing and indentions Double-space everywhere. Indent paragraphs and displayed quotations one-half inch or five to seven spaces.

Paging Begin numbering on the title page, and number consecutively through the end (including the reference list). Provide a header about one-half inch from the top of every page, as shown in the samples on the next two pages. The header consists of the page number on the far right and your full or shortened title on the far left. Type the title in all-capital letters. On the title page only, precede the title with the label Running head and a colon. Omit this label on all other pages.

Title page Include the full title, your name, the course title, the instructor's name, and the date. Type the title on the top half of the page, followed by the identifying information, all centered horizontally and double-spaced.

Abstract Summarize (in a maximum of 120 words) your subject, research method, findings, and conclusions. Put the abstract on a page by itself.

Body Begin with a restatement of the paper's title and then an introduction (not labeled). The introduction concisely presents the problem you researched, your research method, the relevant background (such as related studies), and the purpose of your research.

The **Method** section provides a detailed discussion of how you conducted your research, including a description of the research subjects, any materials or tools you used (such as questionnaires or lab equipment), and the procedure you followed.

The **Results** section summarizes the data you collected, explains how you analyzed them, and presents them in detail, often in tables, graphs, or charts.

The **Discussion** section interprets the data and presents your conclusions. (When the discussion is brief, you may combine it with the previous section under the heading **Results and Discussion**.)

Headings Label the **Method, Results,** and **Discussion** sections with centered first-level headings, and use second- and third-level headings as needed. Double-space all headings.

First-Level Heading

Second-Level Heading

Third-level heading. Run this heading into the text paragraph.

Long quotations Run into your text all quotations of forty words or less, and enclose them in quotation marks. For quotations of more than forty words, set them off from your text by indenting all lines one-half inch or five to seven spaces, double-spacing above and below.

> Echoing the opinions of other Europeans at the time, Freud (1961) had a poor view of Americans:
>
> > The Americans are really too bad. . . . Competition is much more pungent with them, not succeeding means civil death to every one, and they have no private resources apart from their profession, no hobby, games, love or other interests of a cultured person. And success means money. (p. 86)

Do not use quotation marks around a quotation displayed in this way.

41d Sample pages in APA style

Title page

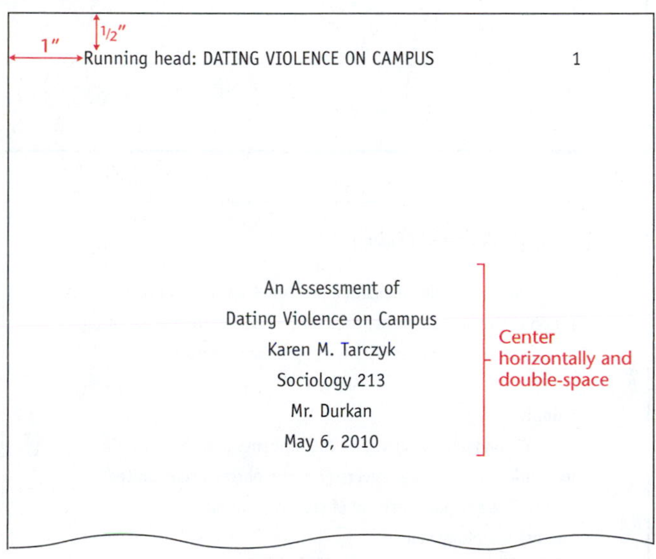

Abstract

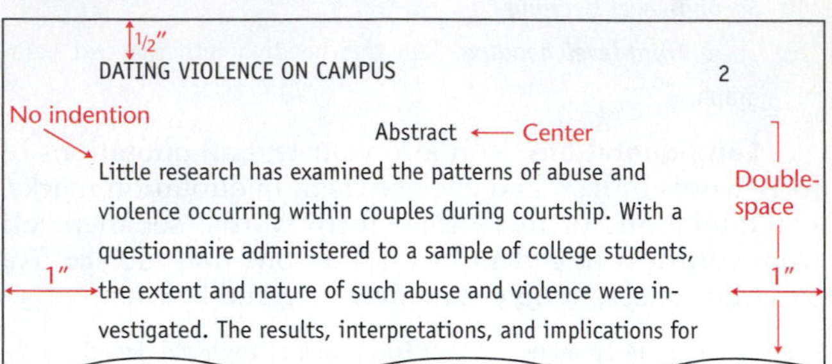
DATING VIOLENCE ON CAMPUS 2

Abstract

Little research has examined the patterns of abuse and violence occurring within couples during courtship. With a questionnaire administered to a sample of college students, the extent and nature of such abuse and violence were investigated. The results, interpretations, and implications for

First page of body

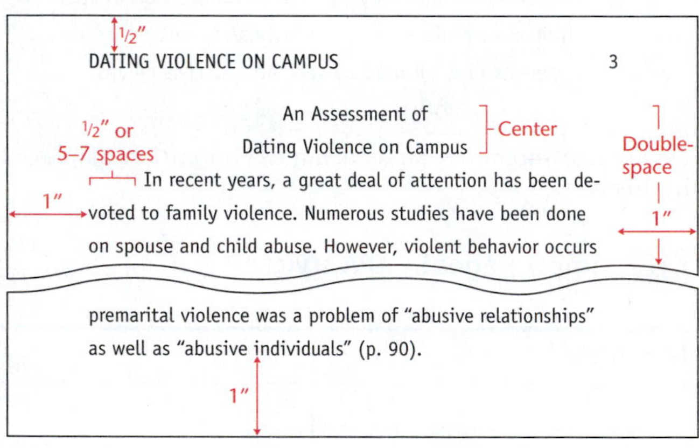
DATING VIOLENCE ON CAMPUS 3

An Assessment of
Dating Violence on Campus

In recent years, a great deal of attention has been devoted to family violence. Numerous studies have been done on spouse and child abuse. However, violent behavior occurs

premarital violence was a problem of "abusive relationships" as well as "abusive individuals" (p. 90).

Later page of body

DATING VIOLENCE ON CAMPUS 4

All the studies indicate a problem that is being neglected. My objective was to gather data on the extent and nature of premarital violence and to discuss possible interpretations.

Method

Sample

Double-space

I conducted a survey of 200 students (134 females, 66 males) at a large state university in the northeastern United States. The sample consisted of students enrolled in an introductory sociology course.

References

DATING VIOLENCE ON CAMPUS 8

References ← Center

Cates, R. L., Rutter, C. H., Karl, J., Linton, M., & Smith, K. (1997). Premarital abuse: A social psychological perspective. *Journal of Family Issues, 13*, 79-90.

½" or 5–7 spaces

Double-space

Cortes, L. (2009). Beyond date rape: Violence during courtship. *Electronic Journal of Intimate Violence, 5*(2). Retrieved from http://www.ejiv.org

1" → Glaser, R., & Rutter, C. H. (Eds.). (1999). Familial violence [Special issue]. *Family Relations, 33*(4). ← 1"

42 Chicago Documentation and Format

Writers in history, art history, philosophy, and other humanities use the note style of documentation from *The Chicago Manual of Style*, 16th ed. (2010), or the student reference adapted from it, *A Manual for Writers of Research Papers, Theses, and Dissertations*, by Kate L. Turabian, 7th ed., revised by Wayne C. Booth, Gregory G. Colomb, and Joseph M. Williams (2007). *The Chicago Manual* has a Web site that answers frequently asked questions about its style: *www.chicagomanualofstyle.org*.

This chapter explains the Chicago note style (below) and Chicago paper format (p. 229).

42a Chicago notes and bibliography

In the Chicago note style, a raised numeral in the text refers the reader to source information in endnotes or footnotes. In these notes, the first citation of each source contains all the information readers need to find the source. Thus your instructor may consider a bibliography optional because it provides much the same information. Ask your instructor whether you should use footnotes or endnotes and whether you should include a bibliography along with the notes.

The examples below show the essentials of a note and a bibliography entry. (See pp. 230–31 for more illustrations.)

Note

6. Martin Gilbert, *Pictorial Atlas of British History* (New York: Dorset Press, 2006), 96.

Bibliography entry

Gilbert, Martin. *Pictorial Atlas of British History*. New York: Dorset Press, 2006.

Treat some features of notes and bibliography entries the same:

- Single-space each note or entry, and double-space between them.
- Italicize the titles of books and periodicals.
- Enclose in quotation marks the titles of parts of books or articles in periodicals.
- Do not abbreviate publishers' names, but omit "Inc.," "Co.," and similar abbreviations.
- Do not use "p." or "pp." before page numbers.

Treat other features of notes and bibliography entries differently:

Note	**Bibliography entry**
Start with a number that corresponds to the note number in the text.	Do not begin with a number.
Indent the first line five spaces.	Indent the second and subsequent lines five spaces.
Give the author's name in normal order.	Begin with the author's last name.
Use commas between elements such as author's name and title.	Use periods between elements.
Enclose publication information in parentheses, with no preceding punctuation.	Precede the publication information with a period, and don't use parentheses.
Include the specific page number(s) you borrowed from, omitting "p." or "pp."	Omit page numbers except for parts of books or articles in periodicals.

You can instruct your computer to position footnotes at the bottoms of appropriate pages. It will also automatically number notes and renumber them if you add or delete one or more.

42b Chicago models

The Chicago models for common sources are indexed below. The models show notes and bibliography entries together for easy reference. Be sure to use the correct form—numbered note or unnumbered bibliography entry.

Chicago note and bibliography models

Authors

1. One, two, or three authors

1. Carol Gilligan, *In a Different Voice: Psychological Theory and Women's Development* (Cambridge: Harvard University Press, 1982), 27.

Gilligan, Carol. *In a Different Voice: Psychological Theory and Women's Development*. Cambridge: Harvard University Press, 1982.

1. Dennis L. Wilcox, Phillip H. Ault, and Warren K. Agee, *Public Relations: Strategies and Tactics,* 6th ed. (New York: Irwin, 2005), 182.

Wilcox, Dennis L., Phillip H. Ault, and Warren K. Agee. *Public Relations: Strategies and Tactics*. 6th ed. New York: Irwin, 2005.

2. More than three authors

2. Geraldo Lopez et al., *China and the West* (Boston: Little, Brown, 2004), 461.

Lopez, Geraldo, Judith P. Salt, Anne Ming, and Henry Reisen. *China and the West*. Boston: Little, Brown, 2004.

The Latin abbreviation et al. means "and others."

3. Author not named (anonymous)

3. *The Dorling Kindersley World Reference Atlas* (London: Dorling Kindersley, 2005), 150-51.

The Dorling Kindersley World Reference Atlas. London: Dorling Kindersley, 2005.

Print periodicals: Journals, newspapers, magazines

4. An article in a journal (print)

4. Janet Lever, "Sex Differences in the Games Children Play," *Social Problems* 23 (Spring 1996): 482.

Lever, Janet. "Sex Differences in the Games Children Play." *Social Problems* 23 (Spring 1996): 478-87.

Chic 42b

Provide the issue number if the journal numbers issues:

4. Robert Bee, "The Importance of Preserving Paper-Based Artifacts in a Digital Age," *Library Quarterly* 78, no. 2 (April 2008): 176.

Bee, Robert. "The Importance of Preserving Paper-Based Artifacts in a Digital Age." *Library Quarterly* 78, no. 2 (April 2008): 174-94.

5. An article in a newspaper (print)

5. David Stout, "Blind Win Court Ruling on US Currency," *New York Times,* May 21, 2008, national edition, A23.

Stout, David. "Blind Win Court Ruling on US Currency." *New York Times,* May 21, 2008, national edition, A23.

6. An article in a magazine (print)

6. Amanda Fortini, "Pomegranate Princess," *New Yorker,* March 31, 2008, 94.

Fortini, Amanda. "Pomegranate Princess." *New Yorker,* March 31, 2008, 92-99.

7. A review (print)

7. John Gregory Dunne, "The Secret of Danny Santiago," review of *Famous All over Town,* by Danny Santiago, *New York Review of Books,* August 16, 1994, 25.

Dunne, John Gregory. "The Secret of Danny Santiago." Review of *Famous All over Town,* by Danny Santiago. *New York Review of Books,* August 16, 1994, 17-27.

Print books

8. Basic format for a book (print)

8. Barbara Ehrenreich, *Dancing in the Streets: A History of Collective Joy* (New York: Henry Holt, 2006), 97-117.

Ehrenreich, Barbara. *Dancing in the Streets: A History of Collective Joy.* New York: Henry Holt, 2006.

9. A book with an editor (print)

9. Hendrick Ruitenbeek, ed., *Freud as We Knew Him* (Detroit: Wayne State University Press, 1973), 64.

Ruitenbeek, Hendrick, ed. *Freud as We Knew Him.* Detroit: Wayne State University Press, 1973.

10. A book with an author and an editor (print)

10. Lewis Mumford, *The City in History,* ed. Donald L. Miller (New York: Pantheon, 1986), 216-17.

Mumford, Lewis. *The City in History*. Edited by Donald L. Miller. New York: Pantheon, 1986.

11. A translation (print)

11. Dante Alighieri, *The Inferno,* trans. John Ciardi (New York: New American Library, 1971), 51.

Alighieri, Dante. *The Inferno*. Translated by John Ciardi. New York: New American Library, 1971.

12. A later edition (print)

12. Dwight L. Bolinger, *Aspects of Language,* 3rd ed. (New York: Harcourt Brace Jovanovich, 1981), 20.

Bolinger, Dwight L. *Aspects of Language*. 3rd ed. New York: Harcourt Brace Jovanovich, 1981.

13. A work in more than one volume (print)

Citation of one volume without a title:

13. Abraham Lincoln, *The Collected Works of Abraham Lincoln,* ed. Roy P. Basler (New Brunswick: Rutgers University Press, 1953), 5:426-28.

Lincoln, Abraham. *The Collected Works of Abraham Lincoln*. Edited by Roy P. Basler. Vol. 5. New Brunswick: Rutgers University Press, 1953.

Citation of one volume with a title:

13. Linda B. Welkin, *The Age of Balanchine,* vol. 3 of *The History of Ballet* (New York: Columbia University Press, 1999), 56.

Welkin, Linda B. *The Age of Balanchine*. Vol. 3 of *The History of Ballet.* New York: Columbia University Press, 1999.

14. A selection from an anthology (print)

14. Rosetta Brooks, "Streetwise," in *The New Urban Landscape,* ed. Richard Martin (New York: Rizzoli, 2005), 38-39.

Brooks, Rosetta. "Streetwise." In *The New Urban Landscape,* ed. Richard Martin, 37-60. New York: Rizzoli, 2005.

15. A work in a series (print)

15. Ingmar Bergman, *The Seventh Seal,* Modern Film Scripts 12 (New York: Simon and Schuster, 1995), 27.

Bergman, Ingmar. *The Seventh Seal*. Modern Film Scripts 12. New York: Simon and Schuster, 1995.

16. An article in a reference work (print)

16. *Merriam-Webster's Collegiate Dictionary,* 11th ed., s.v. "reckon."

Merriam-Webster's Collegiate Dictionary. 11th ed. S.v. "reckon."

Use the abbreviation s.v. (Latin *sub verbo,* "under the word") for reference works that are alphabetically arranged. Well-known works like the one listed here do not need publication information except for edition number.

Chic 42b

Web and other electronic sources

The *Chicago Manual*'s models for documenting electronic sources mostly begin as those for print sources do. Then you add electronic publication information that will help readers locate the source, such as a URL or a Digital Object Identifier (DOI), a unique identifier that many publishers assign to journal articles and other documents. If an article from a journal, magazine, or newspaper has a DOI, include it as shown in models 17 and 20. Otherwise give the URL.

For Web pages and other electronic sources that are likely to change, the *Chicago Manual* suggests including the date of the most recent update in a statement beginning last modified (see model 22). If no date is available, give the date of your access (see model 23).

Note Chicago style allows many ways to break URLs between the end of one line and the beginning of the next: after a colon or double slash and before a single slash, period, comma, hyphen, and most other marks. *Do not* break after a hyphen or add any hyphens.

17. An article in a journal (Web)

17. Andrew Palfrey, "Choice of Mates in Identical Twins," *Modern Psychology* 4, no. 1 (Fall 2003): 28, doi:10.1080/143257962345987215.

Palfrey, Andrew. "Choice of Mates in Identical Twins." *Modern Psychology* 4, no. 1 (Fall 2003): 26-40. doi:10.1080/143257962345987215.

Give a DOI if one is available (as here) or a URL if not (next two models).

18. An article in a magazine (Web)

18. Nina Shen Rastogi, "Peacekeepers on Trial," *Slate,* May 28, 2008, http://www.slate.com/id/2192272.

Rastogi, Nina Shen. "Peacekeepers on Trial." *Slate,* May 28, 2008. http://www.slate.com/id/2192272.

19. An article in a newspaper (Web)

19. Elissa Gootman, "Gifted Programs in the City Are Less Diverse," *New York Times,* June 19, 2008, http://www.nytimes.com/2008/06/19/nyregion/19gifted.html.

Gootman, Elissa. "Gifted Programs in the City Are Less Diverse." *New York Times,* June 19, 2008. http://www.nytimes.com/2008/06/19/nyregion/19gifted.html.

20. An article in an online database (Web)

20. Jonathan Dickens, "Social Policy Approaches to Intercountry Adoption," *International Social Work* 52, no. 5 (September 2009): 600, doi:10.1177/0020872809337678.

Dickens, Jonathan. "Social Policy Approaches to Intercountry Adoption." *International Social Work* 52, no. 5 (September 2009): 595-607. doi:10.1177/0020872809337678.

If a database article has neither a DOI nor a stable URL, end with the name of the database.

21. A book (Web)

21. Jane Austen, *Emma*, ed. R. W. Chapman (1816; Oxford: Clarendon, 1926; Oxford Text Archive, 2004), chap. 1, http://ota.ahds.ac.uk/Austen/Emma.1519.

Austen, Jane. *Emma*. Edited by R. W. Chapman. 1816. Oxford: Clarendon, 1926. Oxford Text Archive, 2004. http://ota.ahds.ac.uk/Austen/Emma.1519.

Provide print publication information, if any.

22. An article in a reference work (Web)

22. *Wikipedia,* s.v. "Wuhan," last modified July 16, 2010, http://en.wikipedia.org/wiki/Wuhan.

Wikipedia. S.v. "Wuhan." Last modified July 16, 2010. http://en.wikipedia.org/wiki/Wuhan.

23. A Web page

23. "Toyota Safety," Toyota Motor Sales, accessed July 23, 2010, http://www.toyota.com/safety.

Toyota Motor Sales. "Toyota Safety." Accessed July 23, 2010. http://www.toyota.com/safety.

24. An audio or visual source (Web)

A work of art:

24. Jackson Pollock, *Shimmering Substance,* 1946, Museum of Modern Art, New York, http://moma.org/collection/conservation/pollock/shimmering_substance.html.

Pollock, Jackson. *Shimmering Substance.* 1946. Museum of Modern Art, New York. http://moma.org/collection/conservation/pollock/shimmering_substance.html.

A sound recording:

24. Ronald W. Reagan, "State of the Union Address," January 26, 1982, Vincent Voice Library, Digital and Multimedia Center, University of Michigan, http://www.lib.msu.edu/vincent/presidents/reagan.html.

Reagan, Ronald W. "State of the Union Address." January 26, 1982. Vincent Voice Library. Digital and Multimedia Center, University of Michigan. http://www.lib.msu.edu/vincent/presidents/reagan.html.

A film or film clip:

24. Leslie J. Stewart, *96 Ranch Rodeo and Barbecue* (1951); 16mm; from Library of Congress, *Buckaroos in Paradise: Ranching Culture in Northern Nevada, 1945-1982,* MPEG, http://memory.loc.gov/cgi-bin/query.

Stewart, Leslie J. 96 *Ranch Rodeo and Barbecue*. 1951; 16 mm. From Library of Congress, *Buckaroos in Paradise: Ranching Culture in Northern Nevada, 1945-1982*. MPEG, http://memory.loc.gov/cgi-bin/query.

25. A message posted to a blog or discussion group (Web)

25. Chris Horner, "EU Emissions," *Cooler Heads Blog,* June 18, 2008, http://www.globalwarming.org/node/2362.

Horner, Chris. "EU Emissions." *Cooler Heads Blog*. June 18, 2008. http://www.globalwarming.org/node/2362.

25. Michael Tourville, "European Currency Reform," e-mail to International Finance discussion list, January 6, 2008, http://www.weg.isu.edu/finance-dl/archive/46732.

Tourville, Michael. "European Currency Reform." E-mail to International Finance discussion list. January 6, 2008. http://www.weg.isu.edu/finance-dl/archive/46732.

26. Electronic mail

26. Elizabeth Bailey, "Re: London," e-mail message to author, May 4, 2010.

Bailey, Elizabeth. "Re: London." E-mail message to author. May 4, 2010.

27. A work on CD-ROM or DVD-ROM

27. *The American Heritage Dictionary of the English Language*, 4th ed. (Boston: Houghton Mifflin, 2000), CD-ROM.

The American Heritage Dictionary of the English Language. 4th ed. Boston: Houghton Mifflin, 2000. CD-ROM.

Other sources

28. A government publication (print)

28. House Comm. on Ways and Means, *Medicare Payment for Outpatient Physical and Occupational Therapy Services*, 110th Cong., 1st sess., H.R. Doc. 772, 18-19 (2007).

House Comm. on Ways and Means. *Medicare Payment for Outpatient Physical and Occupational Therapy Services*. 110th Cong. 1st sess. H.R. Doc. 772 (2007).

28. Hawaii Department of Education, *Kauai District Schools, Profile 2007-08* (Honolulu, 2008), 38.

Hawaii. Department of Education. *Kauai District Schools, Profile 2007-08*. Honolulu, 2008.

29. A published letter (print)

29. Mrs. Laura E. Buttolph to Rev. and Mrs. C. C. Jones, June 20, 1857, in *The Children of Pride: A True Story of Georgia and the Civil War*, ed. Robert Manson Myers (New Haven, CT: Yale University Press, 1972), 334.

Buttolph, Laura E. Mrs. Laura E. Buttolph to Rev. and Mrs. C. C. Jones, June 20, 1857. In *The Children of Pride: A True Story of Georgia and the Civil War*, edited by Robert Manson Myers. New Haven, CT: Yale University Press, 1972.

30. A published or broadcast interview

30. Junot Diaz, interview by Terry Gross, *Fresh Air*, NPR, October 18, 2010.

Diaz, Junot. Interview by Terry Gross. *Fresh Air*. NPR. October 18, 2010.

31. A personal letter or interview

31. Ann E. Packer, letter to author, June 15, 2009.

Packer, Ann E. Letter to author. June 15, 2009.

31. Andrew Stern, interview by author, December 19, 2009.

Stern, Andrew. Interview by author. December 19, 2009.

32. A work of art

32. John Singer Sargent, *In Switzerland,* 1908, Metropolitan Museum of Art, New York.

Sargent, John Singer. *In Switzerland.* 1908. Metropolitan Museum of Art, New York.

33. A film, DVD, or video recording

33. George Balanchine, *Serenade,* San Francisco Ballet, performed February 2, 2000 (New York: PBS Video, 2006), DVD.

Balanchine, George. *Serenade*. San Francisco Ballet. Performed February 2, 2000. New York: PBS Video, 2006. DVD.

34. A sound recording

34. Philip Glass, *String Quartet no. 5,* with Kronos Quartet, recorded 1991, Nonesuch 79356-2, 1995, compact disc.

Glass, Philip. *String Quartet no. 5.* Kronos Quartet. Recorded 1991. Nonesuch 79356-2, 1995, compact disc.

Shortened notes

To streamline documentation, Chicago style recommends shortened notes for sources that are fully cited elsewhere, either in a complete bibliography or in previous notes. Ask your instructor whether your paper should include a bibliography and, if so, whether you may use shortened notes for first references to sources as well as for subsequent references.

A shortened note contains the author's last name, the work's title (minus any initial *A*, *An*, or *The*), and the page number. Reduce long titles to four or fewer key words.

Complete note

4. Janet Lever, "Sex Differences in the Games Children Play," *Social Problems* 23 (Spring 1996): 482.

Complete bibliography entry

Lever, Janet. "Sex Differences in the Games Children Play." *Social Problems* 23 (Spring 1996): 478-87.

Shortened note

12. Lever, "Sex Differences," 483.

You may use the Latin abbreviation ibid. (meaning "in the same place") to refer to the same source cited in the preceding note. Give a page number if it differs from that in the preceding note.

12. Lever, "Sex Differences," 483.

13. Gilligan, *In a Different Voice,* 92.

14. Ibid., 93.

15. Lever, "Sex Differences," 483.

Chicago style allows for in-text parenthetical citations when you cite one or more works repeatedly. In the following example, the raised number 2 refers to the source information in a note; the number in parentheses is a page number in the same source.

> British rule, observes Stuart Cary Welch, "seemed as permanent as Mount Everest."[2] Most Indians submitted, willingly or not, to British influence in every facet of life (42).

42c Chicago paper format

The following guidelines come mainly from Turabian's *Manual for Writers*, which offers more specific advice than *The Chicago Manual* on the format of students' papers. See the next two pages for illustrations of the following elements. And see pages 22–25 for advice on type fonts, lists, illustrations, and other elements of document design.

Margins and spacing Use minimum one-inch margins on all pages of the body. (The first page of endnotes or the bibliography begins two inches from the top; see p. 231.) Double-space your own text and between notes and bibliography entries; single-space displayed quotations (see below) and each note and bibliography entry.

Paging Number pages consecutively from the first text page through the end (endnotes or bibliography). Use Arabic numerals (1, 2, 3) in the upper right corner.

Title page On an unnumbered title page provide the title of the paper, your name, the course title, your instructor's name, and the date. Use all-capital letters for the paper's title, and center everything horizontally. Single-space between adjacent lines, and add extra space below the title as shown on the next page.

Poetry and long prose quotations Display certain quotations separately from your text: three or more lines of poetry and two or more sentences of prose. Indent a displayed quotation four spaces from the left, single-space the quotation, and double-space above and below it. *Do not add quotation marks*.

> Gandhi articulated the principles of his movement in 1922:
>
> > I discovered that pursuit of truth did not permit violence being inflicted on one's opponent, but that he must be weaned from error by patience and sympathy. For what appears to be truth to one may appear to be error to the other.[6]

42d Sample pages in Chicago style

Title page

INDIAN NATIONALISM IN INDIAN ART
AFTER WORLD WAR I

Single-space

Reyna P. Dixon
Art History 236
Ms. Parikh
December 16, 2009

Single-space

First page of paper with footnotes

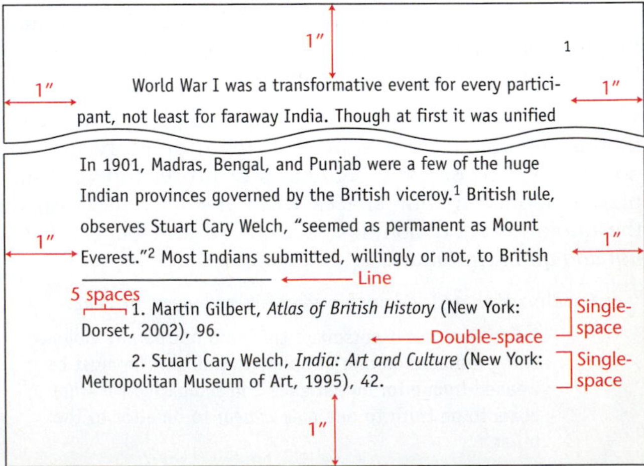

Endnotes

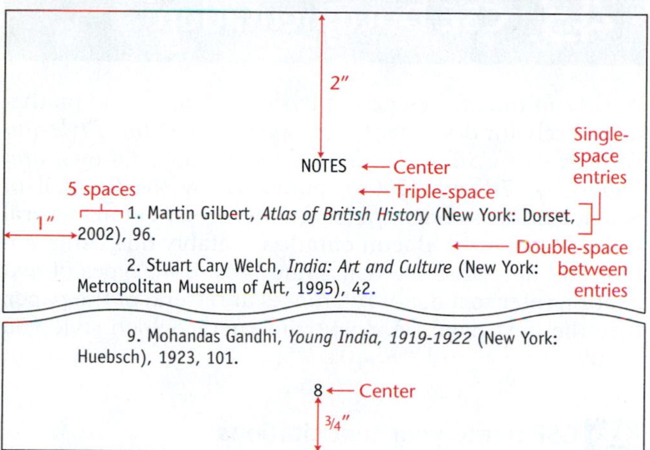

Bibliography

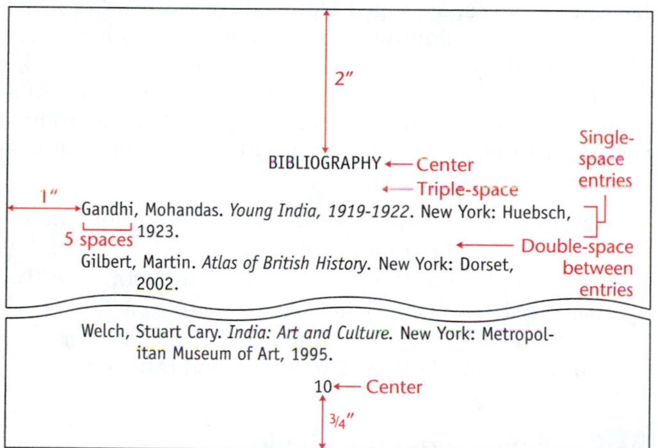

43 CSE Documentation

Writers in the life sciences, physical sciences, and mathematics rely for documentation style on *Scientific Style and Format: The CSE Style Manual for Authors, Editors, and Publishers,* 7th ed. (2006), published by the Council of Science Editors. *Scientific Style and Format* details several styles of scientific documentation, notably one using author and date and one using numbers. Both types of text citation refer to a list of references at the end of the paper. (See the next page.) Ask your instructor which style you should use.

43a CSE name-year text citations

In the CSE name-year style, parenthetical text citations provide the last name of the author being cited and the source's year of publication. At the end of the paper, a list of references, arranged alphabetically by authors' last names, provides complete information on each source. (See the next page.)

The CSE name-year style closely resembles the APA name-year style detailed on pages 200–02. You can follow the APA examples for in-text citations, with three differences:

- Do not use a comma to separate the author's name and the date: (Baumrind 1968, p. 34).
- Separate two authors' names with and (not "&"): (Pepinsky and DeStefano 1997).
- For sources with three or more authors, give the first author's name followed by et al. ("and others").

CSE
43b

43b CSE numbered text citations

In the CSE number style, raised numbers in the text refer to a numbered list of references at the end of the paper.

Two standard references[1,2] use this term.

These forms of immunity have been extensively researched.[3]

Assignment of numbers The number for each source is based on the order in which you cite the source in the text: the first cited source is 1, the second is 2, and so on.

mycomplab

Visit *mycomplab.com* for more help with CSE documentation.

Reuse of numbers When you cite a source you have already cited and numbered, use the original number again. This reuse is the key difference between the CSE numbered citations and numbered references to footnotes or endnotes.

Citation of two or more sources When you cite two or more sources at once, arrange their numbers in sequence and separate them with a comma and no space, as in the first of the preceding examples.

43c CSE reference list

For both the name-year and the number styles of in-text citation, provide a list, titled References, of all sources you have cited. Center this heading about an inch from the top of the page, and double-space beneath it.

Spacing Single-space each entry, and double-space between entries.

Arrangement In the name-year style, arrange entries alphabetically by authors' last names. In the number style, arrange entries in numerical order—that is, in order of their citation in the text.

Format In the name-year style, type all lines of entries at the left margin—do not indent. In the number style, begin the first line of each entry at the left margin and indent subsequent lines.

Authors List each author's name with the last name first, followed by initials for first and middle names. Do not use a comma between an author's last name and initials, and do not use periods or space with the initials. Do use a comma to separate authors' names.

Placement of dates In the name-year style, the date follows the author's or authors' names. In the number style, the date follows the publication information (for a book) or the periodical title (for a journal, magazine, or newspaper).

Journal titles Do not underline or italicize journal titles. For titles of two or more words, abbreviate words of six or more letters (without periods) and omit most prepositions,° articles,° and conjunctions.° Capitalize each word. For example, *Journal of Chemical and Biochemical Studies* becomes J Chem Biochem Stud.

Book and article titles Do not underline, italicize, or use quotation marks around a book or an article title. Capitalize only the first word and any proper nouns. See model 2 on page 235.

Publication information for journal articles The name-year and number styles differ in the placement of the

°See Glossary of Terms, page 249.

publication date (see the previous page). However, both styles end with the journal's volume number, any issue number in parentheses, a colon, and the inclusive page numbers of the article, run together without space: 28:329-30 or 62(2):26-40.

The following examples show both a name-year reference and a number reference for each type of source.

Authors

1. One author

Gould SJ. 1987. Time's arrow, time's cycle. Cambridge (MA): Harvard University Press.

CSE references

1. Gould SJ. Time's arrow, time's cycle. Cambridge (MA): Harvard University Press; 1987.

2. Two to ten authors

Hepburn PX, Tatin JM, Tatin JP. 2008. Human physiology. New York (NY): Columbia University Press.

2. Hepburn PX, Tatin JM, Tatin JP. Human physiology. New York (NY): Columbia University Press; 2008.

3. More than ten authors

Evans RW, Bowditch L, Dana KL, Drummond A, Wildovitch WP, Young SL, Mills P, Mills RR, Livak SR, Lisi OL, et al. 2004. Organ transplants: ethical issues. Ann Arbor (MI): University of Michigan Press.

3. Evans RW, Bowditch L, Dana KL, Drummond A, Wildovitch WP, Young SL, Mills P, Mills RR, Livak SR, Lisi OL, et al. Organ transplants: ethical issues. Ann Arbor (MI): University of Michigan Press; 2004.

4. Author not named

Health care for children with diabetes. 2008. New York (NY): US Health Care.

4. Health care for children with diabetes. New York (NY): US Health Care; 2008.

5. Two or more cited works by the same author(s) published in the same year

Gardner H. 1973a. The arts and human development. New York (NY): Wiley.

Gardner H. 1973b. The quest for mind: Piaget, Lévi-Strauss, and the structuralist movement. New York (NY): Knopf.

(The number style does not require such forms.)

Print periodicals: Journals, newspapers, magazines

CSE 43c

6. An article in a journal (print)

Kim P. 2006. Medical decision making for the dying. Milbank Quar. 64(2):26-40.

6. Kim P. Medical decision making for the dying. Milbank Quar. 2006;64(2):26-40.

If a journal article has a Digital Object Identifier (DOI), you may include the number at the end of the entry for readers' convenience. (See p. 209 for more on DOIs.)

7. An article in a newspaper (print)

Stout D. 2008 May 28. Blind win court ruling on US currency. New York Times (National Ed.). Sect. A:23 (col. 3).

7. Stout D. Blind win court ruling on US currency. New York Times (National Ed.). 2008 May 28;Sect. A:23 (col. 3).

8. An article in a magazine (print)

Wilkinson A. 2008 June 2. Crime fighting of the future. New Yorker. 26-33.

8. Wilkinson A. Crime fighting of the future. New Yorker. 2008 June 2:26-33.

Print books

9. Basic format for a book (print)

Wilson EO. 2004. On human nature. Cambridge (MA): Harvard University Press.

9. Wilson EO. On human nature. Cambridge (MA): Harvard University Press; 2004.

10. A book with an editor (print)

Jonson P, editor. 2008. Anatomy yearbook 2008. Los Angeles (CA): Anatco.

10. Jonson P, editor. Anatomy yearbook 2008. Los Angeles (CA): Anatco; 2008.

11. A selection from a book (print)

Krigel R, Laubenstein L, Muggia F. 2005. Kaposi's sarcoma. In: Ebbeson P, Biggar RS, Melbye M, editors. AIDS: a basic guide for clinicians. 2nd ed. Philadelphia (PA): Saunders. p. 100-26.

11. Kriegel R, Laubenstein L, Muggia F. Kaposi's sarcoma. In: Ebbeson P, Biggar RS, Melbye M, editors. AIDS: a basic guide for clinicians. 2nd ed. Philadelphia (PA): Saunders; 2005. p. 100-26.

Web and other electronic sources

CSE references to electronic sources require additions to the basic print formats:

- **Give the medium you used to find the source,** in brackets: [Internet], [DVD], and so on.
- **Give the date you accessed the source preceded by cited,** in brackets: [cited 2009 Dec 7].
- **Give the URL of an Internet source.** Use an availability statement that starts with Available from: and ends with the URL. If you must break a URL from one line to the next, do so only before punctuation such as a period or a slash and do not hyphenate. Do not add a period at the end of a URL.

If an article has a Digital Object Identifier (DOI), you may include the number at the end of the entry for readers' convenience. (See p. 209 for more on DOIs.)

12. An article in a journal (Web)

Grady GF. 2007. The here and now of hepatitis B immunization. Today's Med [Internet]. [cited 2009 Dec 7];6(2):39-41. Available from: http://www.fmrt.org/todaysmedicine/Grady050293.pdf6

12. Grady GF. The here and now of hepatitis B immunization. Today's Med [Internet]. 2007 [cited 2009 Dec 7];6(2):39-41. Available from: http://www.fmrt.org/todaysmedicine/Grady050293.pdf6

13. An article in a database (Web)

McAskill MR, Anderson TJ, Jones RD. 2005. Saccadic adaptation in neurological disorders. Prog Brain Res. 140:417-431. PubMed [Internet]. Bethesda (MD): National Library of Medicine; [cited 2010 Mar 6]. Available from: http://www.ncbi.nlm.nih.gov/PubMed

13. McAskill MR, Anderson TJ, Jones RD. Saccadic adaptation in neurological disorders. Prog Brain Res. 2005;140:417-431. PubMed [Internet]. Bethesda (MD): National Library of Medicine; [cited 2010 Mar 6]. Available from: http://www.ncbi.nlm.nih.gov/PubMed

Provide information on the database: title, [Internet], place of publication, and publisher. (If the database author is different from the publisher, give the author's name before the title.) If you see a date of publication or a copyright date for the database, give it after the publisher's name.

14. A book (Web)

Ruch BJ, Ruch DB. 2007. Homeopathy and medicine: resolving the conflict [Internet]. New York (NY): Albert Einstein College of Medicine [cited 2010 Jan 28]. Available from: http://www.einstein.edu/medicine/books/ruch.html

14. Ruch BJ, Ruch DB. Homeopathy and medicine: resolving the conflict [Internet]. New York (NY): Albert Einstein College of Medicine; 2007 [cited 2010 Jan 28]. Available from: http://www.einstein.edu/medicine/books/ruch.html

15. A Web site

American Medical Association [Internet]. 2009. Chicago (IL): American Medical Association; [cited 2009 Nov 26]. Available from: http://ama-assn.org

15. American Medical Association [Internet]. Chicago (IL): American Medical Association; 2009 [cited 2009 Nov 26]. Available from: http://ama-assn.org

16. A message posted to a discussion list

Stalinsky Q. 2007 Aug 16. Reconsidering the hormone-replacement study. Woman Physicians Congress [discussion list on the Internet]. Chicago (IL): American Medical Association; [cited 2010 Aug 17]. Available from: ama-wpc@ama-assn.org

16. Stalinsky Q. Reconsidering the hormone-replacement study. Woman Physicians Congress [discussion list on the Internet]. Chicago (IL): American Medical Association; 2007 Aug 16 [cited 2010 Aug 17]. Available from: ama-wpc@ama-assn.org

17. A personal online communication (text citation)

One member of the research team has expressed reservation about the study design (personal communication from L. Kogod, 2010 Feb 6; unreferenced).

A personal letter or e-mail message should be cited in your text, not in your reference list. The format is the same for both the name-year and the number styles.

18. A document on CD-ROM or DVD-ROM

Reich WT, editor. 2010. Encyclopedia of bioethics [DVD-ROM]. New York (NY): Co-Health.

18. Reich WT, editor. Encyclopedia of bioethics [DVD-ROM]. New York (NY): Co-Health; 2010.

Other sources

19. A report written and published by the same organization

Warnock M. 2006. Report of the Committee on Fertilization and Embryology. Waco (TX): Baylor University Department of Embryology. Report No.: BU/DE.4261.

19. Warnock M. Report of the Committee on Fertilization and Embryology. Waco (TX): Baylor University Department of Embryology; 2006. Report No.: BU/DE.4261.

20. A report written and published by different organizations

Hackney, JD (Rancho Los Amigos Hospital, Downey, CA). 2007. Effect of atmospheric pollutants on human physiologic function. Washington (DC): Environmental Protection Agency (US). Report No.: R-801396.

CSE 43c

20. Hackney, JD (Rancho Los Amigos Hospital, Downey, CA). Effect of atmospheric pollutants on human physiologic function. Washington (DC): Environmental Protection Agency (US); 2007. Report No.: R-801396.

21. An audio or visual recording

Cell mitosis [DVD-ROM]. 2010. White Plains (NY): Teaching Media.

21. Cell mitosis [DVD-ROM]. White Plains (NY): Teaching Media; 2010.

Glossary of Usage

This glossary provides notes on words or phrases that often cause problems for writers. The recommendations for standard written English are based on current dictionaries and usage guides. Items labeled *nonstandard* should be avoided in final drafts of academic and business writing. Those labeled *colloquial* and *slang* appear in some informal writing and may occasionally be used for effect in more formal academic and career writing. (Words and phrases labeled *colloquial* include those labeled *informal* by many dictionaries.) See Chapter 9 for more on levels of language.

a, an Use *a* before words beginning with consonant sounds: *a historian, a one-o'clock class, a university.* Use *an* before words that begin with vowel sounds, including silent *h*'s: *an organism, an L, an honor.*

The article before an abbreviation depends on how the abbreviation is read: *She was once an AEC aide* (*AEC* is read as three separate letters); *Many Americans opposed a SALT treaty* (*SALT* is read as one word, *salt*).

See also pp. 72–74 on the uses of *a/an* versus *the.*

accept, except *Accept* is a verb° meaning "to receive." *Except* is usually a preposition° or conjunction° meaning "but for" or "other than"; when it is used as a verb, it means "to leave out." *I can accept all your suggestions except the last one. I'm sorry you excepted my last suggestion from your list.*

advice, advise *Advice* is a noun,° and *advise* is a verb.° *Take my advice; do as I advise you.*

affect, effect Usually *affect* is a verb° meaning "to influence," and *effect* is a noun° meaning "result": *The drug did not affect his driving; in fact, it seemed to have no effect at all.* (Note that *effect* occasionally is used as a verb meaning "to bring about": *Her efforts effected a change.* And *affect* is used in psychology as a noun meaning "feeling or emotion": *One can infer much about affect from behavior.*)

all, always, never, no one These absolute words often exaggerate a situation in which *many, often, rarely,* or *few* is more accurate.

all ready, already *All ready* means "completely prepared," and *already* means "by now" or "before now": *We were all ready to go to the movie, but it had already started.*

all right *All right* is always two words. *Alright* is an error.

all together, altogether *All together* means "in unison," or "gathered in one place." *Altogether* means "entirely." *It's not altogether true that our family never spends vacations all together.*

Usage

°See Glossary of Terms, page 249.

allusion, illusion An *allusion* is an indirect reference, and an *illusion* is a deceptive appearance: *Paul's constant allusions to Shakespeare created the illusion that he was an intellectual.*

a lot *A lot* is always two words, used informally to mean "many." *Alot* is a common misspelling.

always See *all, always, never, no one*.

among, between In general, use *between* only for relationships of two and *among* for more than two.

amount, number Use *amount* with a singular noun that names something not countable (a noncount noun°): *The amount of food varies.* Use *number* with a plural noun that names more than one of something countable (a count noun°): *The number of calories must stay the same.*

and/or *And/or* indicates three options: one or the other or both (*The decision is made by the mayor and/or the council*). If you mean all three options, *and/or* is appropriate. Otherwise, use *and* if you mean both, *or* if you mean either.

anxious, eager *Anxious* means "nervous" or "worried" and is usually followed by *about. Eager* means "looking forward" and is usually followed by *to. I've been anxious about getting blisters. I'm eager* [not *anxious*] *to get new cross-training shoes.*

anybody, any body; anyone, any one *Anybody* and *anyone* are indefinite pronouns;° *any body* is a noun° modified by *any; any one* is a pronoun° or adjective° modified by *any. How can anybody communicate with any body of government? Can anyone help Amy? She has more work than any one person can handle.*

any more, anymore *Any more* means "no more"; *anymore* means "now." Both are used in negative constructions: *He doesn't want any more. She doesn't live here anymore.*

anyways, anywheres Nonstandard for *anyway* and *anywhere.*

are, is Use *are* with a plural subject° (*books are*), *is* with a singular subject (*book is*). See p. 63.

as *As* may be vague or ambiguous when it substitutes for *because, since,* or *while*: *As we were stopping to rest, we decided to eat lunch.* (Does *as* mean "while" or "because"?) *As* should never be used as a substitute for *whether* or *who. I'm not sure whether* [not *as*] *we can make it. That's the man who* [not *as*] *gave me directions.*

Usage

as, like See *like, as*.

at this point in time Wordy for *now, at this point,* or *at this time.*

awful, awfully Strictly speaking, *awful* means "inspiring awe." As intensifiers meaning "very" or "extremely" (*He tried awfully hard*), *awful* and *awfully* should be avoided in formal speech or writing.

°See Glossary of Terms, page 249.

a while, awhile *Awhile* is an adverb;° *a while* is an article° and a noun.° *I will be gone awhile* [not *a while*]. *I will be gone for a while* [not *awhile*].

bad, badly In formal speech and writing, *bad* should be used only as an adjective;° the adverb° is *badly. He felt bad because his tooth ached badly*. In *He felt bad*, the verb *felt* is a linking verb° and the adjective *bad* modifies the subject° *he*, not the verb *felt*. See also pp. 70–71.

being as, being that Colloquial for *because*, the preferable word in formal speech or writing: *Because* [not *Being as*] *the world is round, Columbus never did fall off the edge.*

beside, besides *Beside* is a preposition° meaning "next to." *Besides* is a preposition meaning "except" or "in addition to" as well as an adverb° meaning "in addition." *Besides, several other people besides you want to sit beside Dr. Christensen.*

between, among See *among, between.*

bring, take Use *bring* only for movement from a farther place to a nearer one and *take* for any other movement. *First, take these books to the library for renewal, then take them to Mr. Daniels. Bring them back to me when he's finished.*

can, may Strictly, *can* indicates capacity or ability, and *may* indicates permission: *If I may talk with you a moment, I believe I can solve your problem.*

climatic, climactic *Climatic* comes from *climate* and refers to weather: *Recent droughts may indicate a climatic change. Climactic* comes from *climax* and refers to a dramatic high point: *During the climactic duel between Hamlet and Laertes, Gertrude drinks poisoned wine.*

complement, compliment To *complement* something is to add to, complete, or reinforce it: *Her yellow blouse complemented her black hair.* To *compliment* something is to make a flattering remark about it: *He complimented her on her hair. Complimentary* can also mean "free": *complimentary tickets.*

conscience, conscious *Conscience* is a noun° meaning "a sense of right and wrong"; *conscious* is an adjective° meaning "aware" or "awake." *Though I was barely conscious, my conscience nagged me.*

continual, continuous *Continual* means "constantly recurring": *Most movies on television are continually interrupted by commercials. Continuous* means "unceasing": *Some cable channels present movies continuously without commercials.*

could of See *have, of.*

criteria The plural of *criterion* (meaning "standard for judgment"): *Our criteria are strict. The most important criterion is a sense of humor.*

data The plural of *datum* (meaning "fact"). Though *data* is often used with a singular verb, many readers prefer the plural verb and it is always correct: *The data fail* [not *fails*] *to support the hypothesis.*

°See Glossary of Terms, page 249.

device, devise *Device* is the noun,° and *devise* is the verb:° *Can you devise some device for getting his attention?*

different from, different than *Different from* is preferred: *His purpose is different from mine.* But *different than* is widely accepted when a construction using *from* would be wordy: *I'm a different person now than I used to be* is preferable to *I'm a different person now from the person I used to be.*

disinterested, uninterested *Disinterested* means "impartial": *We chose Pete, as a disinterested third party, to decide who was right. Uninterested* means "bored" or "lacking interest": *Unfortunately, Pete was completely uninterested in the question.*

don't *Don't* is the contraction for *do not,* not for *does not*: *I don't care, you don't care,* and *he doesn't* [not *don't*] *care.*

due to *Due* is an adjective° or noun;° thus *due to* is always acceptable as a subject complement:° *His gray hairs were due to age.* Many object to *due to* as a preposition° meaning "because of" (*Due to the holiday, class was canceled*). A rule of thumb is that *due to* is always correct after a form of the verb *be* but questionable otherwise.

eager, anxious See *anxious, eager.*

effect See *affect, effect.*

elicit, illicit *Elicit* is a verb° meaning "bring out" or "call forth." *Illicit* is an adjective° meaning "unlawful." *The crime elicited an outcry against illicit drugs.*

emigrate, immigrate *Emigrate* means "to leave one place and move to another": *The Chus emigrated from Korea. Immigrate* means "to move into a place where one was not born": *They immigrated to the United States.*

enthused Sometimes used colloquially as an adjective° meaning "showing enthusiasm." The preferred adjective is *enthusiastic*: *The coach was enthusiastic* [not *enthused*] *about the team's victory.*

etc. *Etc.*, the Latin abbreviation for "and other things," should be avoided in formal writing and should not be used to refer to people. When used, it should not substitute for precision, as in *The government provides health care, etc.*, and it should not end a list beginning *such as* or *for example.*

Usage

everybody, every body; everyone, every one *Everybody* and *everyone* are indefinite pronouns:° *Everybody* [or *Everyone*] *knows Tom steals. Every one* is a pronoun° modified by *every,* and *every body* is a noun° modified by *every.* Both refer to each thing or person of a specific group and are typically followed by *of*: *The game commissioner has stocked every body of fresh water in the state with fish, and now every one of our rivers is a potential trout stream.*

everyday, every day *Everyday* is an adjective° meaning "used daily" or "common"; *every day* is a noun° modified by *every*: *Everyday problems tend to arise every day.*

°See Glossary of Terms, page 249.

everywheres Nonstandard for *everywhere.*

except See *accept, except.*

explicit, implicit *Explicit* means "stated outright": *I left explicit instructions. Implicit* means "implied, unstated": *We had an implicit understanding.*

farther, further *Farther* refers to additional distance (*How much farther is it to the beach?*), and *further* refers to additional time, amount, or other abstract matters (*I don't want to discuss this any further*).

feel Avoid this word in place of *think* or *believe: She thinks* [not *feels*] *that the law should be changed.*

fewer, less *Fewer* refers to individual countable items (a plural count noun°), *less* to general amounts (a noncount noun,° always singular): *Skim milk has fewer calories than whole milk. We have less milk left than I thought.*

further See *farther, further.*

get *Get* is easy to overuse; watch out for it in expressions such as *it's getting better* (substitute *improving*), *we got done* (substitute *finished*), and *the mayor has got to* (substitute *must*).

good, well *Good* is an adjective,° and *well* is nearly always an adverb:° *Larry's a good dancer. He and Linda dance well together. Well* is properly used as an adjective only to refer to health: *You look well.* (*You look good,* in contrast, means "Your appearance is pleasing.") See also p. 70.

hanged, hung Though both are past-tense forms° of *hang, hanged* is used to refer to executions and *hung* is used for all other meanings: *Tom Dooley was hanged* [not *hung*] *from a white oak tree. I hung* [not *hanged*] *the picture you gave me.*

have, of Use *have,* not *of,* after helping verbs° such as *could, should, would, may,* and *might: You should have* [not *should of*] *told me.*

he, she; he/she Convention has allowed the use of *he* to mean "he or she," but most writers today consider this usage inaccurate and unfair because it excludes females. The construction *he/she,* one substitute for *he,* is awkward and objectionable to many readers. The better choice is to recast the sentence in the plural, to rephrase, or to use *he or she*. For instance: *After infants learn to creep, they progress to crawling. After learning to creep, the infant progresses to crawling. After the infant learns to creep, he or she progresses to crawling.* See also pp. 45 and 67.

herself, himself See *myself, herself, himself, yourself.*

hisself Nonstandard for *himself.*

hopefully *Hopefully* means "with hope": *Freddy waited hopefully*. The use of *hopefully* to mean "it is to be hoped," "I hope," or "let's hope" is now very common; but try to avoid it in writing because many readers continue to object strongly to the usage.

°See Glossary of Terms, page 249.

idea, ideal An *idea* is a thought or conception. An *ideal* (noun°) is a model of perfection or a goal. *Ideal* should not be used in place of *idea*: *The idea* [not *ideal*] *of the play is that our ideals often sustain us.*

if, whether For clarity, use *whether* rather than *if* when you are expressing an alternative: *If I laugh hard, people can't tell whether I'm crying.*

illicit See *elicit, illicit.*

illusion See *allusion, illusion.*

immigrate See *emigrate, immigrate.*

implicit See *explicit, implicit.*

imply, infer Writers or speakers *imply,* meaning "suggest": *Jim's letter implies he's having a good time.* Readers or listeners *infer,* meaning "conclude": *From Jim's letter I infer he's having a good time.*

irregardless Nonstandard for *regardless.*

is, are See *are, is.*

is when, is where These are faulty constructions in sentences that define: *Adolescence is a stage* [not *is when a person is*] *between childhood and adulthood. Socialism is a system in which* [not *is where*] *government owns the means of production.*

its, it's *Its* is the pronoun° *it* in the possessive case:° *That plant is losing its leaves. It's* is a contraction for *it is* or *it has: It's* [*It is*] *likely to die. It's* [*It has*] *got a fungus.* See also p. 93.

kind of, sort of, type of In formal speech and writing, avoid using *kind of* or *sort of* to mean "somewhat": *He was rather* [not *kind of*] *tall.*

Kind, sort, and *type* are singular: *This kind of dog is easily trained.* Errors often occur when these singular nouns are combined with the plural adjectives° *these* and *those*: *These kinds* [not *kind*] *of dogs are easily trained. Kind, sort,* and *type* should be followed by *of* but not by *a*: *I don't know what type of* [not *type* or *type of a*] *dog that is.*

Don't use *kind of, sort of,* or *type of* unless the word *kind, sort,* or *type* is important: *That was a strange* [not *strange sort of*] *statement.*

lay, lie *Lay* means "put" or "place" and takes a direct object:° *We could lay the tablecloth in the sun.* Its main forms are *lay, laid, laid. Lie* means "recline" or "be situated" and does not take an object: *I lie awake at night. The town lies east of the river.* Its main forms are *lie, lay, lain.*

Usage

less See *fewer, less.*

lie, lay See *lay, lie.*

like, as In formal speech and writing, *like* should not introduce a main clause.° The preferred choice is *as* or *as if: The plan succeeded as* [not *like*] *we hoped.* Use *like* only before a word or phrase: *Other plans like it have failed.*

°See Glossary of Terms, page 249.

literally This word means "actually" or "just as the words say," and it should not be used to intensify expressions whose words are not to be taken at face value. The sentence *He was literally climbing the walls* describes a person behaving like an insect, not a person who is restless or anxious. For the latter meaning, *literally* should be omitted.

lose, loose *Lose* means "mislay": *Did you lose a brown glove? Loose* usually means "unrestrained" or "not tight": *Ann's canary got loose*.

may, can See *can, may.*

may be, maybe *May be* is a verb,° and *maybe* is an adverb° meaning "perhaps": *Tuesday may be a legal holiday. Maybe we won't have classes.*

may of See *have, of.*

media *Media* is the plural of *medium* and takes a plural verb.° *All the news media are increasingly visual.* The singular verb is common, even in the media, but many readers prefer the plural verb and it is always correct.

might of See *have, of.*

must of See *have, of.*

myself, herself, himself, yourself The *-self* pronouns° refer to or intensify another word or words: *Paul did it himself; Jill herself said so.* In formal speech or writing, avoid using the *-self* pronouns in place of personal pronouns:° *No one except me* [not *myself*] *saw the accident. Michiko and I* [not *myself*] *planned the ceremony.*

never, no one See *all, always, never, no one*.

nowheres Nonstandard for *nowhere.*

number See *amount, number.*

of, have See *have, of.*

OK, O.K., okay All three spellings are acceptable, but avoid this colloquial term in formal speech and writing.

people, persons Except when emphasizing individuals, prefer *people* to *persons: We the people of the United States . . . ; Will the person or persons who saw the accident please notify. . . .*

percent (per cent), percentage Both these terms refer to fractions of one hundred. *Percent* always follows a number (*40 percent of the voters*), and the word should be used instead of the symbol (%) in nontechnical writing. *Percentage* usually follows an adjective (*a high percentage*).

persons See *people, persons.*

phenomena The plural of *phenomenon* (meaning "perceivable fact" or "unusual occurrence"): *Many phenomena are not recorded. One phenomenon is attracting attention.*

plus *Plus* is standard as a preposition° meaning "in addition to": *His income plus mine is sufficient.* But *plus* is colloquial

°See Glossary of Terms, page 249.

as a conjunctive adverb:° *Our organization is larger than theirs; moreover* [not *plus*], *we have more money.*

precede, proceed *Precede* means "come before": *My name precedes yours in the alphabet. Proceed* means "move on": *We were told to proceed to the waiting room.*

prejudice, prejudiced *Prejudice* is a noun;° *prejudiced* is an adjective.° Do not drop the *-d* from *prejudiced*: *I knew that my grandparents were prejudiced* [not *prejudice*].

principal, principle *Principal* is an adjective° meaning "foremost" or "major," a noun° meaning "chief official," or, in finance, a noun meaning "capital sum." *Principle* is a noun only, meaning "rule" or "axiom." *Her principal reasons for confessing were her principles of right and wrong.*

proceed, precede See *precede, proceed.*

raise, rise *Raise* means "lift" or "bring up" and takes a direct object:° *The Kirks raise cattle.* Its main forms are *raise, raised, raised. Rise* means "get up" and does not take an object: *They must rise at dawn.* Its main forms are *rise, rose, risen.*

real, really In formal speech and writing, *real* should not be used as an adverb;° *really* is the adverb and *real* an adjective.° *Popular reaction to the announcement was really* [not *real*] *enthusiastic.*

reason is because Although colloquially common, this construction should be avoided in formal speech and writing. Use a *that* clause after *reason is*: *The reason he is absent is that* [not *is because*] *he is sick.* Or: *He is absent because he is sick.*

respectful, respective *Respectful* means "full of (or showing) respect": *Be respectful of other people. Respective* means "separate": *The French and the Germans occupied their respective trenches.*

rise, raise See *raise, rise.*

sensual, sensuous *Sensual* suggests sexuality; *sensuous* means "pleasing to the senses." *Stirred by the sensuous scent of meadow grass and flowers, Cheryl and Paul found their thoughts turning sensual.*

set, sit *Set* means "put" or "place" and takes a direct object:° *He sets the pitcher down.* Its main forms are *set, set, set. Sit* means "be seated" and does not take an object: *She sits on the sofa.* Its main forms are *sit, sat, sat.*

should of See *have, of.*

since *Since* mainly relates to time: *I've been waiting since noon.* But *since* can also mean "because": *Since you ask, I'll tell you.* Revise sentences in which the word could have either meaning, such as *Since you left, my life is empty.*

sit, set See *set, sit.*

somebody, some body; someone, some one *Somebody* and *someone* are indefinite pronouns;° *some body* is a noun° mod-

°See Glossary of Terms, page 249.

ified by *some*; and *some one* is a pronoun° or an adjective° modified by *some*. *Somebody ought to invent a shampoo that will give hair some body. Someone told James he should choose some one plan and stick with it.*

somewheres Nonstandard for *somewhere*.

sort of, sort of a See *kind of, sort of, type of*.

supposed to, used to In both these expressions, the *-d* is essential: *I used to* [not *use to*] *think so. He's supposed to* [not *suppose to*] *meet us.*

sure and, sure to; try and, try to *Sure to* and *try to* are the correct forms: *Be sure to* [not *sure and*] *buy milk. Try to* [not *Try and*] *find some decent tomatoes.*

take, bring See *bring, take*.

than, then *Than* is a conjunction° used in comparisons, *then* an adverb° indicating time: *Holmes knew then that Moriarty was wilier than he had thought.*

that, which *That* always introduces essential° clauses: *Use the lettuce that Susan bought* (the clause limits *lettuce* to a particular lettuce). *Which* can introduce both essential and nonessential° clauses, but many writers reserve *which* only for nonessential clauses: *The leftover lettuce, which is in the refrigerator, would make a good salad* (the clause simply provides more information about the lettuce we already know of). Essential clauses are not set off by commas; nonessential clauses are. See also pp. 86–87.

that, who, which Use *that* to refer to most animals and to things: *The animals that escaped included a zebra. The rocket that failed cost millions.* Use *who* to refer to people and to animals with names: *Dorothy is the girl who visits Oz. Her dog, Toto, who accompanies her, gives her courage.* Use *which* only to refer to animals and things: *The river, which runs a thousand miles, empties into the Indian Ocean.*

their, there, they're *Their* is the possessive° form of *they*: *Give them their money. There* indicates place (*I saw her standing there*) or functions as an expletive° (*There is a hole behind you*). *They're* is a contraction° for *they are: They're going fast.*

theirselves Nonstandard for *themselves*.

then, than See *than, then*.

these, this *These* is plural; *this* is singular. *This pear is ripe, but these pears are not.*

these kind, these sort, these type, those kind See *kind of, sort of, type of*.

thru A colloquial spelling of *through* that should be avoided in all academic and business writing.

to, too, two *To* is a preposition;° *too* is an adverb° meaning "also" or "excessively"; and *two* is a number. *I too have been to Europe two times.*

°See Glossary of Terms, page 249.

toward, towards Both are acceptable, though *toward* is preferred. Use one or the other consistently.

try and, try to See *sure and, sure to; try and, try to.*

type of See *kind of, sort of, type of.*

uninterested See *disinterested, uninterested.*

unique *Unique* means "the only one of its kind" and so cannot sensibly be modified with words such as *very* or *most*: *That was a unique* [not *a very unique* or *the most unique* *movie.*

used to See *supposed to, used to.*

weather, whether The *weather* is the state of the atmosphere. *Whether* introduces alternatives. *The weather will determine whether we go or not.*

well See *good, well.*

whether, if See *if, whether.*

which, that See *that, which.*

who, which, that See *that, who, which.*

who, whom *Who* is the subject of a sentence or clause:° *We know who will come. Whom* is the object° of a verb° or preposition:° *We know whom we invited*.

who's, whose *Who's* is the contraction° of *who is* or *who has*: *Who's* [*Who is*] *at the door? Jim is the only one who's* [*who has*] *passed. Whose* is the possessive° form of *who*: *Whose book is that?*

would be Often used instead of *is* or *are* to soften statements needlessly: *One example is* [not *would be*] *gun-control laws*.

would have Avoid this construction in place of *had* in clauses that begin *if*: *If the tree had* [not *would have*] *withstood the fire, it would have been the oldest in town.*

would of See *have, of.*

you In all but very formal writing, *you* is generally appropriate as long as it means "you, the reader." In all writing, avoid indefinite uses of *you,* such as *In one ancient tribe your first loyalty was to your parents.*

your, you're *Your* is the possessive° form of *you: Your dinner is ready. You're* is the contraction° of *you are: You're late.*

yourself See *myself, herself, himself, yourself.*

°See Glossary of Terms, page 249.

Glossary of Terms

This glossary defines the terms and concepts of basic English grammar, including every term marked ° in the text.

absolute phrase A phrase that consists of a noun° or pronoun° plus the *-ing* or *-ed* form of a verb° (a participle°): *Our accommodations arranged, we set out on our trip. They will hire a local person, other things being equal.*

active voice The verb form° used when the sentence subject° names the performer of the verb's action: *The drillers used a rotary blade.* For more, see *voice.*

adjective A word used to modify a noun° or pronoun:° *beautiful morning, ordinary one, good spelling.* Contrast *adverb.* Nouns, word groups, and some verb° forms may also serve as adjectives: *book sale; sale of old books; the sale, which occurs annually; increasing profits.*

adverb A word used to modify a verb,° an adjective,° another adverb, or a whole sentence: *warmly greet* (verb), *only three people* (adjective), *quite seriously* (adverb), *Fortunately, she is employed* (sentence). Word groups may also serve as adverbs: *drove by a farm, plowed the field when the earth thawed.*

agreement The correspondence of one word to another in person,° number,° or gender.° Mainly, a verb° must agree with its subject° (*The chef orders eggs*), and a pronoun° must agree with its antecedent° (*The chef surveys her breakfast*). See also pp. 60–63 and 66–67.

antecedent The word a pronoun° refers to: *Jonah, who is not yet ten, has already chosen the college he will attend* (*Jonah* is the antecedent of the pronouns *who* and *he*).

appositive A word or word group appearing next to a noun° or pronoun° that renames or identifies it and is equivalent to it: *My brother Michael, the best horn player in town, won the state competition* (*Michael* identifies which brother is being referred to; *the best horn player in town* renames *My brother Michael*).

article The words *a, an,* and *the.* A kind of determiner,° an article always signals that a noun follows. See p. 239 for how to choose between *a* and *an.* See pp. 72–74 for the rules governing *a/an* and *the.*

auxiliary verb See *helping verb.*

case The form of a pronoun° or noun° that indicates its function in the sentence. Most pronouns have three cases. The **subjective case** is for subjects° and subject complements:° *I, you, he, she, it, we, they, who, whoever.* The **objective case** is for objects:° *me, you, him, her, it, us, them, whom, whomever.*

°Defined in this glossary.

The **possessive case** is for ownership: *my/mine, your/yours, his, her/hers, its, our/ours, their/theirs, whose.* Nouns use the subjective form (*dog, America*) for all cases except the possessive (*dog's, America's*).

clause A group of words containing a subject° and a predicate.° A **main clause** can stand alone as a sentence: *We can go to the movies*. A **subordinate clause** cannot stand alone as a sentence: *We can go if Julie gets back on time*. For more, see *subordinate clause.*

collective noun A word with singular form that names a group of individuals or things: for instance, *team, army, family, flock, group.* A collective noun generally takes a singular verb and a singular pronoun: *The army is prepared for its role.* See also pp. 62 and 67.

comma splice A sentence error in which two sentences (main clauses°) are separated by a comma without *and, but, or, nor,* or another coordinating conjunction.° Splice: *The book was long, it contained useful information.* Revised: *The book was long; it contained useful information.* Or: *The book was long, and it contained useful information.* See pp. 79–81.

comparison The form of an adjective° *or* adverb° that shows its degree of quality or amount. The **positive** is the simple, uncompared form: *gross, clumsily.* The **comparative** compares the thing modified to at least one other thing: *grosser, more clumsily.* The **superlative** indicates that the thing modified exceeds all other things to which it is being compared: *grossest, most clumsily.* The comparative and superlative are formed either with the endings *-er/-est* or with the words *more/most* or *less/least.*

complement See *subject complement.*

complex sentence See *sentence.*

compound-complex sentence See *sentence.*

compound construction Two or more words or word groups serving the same function, such as a compound subject° (*Harriet and Peter poled their barge down the river*), a compound predicate° (*The scout watched and waited*), or a compound sentence° (*He smiled, and I laughed*).

compound sentence See *sentence.*

conditional statement A statement expressing a condition contrary to fact and using the subjunctive mood° of the verb: *If she were mayor, the unions would cooperate.*

conjunction A word that links and relates parts of a sentence. See *coordinating conjunction* (*and, but,* etc.), *correlative conjunction* (*either . . . or, both . . . and,* etc.), and *subordinating conjunction* (*because, if,* etc.).

conjunctive adverb An adverb° that can relate two main clauses° in a single sentence: *We had hoped to own a house by now; however, prices are still too high.* The main clauses are separated by a semicolon or a period. Some common con-

Terms

°Defined in this glossary.

junctive adverbs: *accordingly, also, anyway, besides, certainly, consequently, finally, further, furthermore, hence, however, in addition, incidentally, indeed, instead, likewise, meanwhile, moreover, namely, nevertheless, next, nonetheless, now, otherwise, rather, similarly, still, then, thereafter, therefore, thus, undoubtedly.*

contraction A condensed expression, with an apostrophe replacing the missing letters: for example, *doesn't* (*does not*), *we'll* (*we will*).

coordinating conjunction A word linking words or word groups serving the same function: *The dog and cat sometimes fight, but they usually get along.* The coordinating conjunctions are *and, but, or, nor, for, so, yet.*

coordination The linking of words or word groups that are of equal importance, usually with a coordinating conjunction.° *He and I laughed, but she was not amused.* Contrast *subordination.*

correlative conjunction Two or more connecting words that work together to link words or word groups serving the same function: *Both Michiko and June signed up, but neither Stan nor Carlos did.* The correlatives include *both . . . and, just as . . . so, not only . . . but also, not . . . but, either . . . or, neither . . . nor, whether . . . or, as . . . as.*

count noun A word that names a person, place, or thing that can be counted (and so may appear in plural form): *camera/cameras, river/rivers, child/children.*

dangling modifier A modifier that does not sensibly describe anything in its sentence. Dangling: *Having arrived late, the concert had already begun.* Revised: *Having arrived late, we found that the concert had already begun.* See p. 76.

determiner A word such as *a, an, the, my,* and *your* that indicates that a noun follows. See also *article.*

direct address A construction in which a word or phrase indicates the person or group spoken to: *Have you finished, John? Farmers, unite.*

direct object A noun° or pronoun° that identifies who or what receives the action of a verb:° *Education opens doors.* For more, see *object* and *predicate.*

direct question A sentence asking a question and concluding with a question mark: *Do they know we are watching?* Contrast *indirect question.*

direct quotation Repetition of what someone has written or said, using the exact words of the original and enclosing them in quotation marks: *Feinberg writes, "The reasons are both obvious and sorry."*

double negative A nonstandard form consisting of two negative words used in the same construction so that they effectively cancel each other: *I don't have no money.* Rephrase as *I have no money* or *I don't have any money.* See also p. 72.

°Defined in this glossary.

ellipsis The omission of a word or words from a quotation, indicated by the three spaced periods of an **ellipsis mark:** *"all . . . are created equal."* See also pp. 99–101.

essential element A word or word group that is necessary to the meaning of the sentence because it limits the word it refers to: removing it would leave the meaning unclear or too general. Essential elements are *not* set off by commas: *Dorothy's companion the Scarecrow lacks a brain. The man who called about the apartment said he'd try again.* Contrast *nonessential element*. See also pp. 86–87.

expletive construction A sentence that postpones the subject° by beginning with *there* or *it* and a form of *be: It is impossible to get a ticket. There are no more seats available.*

first person See *person.*

fused sentence (run-on sentence) A sentence error in which two complete sentences (main clauses°) are joined with no punctuation or connecting word between them. Fused: *I heard his lecture it was dull.* Revised: *I heard his lecture; it was dull.* See pp. 79–81.

future perfect tense The verb tense expressing an action that will be completed before another future action: *They will have heard by then.* For more, see *tense.*

future tense The verb tense expressing action that will occur in the future: *They will hear soon.* For more, see *tense.*

gender The classification of nouns° or pronouns° as masculine (*he, boy*), feminine (*she, woman*), or neuter (*it, computer*).

generic *he* *He* used to mean *he or she.* Avoid *he* when you intend either or both genders. See pp. 45 and 67.

generic noun A noun° that does not refer to a specific person or thing: *Any person may come. A student needs good work habits. A school with financial problems may shortchange its students.* A singular generic noun takes a singular pronoun° (*he, she,* or *it*). See also *indefinite pronoun* and pp. 66–67.

gerund A verb form that ends in *-ing* and functions as a noun:° *Working is all right for killing time.* For more, see *verbals and verbal phrases.*

gerund phrase See *verbals and verbal phrases.*

helping verb (auxiliary verb) A verb° used with another verb to convey time, possibility, obligation, and other meanings: *You should write a letter. You have written other letters.* The **modals** are the following: *be able to, be supposed to, can, could, had better, had to, may, might, must, ought to, shall, should, used to, will, would.* The other helping verbs are forms of *be, have,* and *do.* See also pp. 51–53.

idiom An expression that is peculiar to a language and that may not make sense if taken literally: for example, *bide your time, by and large,* and *put up with.*

imperative See *mood.*

°Defined in this glossary.

indefinite pronoun A word that stands for a noun° and does not refer to a specific person or thing. A few indefinite pronouns are plural (*both, few, many, several*) or may be singular or plural (*all, any, more, most, none, some*). But most are only singular: *anybody, anyone, anything, each, either, everybody, everyone, everything, neither, nobody, no one, nothing, one, somebody, someone, something*. The singular indefinite pronouns take singular verbs and are referred to by singular pronouns: *Something makes its presence felt.* See also *generic noun* and pp. 61–62 and 66–67.

indicative See *mood.*

indirect object A noun° or pronoun° that identifies to whom or what something is done: *Give them the award.* For more, see *object* and *predicate.*

indirect question A sentence reporting a question and ending with a period: *Writers wonder whether their work must always be lonely.* Contrast *direct question.*

indirect quotation A report of what someone has written or said, but not using the exact words of the original and not enclosing the words in quotation marks. Quotation: *"Events have controlled me."* Indirect quotation: *Lincoln said that events had controlled him*.

infinitive A verb form° consisting of the verb's dictionary form plus *to: to swim, to write.* For more, see *verbals and verbal phrases.*

infinitive phrase See *verbals and verbal phrases.*

intensive pronoun See *pronoun.*

interjection A word standing by itself or inserted in a construction to exclaim: *Hey! What the heck did you do that for?*

interrogative pronoun A word that begins a question and serves as the subject° or object° of the sentence. The interrogative pronouns are *who, whom, whose, which,* and *what. Who received the flowers? Whom are they for?*

intransitive verb A verb° that does not require a following word (direct object°) to complete its meaning: *Mosquitoes buzz. The hospital may close*. For more, see *predicate.*

irregular verb See *verb forms.*

linking verb A verb that links, or connects, a subject° and a word that renames or describes the subject (a subject complement°): *They are golfers. You seem lucky.* The linking verbs are the forms of *be,* the verbs of the senses (*look, sound, smell, feel, taste*), and a few others (*appear, become, grow, prove, remain, seem, turn*). For more, see *predicate.*

main clause A word group that contains a subject° and a predicate,° does not begin with a subordinating word, and may stand alone as a sentence: *The president was not overbearing.* For more, see *clause.*

°Defined in this glossary.

main verb The part of a verb phrase° that carries the principal meaning: *had been walking, could happen, was chilled.* Contrast *helping verb.*

misplaced modifier A modifier whose position makes unclear its relation to the rest of the sentence. Misplaced: *The children played with firecrackers that they bought illegally in the field.* Revised: *The children played in the field with firecrackers that they bought illegally.*

modal See *helping verb.*

modifier Any word or word group that limits or qualifies the meaning of another word or word group. Modifiers include adjectives° and adverbs° as well as words and word groups that act as adjectives and adverbs.

mood The form of a verb° that shows how the speaker views the action. The **indicative mood,** the most common, is used to make statements or ask questions: *The play will be performed Saturday. Did you get tickets?* The **imperative mood** gives a command: *Please get good seats. Avoid the top balcony.* The **subjunctive mood** expresses a wish, a condition contrary to fact, a recommendation, or a request: *I wish George were coming with us. If he were here, he'd come. I suggested that he come. The host asked that he be here.*

noncount noun A word that names a person, place, or thing and that is not considered countable in English (and so does not appear in plural form): *confidence, information, silver, work.* See pp. 73–74 for a longer list.

nonessential element A word or word group that does not limit the word it refers to and that is not necessary to the meaning of the sentence. Nonessential elements are usually set off by commas: *Sleep, which we all need, occupies a third of our lives. His wife, Patricia, is a chemist.* Contrast *essential element.* See also pp. 86–87.

nonrestrictive element See *nonessential element.*

noun A word that names a person, place, thing, quality, or idea: *Maggie, Alabama, clarinet, satisfaction, socialism.* See also *collective noun, count noun, generic noun, noncount noun,* and *proper noun.*

noun clause See *subordinate clause.*

number The form of a word that indicates whether it is singular or plural. Singular: *I, he, this, child, runs, hides.* Plural: *we, they, these, children, run, hide.*

object A noun° or pronoun° that receives the action of or is influenced by another word. A **direct object** receives the action of a verb° or verbal° and usually follows it: *We watched the stars.* An **indirect object** tells for or to whom something is done: *Reiner bought us tapes.* An **object of a preposition** usually follows a preposition:° *They went to New Orleans.*

Terms

°Defined in this glossary.

objective case The form of a pronoun° when it is the object° of a verb° (*call him*) or the object of a preposition° (*for us*). For more, see *case*.

object of preposition See *object*.

parallelism Similarity of form between two or more coordinated elements: *Rising prices and declining incomes left many people in bad debt and worse despair*. See also pp. 37–38.

parenthetical expression A word or construction that interrupts a sentence and is not part of its main structure, called *parenthetical* because it could (or does) appear in parentheses: *Mary Cassatt (1845–1926) was an American painter. Her work, incidentally, is in the museum.*

participial phrase See *verbals and verbal phrases*.

participle See *verbals and verbal phrases*.

particle A preposition° or adverb° in a two-word verb: *catch on, look up*.

parts of speech The classes of words based on their form, function, and meaning: nouns, pronouns, verbs, adjectives, adverbs, conjunctions, prepositions, and interjections. See separate entries for each part of speech.

passive voice The verb form° used when the sentence subject° names the receiver of the verb's action: *The mixture was stirred*. For more, see *voice*.

past participle The *-ed* form of most verbs:° *fished, hopped*. The past participle may be irregular: *begun, written*. For more, see *verbals and verbal phrases* and *verb forms*.

past perfect tense The verb tense expressing an action that was completed before another past action: *No one had heard that before*. For more, see *tense*.

past tense The verb tense expressing action that occurred in the past: *Everyone laughed*. For more, see *tense*.

past-tense form The verb form used to indicate action that occurred in the past, usually created by adding *-d* or *-ed* to the verb's dictionary form (*smiled*) but created differently for most irregular verbs (*began, threw*). For more, see *verb forms*.

perfect tenses The verb tenses indicating action completed before another specific time or action: *have walked, had walked, will have walked*. For more, see *tense*.

person The form of a verb° or pronoun° that indicates whether the subject is speaking, spoken to, or spoken about. In the **first person** the subject is speaking: *I am, we are*. In the **second person** the subject is spoken to: *you are*. In the **third person** the subject is spoken about: *he/she/it is, they are*.

personal pronoun *I, you, he, she, it, we,* or *they:* a word that substitutes for a specific noun° or other pronoun. For more, see *case*.

Terms

°Defined in this glossary.

phrase A group of related words that lacks a subject° or a predicate° or both: *She ran into the field. She tried to jump the fence.* See also *absolute phrase, prepositional phrase, verbals and verbal phrases.*

plain form The dictionary form of a verb: *buy, make, run, swivel.* For more, see *verb forms.*

plural More than one. See *number.*

positive form See *comparison.*

possessive case The form of a noun° or pronoun° that indicates its ownership of something else: *men's attire, your briefcase.* For more, see *case.*

possessive pronoun A word that replaces a noun° or other pronoun° and shows ownership: *The cat chased its tail.* The possessive pronouns are *my, our, your, his, her, its, their, whose.*

predicate The part of a sentence that makes an assertion about the subject.° The predicate may consist of an intransitive verb° (*The earth trembled*), a transitive verb° plus direct object° (*The earthquake shook buildings*), a linking verb° plus subject complement° (*The result was chaos*), a transitive verb plus indirect object° and direct object (*The government sent the city aid*), or a transitive verb plus direct object and object complement (*The citizens considered the earthquake a disaster*).

preposition A word that forms a noun° or pronoun° (plus any modifiers) into a **prepositional phrase**: *about love, down the steep stairs.* The common prepositions: *about, above, according to, across, after, against, along, along with, among, around, as, at, because of, before, behind, below, beneath, beside, between, beyond, by, concerning, despite, down, during, except, except for, excepting, for, from, in, in addition to, inside, in spite of, instead of, into, like, near, next to, of, off, on, onto, out, out of, outside, over, past, regarding, since, through, throughout, till, to, toward, under, underneath, unlike, until, up, upon, with, within, without.*

prepositional phrase A word group consisting of a preposition° and its object.° Prepositional phrases usually serve as adjectives° (*We saw a movie about sorrow*) or as adverbs° (*We went back for the second show*).

present participle The *-ing* form of a verb:° *swimming, flying.* For more, see *verbals and verbal phrases.*

present perfect tense The verb tense expressing action that began in the past and is linked to the present: *Dogs have buried bones here before.* For more, see *tense.*

present tense The verb tense expressing action that is occurring now, occurs habitually, or is generally true: *Dogs bury bones here often.* For more, see *tense.*

principal parts The three forms of a verb from which its various tenses are created: the **plain form** (*stop, go*), the **past-**

°Defined in this glossary.

tense form (*stopped, went*), and the **past participle** (*stopped, gone*). For more, see *tense* and *verb forms.*

progressive tenses The verb tenses that indicate continuing (progressive) action and use the *-ing* form of the verb: *A dog was barking here this morning.* For more, see *tense.*

pronoun A word used in place of a noun,° such as *I, he, everyone, who,* and *herself.* See also *indefinite pronoun, interrogative pronoun, personal pronoun, possessive pronoun, relative pronoun.*

proper adjective A word formed from a proper noun° and used to modify a noun° or pronoun:° *Alaskan winter.*

proper noun A word naming a specific person, place, or thing and beginning with a capital letter: *David Letterman, Mt. Rainier, Alaska, US Congress.*

regular verb See *verb forms.*

relative pronoun A word that relates a group of words to a noun° or another pronoun.° The relative pronouns are *who, whom, whoever, whomever, which,* and *that. Ask the woman who knows all. This may be the question that stumps her.* For more, see *case.*

restrictive element See *essential element.*

run-on sentence See *fused sentence.*

-*s* form See *verb forms.*

second person See *person.*

sentence A complete unit of thought, consisting of at least a subject° and a predicate° that are not introduced by a subordinating word. A **simple sentence** contains one main clause:° *I'm leaving.* A **compound sentence** contains at least two main clauses: *I'd like to stay, but I'm leaving.* A **complex sentence** contains one main clause and at least one subordinate clause:° *If you let me go now, you'll be sorry.* A **compound-complex sentence** contains at least two main clauses and at least one subordinate clause: *I'm leaving because you want me to, but I'd rather stay.*

sentence fragment An error in which an incomplete sentence is set off as a complete sentence. Fragment: *She was not in shape for the race. Which she had hoped to win.* Revised: *She was not in shape for the race, which she had hoped to win.* See pp. 77–79.

series Three or more items with the same function: *We gorged on ham, eggs, and potatoes.*

simple sentence See *sentence.*

simple tenses See *tense.*

singular One. See *number.*

split infinitive The usually awkward interruption of an infinitive° and its marker *to* by a modifier: *Management decided to not introduce the new product.* See p. 75.

°Defined in this glossary.

squinting modifier A modifier that could modify the words on either side of it: *The plan we considered seriously worries me.*

subject In grammar, the part of a sentence that names something and about which an assertion is made in the predicate:° *The quick, brown fox jumped lazily* (simple subject); *The quick, brown fox jumped lazily* (complete subject).

subject complement A word that renames or describes the subject° of a sentence, after a linking verb.° *The stranger was a man* (noun°). *He seemed gigantic* (adjective°).

subjective case The form of a pronoun° when it is the subject° of a sentence (*I called*) or a subject complement° (*It was I*). For more, see *case.*

subjunctive See *mood.*

subordinate clause A word group that consists of a subject° and a predicate,° begins with a subordinating word such as *because* or *who,* and is not a question: *They voted for whoever cared the least because they mistrusted politicians.* Subordinate clauses may serve as adjectives° (*The car that hit Fred was blue*), as adverbs° (*The car hit Fred when it ran a red light*), or as nouns° (*Whoever was driving should be arrested*). Subordinate clauses are *not* complete sentences.

subordinating conjunction A word that turns a complete sentence into a word group (a subordinate clause°) that can serve as an adverb° or a noun.° *Everyone was relieved when the meeting ended.* Some common subordinating conjunctions: *after, although, as, as if, as long as, as though, because, before, even if, even though, if, if only, in order that, now that, once, rather than, since, so that, than, that, though, till, unless, until, when, whenever, where, whereas, wherever, while.*

subordination Deemphasizing one element in a sentence by making it dependent on rather than equal to another element. Through subordination, *I left six messages; the doctor failed to call* becomes *Although I left six messages, the doctor failed to call* or *After six messages, the doctor failed to call.*

superlative See *comparison.*

tag question A question attached to the end of a statement and composed of a pronoun,° a helping verb,° and sometimes the word *not: It isn't raining, is it? It is sunny, isn't it?*

tense The verb form that expresses time, usually indicated by endings and by helping verbs. See also *verb forms.*

Present Action that is occurring now, occurs habitually, or is generally true

Simple present Plain form **or -*s* form**	Present progressive *Am, is,* or *are* plus *-ing* form
I *walk.*	I *am walking.*
You/we/they *walk.*	You/we/they *are walking.*
He/she/it *walks.*	He/she/it *is walking.*

Terms

°Defined in this glossary.

Past Action that occurred before now

Simple past Past-tense form	Past progressive *Was* or *were* plus *-ing* form
I/he/she/it *walked.* You/we/they *walked.*	I/he/she/it *was walking.* You/we/they *were walking.*

Future Action that will occur in the future

Simple future *Will* plus plain form	Future progressive *Will be* plus *-ing* form
I/you/he/she/it/we/they *will walk.*	I/you/he/she/it/we/they *will be walking.*

Present perfect Action that began in the past and is linked to the present

Present perfect *Have* or *has* plus past participle	Present perfect progressive *Have been* or *has been* plus *-ing* form
I/you/we/they *have walked.*	I/you/we/they *have been walking.*
He/she/it *has walked.*	He/she/it *has been walking.*

Past perfect Action that was completed before another past action

Past perfect *Had* plus past participle	Past perfect progressive *Had been* plus *-ing* form
I/you/he/she/it/we/they *had walked.*	I/you/he/she/it/we/they *had been walking.*

Future perfect Action that will be completed before another future action

Future perfect *Will have* plus past participle	Future perfect progressive *Will have been* plus *-ing* form
I/you/he/she/it/we/they *will have walked.*	I/you/he/she/it/we/they *will have been walking.*

third person See *person*.

transitional expression A word or phrase that links sentences and shows the relations between them. Transitional expressions can signal various relationships (examples in parentheses): addition or sequence (*also, besides, finally, first, furthermore, in addition, last*); comparison (*also, similarly*); contrast (*even so, however, in contrast, still*); examples (*for example, for instance, that is*); intensification (*indeed, in fact, of course*); place (*below, elsewhere, here, nearby, to the east*); time (*afterward, at last, earlier, immediately, meanwhile, simultaneously*); repetition or summary (*in brief, in other words, in short, in summary, that is*); and cause and effect (*as a result, consequently, hence, therefore, thus*).

transitive verb A verb° that requires a following word (a direct object°) to complete its meaning: *We raised the roof.* For more, see *predicate*.

°Defined in this glossary.

verb A word that expresses an action (*bring, change*), an occurrence (*happen, become*), or a state of being (*be, seem*). A verb is the essential word in a predicate,° the part of a sentence that makes an assertion about the subject.° With endings and helping verbs,° verbs can indicate tense,° mood,° voice,° number,° and person.° For more, see separate entries for each of these aspects as well as *verb forms*.

verbals and verbal phrases **Verbals** are verb forms used as adjectives,° adverbs,° or nouns.° They form **verbal phrases** with objects° and modifiers.° A **present participle** adds *-ing* to the dictionary form of a verb (*living*). A **past participle** usually adds *-d* or *-ed* to the dictionary form (*lived*), although irregular verbs work differently (*begun, swept*). A participle or **participial phrase** usually serves as an adjective: *Strolling shoppers fill the malls*. A **gerund** is the *-ing* form of a verb used as a noun. Gerunds and **gerund phrases** can do whatever nouns can do: *Shopping satisfies needs*. An **infinitive** is the verb's dictionary form plus *to: to live*. Infinitives and **infinitive phrases** may serve as nouns (*To design a mall is a challenge*), as adverbs (*Malls are designed to make shoppers feel safe*), or as adjectives (*The mall supports the impulse to shop*).

A verbal *cannot* serve as the only verb in a sentence. For that, it requires a helping verb:° *Shoppers were strolling*.

verb forms Verbs have five distinctive forms. The **plain form** is the dictionary form: *A few artists live in town today*. The **-s form** adds *-s* or *-es* to the plain form: *The artist lives in town today*. The **past-tense form** usually adds *-d* or *-ed* to the plain form: *Many artists lived in town before this year*. Some verbs' past-tense forms are irregular, such as *began, fell, swam, threw, wrote*. The **past participle** is usually the same as the past-tense form, although, again, some verbs' past participles are irregular (*begun, fallen, swum, thrown, written*). The **present participle** adds *-ing* to the plain form: *A few artists are living in town today*.

Regular verbs are those that add *-d* or *-ed* to the plain form for the past-tense form and past participle. **Irregular verbs** create these forms in irregular ways (see above).

verb phrase A verb° of more than one word that serves as the predicate° of a sentence: *The movie has started*.

voice The form of a verb° that tells whether the sentence subject° performs the action or is acted upon. In the **active voice** the subject acts: *The city controls rents*. In the **passive voice** the subject is acted upon: *Rents are controlled by the city*. See also pp. 59–60.

°Defined in this glossary.

Credits

Allianz Knowledge. Screenshot from *Allianz Knowledge Partnersite* Web site, *www.knowledge.allianz.com.* Reprinted by permission of Allianz Knowledge.

Cunningham, John, and Peter Selby. From "Relighting Cigarettes: How Common Is It?" by John Cunningham and Peter Selby in *Nicotine and Tobacco Research*, Vol. 9, No. 5, May 2007. Copyright © 2007 by Cunningham and Selby. Reprinted by permission of Oxford University Press.

Dickinson, Emily. From "A narrow fellow in the grass" by Emily Dickinson from *The Poems of Emily Dickinson,* edited by Thomas H. Johnson. Copyright © 1951, 1955, 1979, 1983 by the President and Fellows of Harvard College. Reprinted by permission of the publishers and the Trustees of Amherst College from *The Poems of Emily Dickinson,* Thomas H. Johnson, ed., Cambridge, Mass.: The Belknap Press of Harvard University Press.

EBSCO Publishing. From *EBSCOhost Academic Search.* Copyright © 2010 by EBSCO Publishing. Reprinted with permission.

Ethnic NewsWatch Database. Copyright © 2010 by ProQuest. Reprinted by permission of ProQuest LLC.

Jackson, Tim. From "Live Better by Consuming Less?: Is There a 'Double Dividend' in Sustainable Consumption?" by Tim Jackson in *Journal of Industrial Ecology,* Vol. 9, 2005. Copyright © 2005 by Tim Jackson. Reprinted by permission of John Wiley and Sons.

Library Quarterly. From *Library Quarterly*, Vol. 78, No. 2, April 2008. Copyright © 2008. Reprinted by permission of University of Chicago Press.

Makower, Joel. From "Go for the Green: Buying Beer? Sneakers? A Car? The Most Eco-conscious Companies Aren't Always the Most Obvious" by Joel Makower in *Vegetarian Times,* January 2006. Copyright © 2006 by Vegetarian Times. Reprinted with permission.

Molella, Arthur. "Cultures of Innovation" by Arthur Molella, from "Resources" Web page by the Lemelson Center. Copyright © 2010 by the Smithsonian Institution. Reprinted with permission.

Parry, Martin, Jean Palutikof, Clair Hanson, and Jason Lowe. From "Squaring Up to Reality" by Martin Parry, Jean Palutikof, Clair Hanson, and Jason Lowe. Copyright © by Parry et al. Reprinted by permission of *Nature*.

Selwyn, Neil. From "The Social Process of Learning to Use Computers" by Neil Selwyn in *Social Science Computer Review*, Vol. 23, No. 1, Spring 2005. Copyright © 2005 by Neil Selwyn. Reprinted by permission of Sage Publications.

Index

A

D

Index

J

K

L

M

O

S

U

Index

ESL Guide

ESL

Throughout this handbook, the symbol ESL signals topics for students whose first language is not standard American English. These topics can be tricky because they arise from rules in standard English that are quite different in other languages. Many of the topics involve significant cultural assumptions as well.

Whatever your language background, as a college student you are learning the culture of US higher education and the language that is used and shaped by that culture. The process is challenging, even for native speakers of standard American English. It requires not just writing clearly and correctly but also mastering conventions of developing, presenting, and supporting ideas. The challenge is greater if, in addition, you are trying to learn standard English and are accustomed to other conventions. Several habits can help you succeed:

- **Read.** Besides course assignments, read newspapers, magazines, and books in English. The more you read, the more fluently and accurately you'll write.
- **Write.** Keep a journal in which you practice writing in English every day.
- **Talk and listen.** Take advantage of opportunities to hear and use English.
- **Ask questions.** Your instructors, tutors in the writing center, and fellow students can clarify assignments and help you identify and solve writing problems.
- **Don't try for perfection.** No one writes perfectly, and the effort to do so can prevent you from expressing yourself fluently. View mistakes not as failures but as opportunities to learn.
- **Revise first; then edit.** Focus on each essay's ideas, support, and organization before attending to grammar and vocabulary. See the checklist for revising academic writing on page 2.
- **Set editing priorities.** Check first for errors that interfere with clarity, such as problems with word order or subject-verb agreement. The following index can help you identify the topics you need to work on and can lead you to appropriate text discussions.

Detailed Contents

Editing Symbols

Readers may use these symbols to mark editing you should do. Page numbers refer to relevant sections of this handbook.

ab	Faulty abbreviation *112*
ad	Misused adjective or adverb *70*
agr	Error in agreement *60, 66*
ap	Apostrophe needed or misused *92*
appr	Inappropriate word *41*
awk	Awkward construction
cap	Use capital letter *108*
case	Error in pronoun form *63*
cit	Missing source citation or error in citation form
con	Be more concise *34*
coord	Coordination needed *33*
cs	Comma splice *79*
d	Ineffective diction (word choice) *41–48*
det	Add details *40*
dm	Dangling modifier *76*
emph	Emphasis lacking *31*
exact	Inexact word *46*
frag	Sentence fragment *77*
fs	Fused sentence *79*
gr	Error in grammar *49–81*
hyph	Error in use of hyphen *107*
inc	Incomplete construction
ital	Italicize (underline) *110*
k	Awkward construction
lc	Use lowercase letter *108*
mm	Misplaced modifier *74*
mng	Meaning unclear
ms	Error in manuscript (document) form *21*
no cap	Unnecessary capital letter *108*
no ^,	Comma not needed *85*
no ¶	No new paragraph needed
num	Error in use of numbers *113*
p	Error in punctuation *83–102*
^,	Comma *85*
;	Semicolon *89*
:	Colon *91*

'	Apostrophe *92*
" "	Quotation marks *94*
. ? !	Period, question mark, exclamation point *97*
— ( ) . . . [ ] /	Dash, parentheses, ellipsis mark, brackets, slash *98*
par, ¶	Start new paragraph
pass	Ineffective passive voice *32, 59*
pn agr	Error in pronoun-antecedent agreement *66*
ref	Error in pronoun reference *68*
rel?	Relevance unclear
rep	Unnecessary repetition *36*
run-on	Run-on (fused) sentence *79*
shift	Inconsistency *56, 58, 60, 69*
sp	Misspelled word *105*
spec	Be more specific *40, 46*
sub	Subordination needed *34*
t	Error in verb tense *56*
t seq	Error in tense sequence *7*
trans	Transition needed *259*
und	Underline (italicize) *110*
usage	See Glossary of Usage *239*
var	Vary sentence structure *39*
vb	Error in verb form *51*
vb agr	Error in subject-verb agreement *60*
w	Wordy *34*
ww	Wrong word *46*
//	Faulty parallelism *37*
#	Separate with a space
⁀	Close up space
ℊ	Delete
teh	Transpose letters or words
x	Obvious error
^	Something missing
??	Document illegible or meaning unclear

More than 4 million students are using Pearson MyLabs!

Here's how *MyCompLab* can help you save time and improve results:

- **Multimedia Resources:** Get online instruction, audio and video tutorials, and abundant exercises on a wide variety of writing, grammar, and research topics.
- **Skill Building and Progress Tracking:** Use diagnostics, tutorials, and exercise sets to practice key skills, monitor your progress, and improve your grade.
- **Online Assignments, Commenting, and Grading:** Take advantage of composing and course-management features to receive feedback from your instructor and track your assignments, drafts, and graded papers.

Ask your instructor how to order this book with access to *MyCompLab*.

www.mycomplab.com

Longman
is an imprint of
PEARSON

www.pearsonhighered.com

ISBN-13: 978-0-205-71876-4
ISBN-10: 0-205-71876-0
EAN
9 780205 718764